STATEHOOD ON TRIAL
Thoughts on the 1966 Uganda Political Crisis

There are no Sacred Cows here.
Everyone and Everything is Interrogated.
"I hope for nothing. I fear nothing. I am free."
Nikos Kazantzakis

STATEHOOD ON TRIAL
Thoughts on the 1966 Uganda Political Crisis

Revised Edition

Joseph Bossa

Makerere University Press
www.press.mak.ac.ug

Makerere University Press
P.O. Box 7062
Kampala, Uganda

Copyright © 2022 Joseph Bossa

All rights reserved. No part of this publication may be reproduced, stored in a retrieval system, or transmitted in any form or by any means, electronic, mechanical, photocopying, recording or otherwise, without prior written permission from the publishers.

First published as *Thoughouts About the 1966 Political Crisis* by Joseph Bossa, 2015, under ISBN: 978-9970-27-011-8.

All photographs were reproduced with permission from Monitor Publications Ltd. All rights reserved.

ISBN: 978-9913-603-02-7

Table of Contents

Table of Contents v
Acronyms, Abbreviations and Glossary viii
Preface x
Justification for a Revised Edition xiii
Foreword xiv
Chapter 1: IN THE BEGINNING 1
Chapter 2: LANCASTER HOUSE GRAND SETTLEMENT 28
Chapter 3: UPC/KY COALITION GOVERNMENT 34
   Origin and objective of Kabaka Yekka (KY) 35
   1962 Elections 36
   Kabaka Mutesa Becomes President Mutesa: The Duelling Roles ... 37
   Political Dirty Tricks Begin 43
   Kabaka Mutesa Collides with President Mutesa 52
   President Mutesa Confronts Prime Minister Obote 56
Chapter 4: "STRATEGIES" TO RETAIN THE LOST COUNTIES 59
   Mengo's "Strategy" 59
   The Better Strategy 63
Chapter 5: PARTING OF PATHS 67
Chapter 6: SECONDARY FACTORS AND EPISODES THAT STOKED THE CRISIS 70
   Inherited Complicated and Difficult Situation 71
   Power Struggle within UPC 72
   Political Alliances 72
   UPC in Buganda 89
   Definition of Roles and Statuses 97
   Lack of Political Courage and Self-Delusion 99
   Backgrounds and Ideological Orientations 104
   Friendship 111
   Age, Hubris, and Experience 112

Chapter 7: POST-REFERENDUM PLOTS AND MANOEUVRES ... 114
- Mutesa-Ibingira Partnership ... 115
- Obote's Trump Card ... 122
- Parliamentary Option ... 125
- Power Struggle within UPC ... 131

Chapter 8: ERUPTION ... 140
- Prelude to the Attack on Lubiri ... 140
- Attack on Lubiri ... 144
- Battle in Lubiri ... 147

Chapter 9: AFTER-LIFE OF THE CRISIS ... 149
- Abrogation of the 1962 Uganda Independence Constitution ... 150
- Mutesa, His Dependants and Buganda Officials ... 156
- Obote's Fortunes ... 163
- Symbolic Buildings and Spaces ... 165
- Political Landscape ... 166

Chapter 10: WINNERS AND LOSERS ... 168
- At Individual Level ... 168
- Obote's Second Coming ... 174
- At Institutional Level ... 178

Chapter 11: COULD THE CRISIS HAVE BEEN AVERTED? ... 184
- What if the Issue had been Resolved before Independence? ... 186
- What if Obote had not Gone Ahead with the Referundum? ... 187
- What if Mutesa were not Kabaka of Buganda and the president of Uganda at the same time? ... 188
- What if Mutesa had Looked a Little Farther? ... 191
- Absence of Experienced Statesmen ... 194

Chapter 12: LESSONS LEARNT ... 195
- Conflict of Interest ... 195
- Sudden Change of Equilibrium in Parliament ... 196
- Prime Minister vis-à-vis President Conflict ... 196
- Power Struggle within a Political Party ... 197
- Conflict Between Nation and State ... 198

Table of Contents

Inter- and Intra-Territorial Claims and Divisions 200
Chapter 13: STARTING ANEW 202
   A New Constitution 203
   Governance 207
   Coalition Governments and Government of National Unity 223
   Truth-telling and reconciliation 223
Chapter 14: IN CONCLUSION 232
References 238
Appendix 242
Index 243

Acronyms, Abbreviations and Glossary

Baganda	The people of Buganda Kingdom
Bakopi	The people not belonging to the chiefly or nobility class of Buganda Kingdom
Banyoro	The people of Bunyoro Kingdom
Buganda	The kingdom of the Baganda people
Bulange	The Parliament Building of the Buganda Kingdom
Bunyoro	The Kingdom of the Banyoro people
Busuulu	Rent levied by the registered land owner from the land user known as *kibanja* holder
DP	Democratic Party
FDC	Forum for Democratic Change
Kabaka	The king of Buganda
Katikkiro	The prime minister of Buganda Kingdom
Kiganda	Relating to Buganda or Baganda
Kinyoro	Relating to Bunyoro or Banyoro
KY	Kabaka Yekka
Lubiri	The palace of the Kabaka of Buganda
Luganda	The language of the Baganda
Lukiiko	The Parliament of Buganda Kingdom
Mailo	the localised word from the English word "mile" used to refer to freehold land in Buganda
Muganda	A native of Buganda and singular for *Baganda*
Mukopi	An untitled person in Buganda and singular for *bakopi*

Munyoro	A native of Bunyoro and singular for Banyoro
NRA	National Resistance Army
NRM	National Resistance Movement
Omugabe	The king of Ankore Kingdom
Omukama	The king of Bunyoro or Tooro Kingdom
Ssekabaka	A deceased Kabaka/king of Buganda
UNC	Uganda National Congress
UPC	Uganda People's Congress

In different writings, the names of some people and places are variously spelt, among them are: Mutesa for Muteesa, Ocheng for Ocheng, Opoloto for Opolot and Bugangazzi for Bugangaizi. As far as personal names go, the opinion of the author is that the proper spelling of the name is that which its owner considers proper.

Luganda words and phrases appearing in the text are italicised and the English meaning—both literal and metaphorical—is rendered immediately.

Preface

On 24th May 1966, I was a student at Namilyango College. From the hill on which the college stands, I could hear the bellowing sounds of heavy artillery gunfire and I could see the dark smoke rising from Mengo Hill, the seat of Kabaka Mutesa's palace, for the two hills are hardly separated by more than ten miles as the crow flies. I felt in my bones that something momentous was going on. But I could not tell then that it was a pivotal moment. I could not guess that because of what I was hearing and seeing then, future students of Ugandan history would write of "the before 1966" and "the after 1966" epochs.

Since that time, I have tried to make sense of that event. In a way, we can say that this publication has been 50 years in the making. However, I did not start penning down my thoughts until April 2013 when I was requested by Ambassador Emmanuel Sendawula, the Deputy Katikkiro and chairman of the preparatory committee of the 47th anniversary of the attack on the Lubiri, to write a note on behalf of the Uganda Peoples Congress (UPC), the political party that was in power in 1966. The note would be for publication in the annual magazine, *Entanda ya Buganda*. Given the space the article was allotted in the publication, it could only be a highly condensed note.

When I showed it to Mr Olara Otunnu, the party president, his opinion was that the brevity of the note did not do justice either to the subject, the party, or to me as an author. And, Uganda itself, as a country, would be short-changed. He advised me not to issue it but instead take time to write something more comprehensive, which I could publish when opportunity presented itself. I heeded his advice.

Preface

In this book, I try to narrate the important factual events, explain them and, in the case of Mutesa who, fortunately, did us a great service by giving us a written record of what he saw and felt, I assess what he recorded. In a few sections I adopt, without forewarning, the historical fiction style of writing. I do so where I feel it is most suited to enter the interior of the individual or collective minds of the actors in order to illuminate an understanding of what moved them. Because the elements of the 1966 Uganda Political Crisis continue to be misrepresented and misunderstood, this book is my contribution to bringing factual clarity and a different interpretation of events to this episode in Uganda's history.

In this work, I have avoided laying out in full the profiles of the main protagonists. I do hope that their omission will not diminish the appreciation of these reflections by young readers or those meeting those political actors for the first time.

Many people have been kind enough to find time to read one or the other of the different drafts of this work and to avail me their valuable comments on factual and stylistic matters. In no particular order, these include: Mr Olara Otunnu, Professor Phares Mutibwa (over beer at our local *kafunda*—an unlicensed bar—in Muyenga, a Kampala suburb), Mr Jenkins Kiwanuka, Mr Joseph Magala-Nyago, and Mr Patrick Bugembe. I wish to thank all of them most heartily for their time and effort so generously spared.

A few people who availed me their comments withheld their consent to be mentioned here, preferring to retain their independence to savage the work after publication, should they be so inclined. Still, I value their contribution and remain grateful.

I owe an additional debt of gratitude to Mr Olara Otunnu for encouraging me to write everything I know and think about the 1966 crisis and matters incidental thereto. Last but not least, I wish to thank my publishers for their patience in allowing me to make all the changes to the text long after I had submitted the manuscript to them. I now know that even a writing of this modest size is like a painting: it cannot be completed but it is simply abandoned.

However, to none of the people mentioned should be ascribed the errors, inaccuracies and opinions in this work. None of them saw all the drafts of this book. Each version was virtually a different piece. And certainly, apart from my publisher, none saw the last and final version which was submitted to the printer. Therefore, I alone bear full responsibility for all the contents in this writing. As the Swahili speakers would say, *"Kama mbaya, ni mbaya!"* (Come what may!).

Joseph Bossa
Kampala

Justification for a Revised Edition

Any revision of a publication demands a justification. Here is one for issuing this revised edition. First, the reader was warned in the preface to the first edition, even further warned above, that writing is like painting a picture: it is never completed; it is simply abandoned. After resting the essay for one year, I looked at it again. I discovered that, like a painting, it required retouching in some places and correcting errors in others.

This revised edition is a little "tighter" in the sense that this time around, some primary materials, because of their importance, are quoted more fully instead of being paraphrased. It is also longer, so long that I am sure it has gone past an essay to become a book. It is my hope, too, that this revised edition is more reader-friendly than the first in the way it is laid out.

This edition is not a mere tinkering with the title. I hope that those who read the first edition find it worthwhile to read the revised one as well.

That having been said, publishing one's opinions really boils down to self-regard and massaging one's vanity. For other than that, what makes one think that their insights are worth sharing with the rest of humanity (for you never know where the writing may end up)? But then, a person who is completely devoid of ego is not different from a door mat.

I owe an eternal debt of gratitude to my wife, Solomy Balungi Bossa, who, when time and space allowed her to read the revised draft of this work, made exceedingly valuable comments, many of which I took on board. But of course, I accept the credit for all that is good and take responsibility for all that is not so good in this work.

Joseph Bossa

Foreword

It was with great delight that Mr Joseph Bossa, a lawyer and friend, asked me to write this foreword to this interesting work on the political history of Uganda during the first few years of her independence. He appears to have carefully chosen his title—*Statehood on Trial: Thoughts on the 1966 Uganda Political Crisis*. The reader, therefore, expects that Mr Bossa took great care in writing about his subject.

For most African countries, the decade starting in 1960 was a period of attaining independence from colonial rule. The three East African territories under British colonial rule received their independence in succession with Tanganyika (mainland Tanzania) receiving independence in 1961, followed by Uganda in 1962 and Kenya in 1963.

The crisis that is the subject of Bossa's book occurred only four years after the attainment of Uganda's independence. Bossa attributes the crisis partly to the relatively little political experience that the two men at the helm of political power, Sir Edward Mutesa, who was Kabaka of Buganda and constitutional president of Uganda, and Milton Obote, who was the prime minister and head of government since independence. However, Bossa believes most strongly that the "Lost Counties" issue, which simmered throughout the colonial period, reached its peak in 1966.

In 1900, the British colonial rulers had curved away from Bunyoro Kingdom two counties of Buwekula and Bugangazzi and given them to Buganda Kingdom in appreciation of Buganda's official willingness to cooperate with them.

The matter of the two counties—the Lost Counties—was a thorn in the flesh of Uganda Protectorate Government through the entire period of their rule in Uganda. Shortly before the granting of independence, a number of conferences were held in Britain and representatives from Bunyoro Kingdom mounted strong pressure on the colonial government to ensure that the two counties were returned to Bunyoro before independence was granted to Uganda as a whole.

The British knew how controversial the Lost Counties issue had been throughout the colonial period. The British Protectorate Government, therefore, agreed that this matter should be handled by Uganda Government itself two years after attaining independence. A referendum was to be held in which the residents of Buwekula and Bugangazzi would make a decision whether to remain part of Buganda Kingdom or to return to Bunyoro Kingdom.

It is in connection with the issue of holding a referendum in the Lost Counties that the Kabaka of Buganda and president of Uganda at the same time, faced a major conflict of interest. The referendum results showed that the majority of the residents in Buwekula and Bugangazzi opted to return to Bunyoro Kingdom. Kabaka Mutesa II, in his capacity as president of Uganda, was legally supposed to sign the relevant documents that would result in decimating his kingdom. He refused to sign. This was construed by Prime Minister Milton Obote as a failure by the president to fulfil his duties. Eventually, the two counties returned to Bunyoro amid a lot of jubilation on the part of Bunyoro, but very much to the annoyance of the Kabaka of Buganda and his "subjects."

As the issue of the Lost Counties was being handled, there was great unease in the country. It was alleged that Grace Ibingira, then secretary general of Uganda Peoples Congress (UPC), was plotting to take over the leadership of that party from Milton Obote. It was also rumoured that Mutesa had asked the British High Commission to assist him in the event that there was a showdown between him and Obote. In the face of these developments, Obote felt isolated and devastated.

Faced with intelligence that Mutesa had stocked arms in his palace, Prime Minister Obote decided to use force and commanded Colonel Idi Amin to attack the Lubiri (Kabaka's palace) at Mengo. After a fierce battle, Kabaka Mutesa fled to Britain where he died in 1969. A state of emergency was declared over Buganda and was only lifted after the fall of Obote's government on 25th January 1971.

The showdown between Mutesa and Obote was not necessarily because of the difference in their social or ethnic backgrounds. The critical point to examine was who should wield effective power in the country. The Kabaka was not satisfied with being a mere ceremonial president. In any case, the concept of constitutional (non-executive) head of state was alien to Africa. Given these circumstaces, it is difficult to see how a clash could have been avoided.

Bossa is right in bemoaning the fact that Obote did not write any memoirs to let us know why he did what he did. Obote's memoirs would have helped to redress the balance between those who deify and those who demonise him.

I agree with the author's conclusion that the 1966 Crisis should teach Ugandans not to confer too much power in the office of the head of state; this power could be abused. Further, the national Constitution should not be partisan; it should be seen to serve the nation as a whole.

I thank Bossa for this lucid and provocative work on the political history of Uganda. Students of the political history of Uganda will find it informative and thought-provoking. It is also useful to anyone who has ambitions to participate in the governance of this country.

Moses L. Golola, PhD
Former Deputy Executive Director
National Council for Higher Education

Chapter 1

IN THE BEGINNING

In its quest to colonise Uganda, Britain needed to subjugate Bunyoro Kingdom. Britain called upon the military assistance of Buganda Kingdom in order to overcome the resistance of Bunyoro. With the defeat of Bunyoro, Buganda was awarded part of the Bunyoro territory which was formalised in the 1900 Agreement between Britain and Buganda. Part of this territory came to be known as "the Lost Counties."

Though defeated, Bunyoro never ceased demanding the return of these counties but Britain, being the author of the problem, never gave serious consideration to solving the matter. When negotiating the terms of granting independence to Uganda, Bunyoro insisted on the return of the Lost Counties before independence. Buganda insisted on keeping them.

To resolve the impasse, it was decided that the place of the Lost Counties in an independent Uganda—whether to be part of Bunyoro, Buganda or independent of the two as a separate district—would be determined after independence by the people of those counties through a referendum. It was also resolved that after independence, the ceremonial head of state of Uganda would be elected by Parliament from among the traditional leaders of the Ugandan communities.

Sir Edward Mutesa II, the Kabaka of Buganda was elected the first president of Uganda with the political support of Milton Obote, the prime minister, and Uganda Peoples Congress, which political party Obote headed. As we will explain later, Kabaka Mutesa himself and his kingdom, Buganda, had earlier on helped Obote become Uganda's prime minister. The two, and their respective institutions, were thus indebted to one another.

The Uganda Constitution required the president to assent to any law passed by Parliament but also allowed the prime minister to sign it into law if the president failed to do so. Parliament passed a law calling for the holding of the referendum over the Lost Counties. The president declined to assent to it because it was almost a certainty that the people of the counties would vote in favour of being taken back to Bunyoro. The prime minister signed the law, which infuriated the president and the subjects of his kingdom, Buganda.

The referendum proceeded and the result was that the people of the counties voted to be part of Bunyoro, which destroyed the personal relationship between the president and the prime minister. The president joined forces with politicians within the prime minister's party who were plotting to have him removed from leadership, politically, if possible, and militarily, if necessary.

Matters came to a head in May, 1966, when, with an insurrection underway in parts of Buganda against the Central Government, and believing that arms were stocked in the Kabaka's palace, the prime minister abolished the Constitution and, initially, ordered the police to go into the palace to search for and seize the weapons. The Kabaka escaped from the palace and fled into exile. These events have come to constitute what is known as "the 1966 Crisis."

For far too long, the explanation of the 1966 political crisis has been conceded to one side. And such explanation, as has been proffered, has been in terms of Apollo Milton Obote's hatred of Kabaka Mutesa, Buganda and the Baganda. By and large, one side has blocked objective truth from reaching subsequent generations and this side has tried to ease the passage of lies into history. Time is long overdue to balance the accounts. For if we are to hold and express political opinions, let our opinions be founded on facts. At some point, we all must self-examine some of our fundamental political and religious beliefs instead of taking the easy road of just adopting those of our elders. We should also be prepared to change our views when facts justifying change come to light. Received information from elders and ancestors, however venerated those elders may be, will not suffice.

In these pages, we bring everything we know to be true regarding the crisis. This effort is aimed at four categories of readers. The first has virtually no knowledge of, and no opinion about, the 1966 crisis. It may even sound to them like ancient history into which only the most curious of minds delve. The second are those people whose knowledge is based on sketchy information given to them by people they trusted but who themselves were either misinformed, under-informed, or unwilling to discard their prejudices. This is the "I was told by my...." group. The third category, in the secret chambers of their hearts and the deep recesses of their minds, knows what happened, how and why it happened but for a variety of reasons chooses to deliberately and selectively use its knowledge to misinform the first two groups in order to bias them against Obote and UPC, the party he led. This group has, over the years, done their best to fabricate and propagate a notion that this was a clash between two princes: one self-made and another born (similar to the fight in England [1642-49] between Oliver Cromwell and King Charles I). They make it look like the self-made prince, Prime Minister Milton Obote, just woke up one morning and in a fit of sheer malice longly harboured, ordered the Uganda army to attack the palace of the born prince, Kabaka Edward Mutesa. We try to disarm this group in this narrative. This work says, "Wait a minute. It was not as simple as that. Let us have a look at what lies on the other side of the moon." We also venture to write for a fourth category—the generations still unborn.

Our objective is to inform the first group about this pivotal episode in Uganda's history because it largely explains the path Uganda took after that episode. We intend to fill in the second group with the facts to enable them to come to an informed opinion and possibly begin to see the 1966 crisis in a new light. We will try to expose the third group so as to ensure the emancipation of the first and second groups from shackles of misinformation, deliberate or otherwise, under-information and prejudice. We hope future generations will read this work and gain a fair appreciation of this watermark in our history.

The 1966 crisis is a historic fact. We must investigate with care and without prejudice, what happened, when it happened, how it happened, why it happened, who did what, and what the results of what happened were.

We hope that by the end of this writing, the various categories of readers will have learned, unlearned or re-learned some facts about the 1966 crisis so that they will be able to separate opinions from facts and facts from falsehoods and myths, and draw their own conclusions. If by the end, we will have displeased all sides in equal measure, that is a risk we are willing to take in order to protect those who in future will be willing to offer themselves for national leadership.

The bigger part of this work explains the crisis, setting out what we see as its direct and indirect causes and its consequences. Uganda did not fizzle out with the 1966 crisis but lived on. We have attempted to point out what we consider the challenges and recent controversies, not necessarily directly relating to the crisis, which lie ahead and must be addressed in order to take Uganda to a better place. Lest it be forgotten, nation building, and consolidation, is a never-ending task. The Americans refer to their process as seeking to "form a more perfect union." Besides, having done with retrospection, it is proper to look forward and have a peek at the future and try to balance coverage of the past and the near future.

One day in May 1966, three years into independence, the Uganda army clashed with Baganda ex-servicemen of the Second World War loyal to the Kabaka of Buganda who had gathered in his support in his palace at Mengo. The Kabaka managed to escape into exile in London where he died three years later. That clash and the events that followed have come to be dubbed *the 1966 Crisis* by some political commentators and *the 1966 Revolution* by others, including some jurists. For the purposes of this work, we will apply the more commonly used term *the 1966 Crisis* or *the Crisis*, in short.

We have observed that the distinguished authors who have given account of this subject before me have either deliberately shied away from defining the phrase *the 1966 Crisis* or probably assumed it to be self-explanatory, calling for no effort at definition. To the plain Ugandan of a certain age, the 1966 Crisis is understood implicitly to mean the attack by the Uganda army on the Kabaka's palace in May 1966. They may also tend to see and explain it as a personal quarrel between Milton Obote and Edward Mutesa. But if you asked them to give a precise definition of that crisis, they are likely to struggle. They will most probably list a mixture of symbols, causes, incidents and consequences, which constitute the 1966 Crisis; for instance, the gold scandal motion in Parliament, the arrest of five cabinet ministers, the abolition of the 1962 Independence Constitution, the Buganda Lukiiko resolution giving the Uganda government an ultimatum to remove itself from Buganda territory, the army attack on the Kabaka's palace on 24 May 1966, the fleeing of the Kabaka into exile, and the subsequent abolition of not only Buganda but also other kingdoms in Uganda under the 1967 Constitution and thus turning Uganda into a republic.

Calling any of those events the Crisis would be like calling the storming of the fortress of Bastille on 14 July 1789, the French Revolution. That was an event turned into a symbol of the French Revolution and, as such, Bastille Day is still celebrated to date. As far as the 1966 Crisis is concerned, the single most prominent event that can be said to symbolise it is, in the view of many people, the attack on the Lubiri on 24 May 1966.

The need for a definition cannot be over-emphasised. Without a definition of the Crisis and, therefore, in the absence of a scale on which to assess the work, the author may feel a little protected from the critics. But it is unhelpful to today's young people and future generations, let alone non-Ugandan scholars of this period of Uganda's history. Because of the focus it provides, a definition helps the reader to understand, separate and distinguish the causes, incidents, coincidences and consequences of the Crisis. We, therefore, venture to offer one.

Assuming nothing, let us begin with the key word, *crisis*, itself. *Webster's New World Dictionary* defines a crisis, among others, as "a time of great danger or trouble, whose outcome decides whether possible bad consequences will follow." But even more specific for our present situation, *The Concise Oxford Dictionary of Current English* defines a crisis as a "time of danger or suspense in politics, commerce, etc." With that in mind, the 1966 political crisis may be defined as follows:

The 1966 Uganda political crisis was the struggle for the unity of Uganda as a result of the failure of Uganda's political institutions and actors to peacefully resolve the conflict between the Central Government of Uganda and the federal government of the Buganda Kingdom over the jurisdiction, as between the Buganda Kingdom and the Bunyoro Kingdom, the counties of Buyaga and Bugangazzi should fall under.

More broadly, the Crisis was the test of the idea whether the state of Uganda, created by a foreign power out of pre-existing, competing and sometimes warring native nations, could long hold together in one state after the departure of the foreign power. That will be the answer to the question, *what was the 1966 Uganda political crisis about?* long after the names Obote and Mutesa have faded into the mists of time.

The test of the endurance of the country created came when the inter-territorial dispute between two native nations of Buganda and Bunyoro had to be resolved. Would it be resolved peacefully without risk to the continued existence of the country or violently, but the country still escape a break-up? Uganda was lucky that the latter happened, although at a high cost. That is what this writing is about.

More than half a century later, the 1966 Crisis remains one of the most important, perplexing, misunderstood, and divisive historical landmarks we can call to mind since Uganda gained independence. As manifested in the constant demands for *ebyaffe* (what belongs to us) by Buganda, its ramifications continue to impact our politics to this day. For, as a country, we have not yet been able to put it to bed.

Did the Crisis just happen without cause? Was it an accident? Was it inevitable no matter the best efforts and intentions of the human agents? What was/were its cause/causes? Was it brought about by the mistakes and miscalculations of one or both of the main protagonists? Was it fabricated with ill intensions?

Each of the two rival camps—that of Kabaka/President Mutesa on one hand, and that of Prime Minister Obote on the other—views the cause of the Crisis and assigns responsibility for it entirely to the other. For reasons mysterious to the other, the adherents of each hold tenaciously onto emotions fed by what they regard as facts. This work is not intended to whitewash the dark spots of one and/or blacken the bright points of the other. It will be as even-handed to each as much as human foibles allow. Of course, there are moderates in both camps. However, for inexplicable reasons, moderates rarely raise their collective voice high enough to be heard and taken into consideration. So far as UPC itself is concerned, it has been unexpectedly and uncharacteristically shy over the years to present its position in a vigorous manner. We are now faced with a national psychological fix. And as Kennedy (1962) puts it, "An attitude bred into peoples' bones and a part of their national tradition dies hard" (p. 27). What Kennedy called "an attitude ... and a part of their national tradition" may also be referred to as a national historical security or insecurity.

The England, which Kennedy was writing about, was that between the two World Wars (1918-1939). Being an island nation, which for hundreds of years had not been occupied by a foreign power, England had formed a national attitude or a sense of historical security that all it needed to guarantee its security against external enemies was a strong navy, thinking that a threat to its security could only come by way of an attack from the sea. That national historical security prevented it from contemplating air war by an attack from the skies. It did not realise its vulnerability from fighter planes raining down on it bombs in air strikes. Consequently, it was slow to adapt to changed warfare by developing a strong, modern airforce and defences by building sufficient fighter aircraft and anti-aircraft guns and recruiting and training personnel to operate them during the inter-war period. That was one sense in which

In the Beginning

England had "slept" while Germany, which had been defeated in the First World War, was building a formidable airforce. That island mentality is today said to explain England's over cautious attitude in its formulation of its immigration policies.

Germany, although in its present configuration a much younger nation than England, having been clubbed together by Chancellor Otto von Bismarck as recently as 1870, has its own traditional attitude. The hyper-inflation it suffered after World War I formed its attitude as a nation towards economic policies. They are examined from the view point of their likely impact on inflation and unemployment.

Russia's attitude to national security is also shaped by its history. Napoleon's French army in 1812 and Hitler's German army in 1941 and the Poles and Turks before and in between having been stopped at the very gates of Moscow, Russia is very careful to ensure that the states which surround it and which it regards as its buffer do not fall under the control of an expansionary Western European state. That historical insecurity, probably more than anything else, goes to explain the psychology behind Russia's annexation of Crimea in 2014.

The Buganda nation, which pre-dates the Uganda state by over 500 years, has grown an attitude of jealously guarding its kingdom, culture, and language. While it is ready to absorb new traditions and foreign words, it is fearful of itself being assimilated. Thus, it approaches with great caution proposals for wider geographical and closer political integration with other entities. Witness the resistance to the colonial period proposal for East African federation and the introduction of Swahili as the national language. Anyone who wishes to introduce new policies which might conflict with an ingrained national attitude would be advised to proceed with care.

Indeed, people have long memories. Eighty years after the end of the American Civil War, when President Harry Truman invited his Missouri-born and bred mother to the Whitehouse, she was informed upon arrival that she was going to sleep in the Lincoln bed. In that case, she replied, she would rather sleep on the floor. Missouri, her home state, was one of the rebel states which fought to secede from the United States during the civil war in which Lincoln led the successful union government. She had not forgiven him for his leadership or the political party he belonged to, the Republican Party, 80 years (1865-1945) after the war had come to an end. There are people in parts of Uganda who are like Truman's mother with regard to Obote and, to a certain extent, UPC, so many years after the 1966 events. To them, the attack on the Lubiri by Obote and UPC is still in progress, being fought in their heads.

Apart from the fact that it fell under the British sphere of influence as agreed by the colonising powers during the 1884 Berlin Conference in which they partitioned Africa among themselves, Uganda did not exist at the time as a territorial entity for Britain to colonise or protect. Starting with the kingdom of Buganda, mispronounced as *Uganda*, as was handed down to them by the Arabs, the British, through conquest of or contracts with neighbouring kingdoms and chiefdoms, put together an entity they called Uganda. Uganda was, thus, made and not born. The formal and effective colonisation of Uganda, therefore, started under the 1900 Buganda Agreement between the kingdom of Buganda and the British government.

The territory presently known as the Republic of Uganda did not assume its current shape and size until about 1926. It appears that under the 1900 Agreement, Buganda Kingdom had no veto power as to what Britain might do or not do on Buganda territory. So, Britain, the colonial power, established its institutions and installations on land reserved for itself as crown land or land leased from Baganda *mailo* land owners within Buganda territory. In effect, crown land and the land the colonial government had leased in Buganda was not part of Buganda territory. To compound matters further, in terms of the workforce, many Baganda were appointed as local chiefs outside Buganda and many Baganda and non-Baganda were recruited to work within and outside Buganda as Ugandan civil servants.

Buganda was, thus, incorporated into, and became intertwined with Uganda without the general Buganda population being aware of the integration, let alone its implications, and with the Mengo establishment making no effort to make it wiser. However, this is not to say that the Mengo establishment was not aware of the implications of the agreement in regard to the position of Buganda in Uganda. Their principal concern was over land, which the 1900 Agreement had generously taken care of.

In other words, Buganda seems to have been smuggled into Uganda or Uganda smuggled into Buganda, depending on one's point of view. Buganda could not get out of Uganda, even though it has attempted, and Uganda would not let Buganda out. It has not been an easy relationship, especially after independence, as future events would show. Buganda had to be coaxed to remain part of Uganda as Uganda moved forward into independence. And when the time came when it felt that its interests were under threat within a united Uganda, its Lukiiko reputedly passed a resolution expelling Uganda's Central Government from its territory.

The term *Mengo establishment* or *Mengo* in short, where the context so permits, refers to that nebulous group of people in Buganda who, after the 1900 Agreement, were thought to influence or represent the views and took themselves or were deemed to be the custodians of the interests of the Buganda

Kingdom and its people in all matters cultural, political, and economic. The ordinary Baganda have a name for this group; they call them *Ab'e Mengo* (the powerful and influential people of Mengo). Like so many Luganda expressions, the phrase carries certain nuances and, if spoken rather than written, one has to be extremely alert to detect whether the inflection in the voice employed conveys respect and reverence, exasperation and resentment, or plain resignation and indifference. Mengo is also the name of a place which has been the political capital of the Buganda Kingdom since about 1885.

According to Owen Jones (2014), the phrase "the Establishment" was brought into common usage and turned into a household phrase in Britain by Henry Fairlie in a 1955 newspaper article. He defined it as including not only "the centres of official power—though they certainly are part of it"—but "the whole matrix of official and social relations within which power is exercised." More concisely, Owen Jones writes,

> In other words, the Establishment comprised a set of well-connected people who knew each other, mixed in the same circles and had each other's backs. It was not based on official, legal or formal arrangements, but rather on subtle social relationships. (*The Guardian*, 2014)

Every society has an establishment—that segment of people who influence decisions and set the acceptable and unacceptable norms within that society. The Mengo establishment referred to herein became entrenched as a result of the 1900 land allocation in Buganda under that year's agreement. The chiefs of the time and their offspring became the new establishment. It set out to perpetuate itself by, among other things, founding such schools as King's College, Buddo, to impart European education to their sons, who would succeed them as chiefs, and Gayaza High School to prepare the girls who would be the wives to their sons and produce sons who would themselves become chiefs. Of course, that blueprint did not work out perfectly, interlopers having found their way into those schools or founding their own. Since the establishment is not static but evolves by enlisting new categories of people while others drift off, the prevailing Mengo establishment must have changed in composition and spheres of influence from that we have described.

Suffice it to say that it was this establishment which determined which national leader deserved to be *Gandanised* — to be co-opted into the establishment and assimilated as a Muganda by being given a Kiganda name, if he was from outside Buganda but was deemed to be serving the interests of Buganda — or to be *de-Gandanised* — to be stripped of Buganda kinship, and "assigned" another not one's own, if he was a Muganda who was perceived as representing, espousing or promoting interests in conflict with Buganda's. This usually involved playing around the sound or spelling of the subject's name. Thus, for a time, beloved Milton Obote, a Lango, was called *Bwete*, thus "turning" him into a Muganda, and as for out-of-favour Benedicto Kiwanuka, a Muganda, failing to get a fitting twist to his name or coin a new one, they settled for calling him a *Luo of Kenyan origin*. Muwanga, a Muganda, was named *Owanga*, a Ugandan originating from the northern part of the country. Binaisa, another Muganda, became *Bin Isa*, an Arab.

To the establishment, the bottom line was: if you take a political position critical to the interests of Mengo, you are a Muganda if it is favourable. Otherwise, you are not a Muganda. The new name given to a political leader by the establishment is, thus, a badge of honour or dishonour, according to whether one is *Gandanised* or *de-Gandanised*. It is also a certificate of arrival: a confirmation that the person is now regarded as sufficiently influential in society to swing things one way or another; one of the shakers and movers. It is analogous, to a person being depicted in a cartoon form in a newspaper. It is an assumption that the person so portrayed is sufficiently prominent in society to be identified even in a caricature form.

It appears that the business of looking at politicians as either heroes to be assimilated or pariahs to be disowned is not a fashion that is about to run out. What is more, this country appears to have developed a political norm which assumes that a leader cannot be a Ugandan nationalist and pursue Buganda's interests at the same time and vice versa. It is a norm that is extremely restricting to an emerging political leader and, as such, may have excluded able men and women from participating in elective politics. Such a leader takes a huge political risk equivalent to a hen which decides to swallow a black ant *(okutunda omwoyo nga enkoko emira ensanafu)*. It is what made Abu Mayanja, a Muganda politician, declare in the 1950s when he decided to pursue pro-Uganda policies that he had crossed the Rubicon. Crossing the Rubicon is a metaphor for making a commitment involving high risk or reaching a point of no return.

So far as the 1966 Crisis is concerned, for most Baganda, there is no nuance: the ungrateful Obote, and Obote alone, was entirely to blame for it. For us, there is only nuance: there was enough blame to go around. And that is a taboo being broken. But it is a taboo that we cannot help breaking, propelled, as we are, by a hurricane-like, naked-truth-searching force inside me that we cannot resist.

We draw comfort from the fact that, factually, on this matter we are not saying anything Ugandans who follow our politics do not already know. The only difference we are probably making is to dare to say what others only dare to think. The Baganda invented a saying to guard against hypocrisy and sycophancy. They say: *Ensowera ekwagala y'ekugwa ku bbwa*. The literal meaning is that it is the fly that loves you which lands on your wound (the fly's landing on the wound, although hurtful, is a friendly reminder to the sufferer to attend to the wound). The deep meaning is that it is only a true friend that will tell you the bitter truth or give you sincere advice.

Being a Ugandan nationalist and a Buganda nationalist should not be seen as naturally and mutually exclusive. A person aspiring to be a leader, especially one from Buganda, should never be made to feel that he or she has to choose between the two. But truth be told, as of today, a serious Muganda politician walks a tighter political rope than his colleague from elsewhere. It is a burden he can do without.

At independence, partitioning Uganda into Buganda and some other entity or entities by whatever name, as was done between India and Pakistan, was not even contemplated, although the perception remained in Mengo that Uganda was an intruder in Buganda. For example, in October 1960, the Buganda Lukiiko passed a resolution that on 31st December that year Buganda would become an independent state as it was before the 19th century agreements it had signed with the British government. The colonial power ignored the resolution. A rumour has been around for years that on 8 October 1962 the Duke of Kent, who represented the British government at the ceremony of Uganda's independence, handed over to the Mengo government, instruments terminating all agreements that Britain had signed with Buganda. This date has been sporadically celebrated in Mengo since the restoration of Buganda Kingdom to convey to the Baganda that Buganda's independence had been restored before Buganda joined hands with the rest of the other parts of Uganda to form an independent Uganda the following day, that is, 9th October 1962.

It is a narrative put out to emphasise the patronage and protection, erroneously called a special relationship between Buganda and Britain. We were unable to come up with incontrovertible evidence that the duke passed any documents to Buganda officials. One person who was a news reporter with *Uganda Argus*, the leading English paper at the time, gave us the benefit of his memory, although he preferred not to be named. He was present in Bulange when the Lukiiko deliberated the pending independence in the presence of the duke. He was also present in the palace at the dinner hosted in honour of the duke at the Kabaka's palace afterwards. He did not remember any documents being handed to the Buganda officials. On the other hand, a renowned historian, who attended neither function, promised to search in his archives for evidence to confirm to us this event. He had not returned to us by the time of going to press.

The notion that Buganda was special is the wider context within which the 1966 political Crisis may also be viewed. It is worth noting in passing that the psychological and mental confusion among the ordinary Baganda regarding the position of president of Uganda and that of the Kabaka of Buganda, was not helped by nomenclature. When the Arabs were making their way from the East African coast into the hinterland during the middle of the nineteenth century, they asked the people living on the eastern part of Lake Victoria, as it later came to be known, what the land lying on the western side of the lake was called. "Uganda", they replied, for they were unable to say "Buganda." And the people? "Waganda", they said. The British colonialists who followed the Arabs adopted the names conferred by the Arabs and applied them to the rest of the country. Up to today, the Swahili-speaking Kenyans and Tanzanians refer to Ugandans as Waganda, and not everybody in Uganda is amused, some less so than others. Maybe a mistake was made at independence not to give a new name to the new country moving forward.

Like any particular historical event, it may appear difficult to nail down with precision the root cause and when the 1966 Uganda political crisis started. While I acknowledge the uncertainty of pinpointing the causes of some events, there is little doubt in my mind that the genesis of the Crisis goes back to 1897 when, following the defeat of Omukama Kabalega of Bunyoro Kingdom by the advancing British colonial power with the assistance of Buganda chiefs, some counties were hived off from the Bunyoro Kingdom and added to the Buganda Kingdom territory as a form of reward to Buganda and as a penalty to Bunyoro. These were the aforementioned Lost Counties.

There is a school of thought which holds that the Lost Counties were not the main cause of the Crisis; that the importance of the Lost Counties in the Crisis is overblown; that of equal, if not more importance, was the power struggle between Milton Obote, the prime minister and president of UPC, the senior partner party of the coalition government in power on the one hand, and Grace Ibingira, the party's secretary general on the other. This school of thought contends that by the time the Crisis broke out, Buganda's concerns had shifted from the Lost Counties to its federal status in Uganda. This, of course, ignores the fact that the federal issue had been resolved in the 1962 Independence Constitution by the time the referendum on the Lost Counties was held.

It is argued, first, that even at the London independence negotiations conferences, Buganda's major concerns were the position of its Kabaka and Buganda's place (the federal status) in an independent Uganda, not the Lost Counties. We are not comfortable with this argument. It tends to reflect two things about the Buganda delegation or team to the conferences, neither of which is flattering. It shows, first, that Buganda was so self-absorbed that it could not appreciate the demands of other entities with which it was about to form a partnership in a new Uganda. Alternatively, having realised that Buganda being part of Uganda moving forward was unstoppable, it adopted the proverbial ostrich approach to solving an intractable problem by hiding its head in the sand. Lwanga-Lunyiigo's (2007) view is far less charitable. He says, "The Baganda seem to suffer from self-delusion; the 'Lost Counties' issue illustrates this very well" (p. 106). We think the Buganda leaders were better than that. As we will show later, they thought genuinely that they would skirt around the problem after independence.

We are grateful to Professor Phares Mutibwa for enlarging upon the UPC power struggle argument and for giving his permission to reproduce a private note he wrote to us in the course of this writing. He wrote:

> The Lost Counties were not the principal cause of the 1966 Crisis: it was incidental to (or part of) the fundamental cause of the Crisis, namely: the political rivalry between Obote and Ibingira. The role of the Lost Counties was to draw Kabaka Mutesa and Mengo and Ibingira's UPC faction together to fight Obote. The basic issue of the Crisis was the rivalry between Obote and Ibingira for the leadership of the UPC and, by extension, for the leadership of Uganda. The Lost Counties issue was a catalyst in bringing Mengo and Ibingira's group together to confront Obote and his group. There were of course, other players in the plot,

such as Ocheng whose motion was aimed at bringing down Obote (not because of the referendum but because of taking political leadership from him and handing it over to Ibingira's group). In the end, when Ibingira's group lost the battle to Obote, so did Mutesa and Mengo who thus became the victims of a plot which had been hatched outside of Mengo [as an institution] and as early as when Ibingira replaced John Kakonge as UPC's Secretary General in Gulu in 1964. Such are the ironies of history. (Mutibwa, Private note to the author, 2018)

With all deference to the eminent professor, we venture to disagree with him for a number of reasons. In terms of the weight of the parties and causes involved, the UPC leadership rivalry does not compare with the Lost Counties. The Lost Counties pitted two ancient kingdoms against each other. They concerned land and territory, a matter over which wars have been fought since the emergence of nation states. It involved the surrendering of territory by one kingdom to another, something Nsubuga (2013) has rather graphically described as amputation, if done voluntarily. The Lost Counties controversy had a king of a kingdom and president of the country on one side and a prime minister of the country on the other. Let us have a little test. If a film were made of the Crisis, is it conceivable that the Ibingira character would be the lead actor and that of Mutesa the supporting cast? It is difficult to imagine Kabaka Mutesa being a junior partner to UPC Secretary General Ibingira and Mutesa's interests being subordinate to those of Ibingira. In terms of the longevity of the conflict, the issue of the Lost Counties had been simmering since 1897. The Obote-Ibingira rivalry surfaced only in 1964 and by 1966 it had been snuffed out.

The importance of the Lost Counties to both Buganda and Bunyoro cannot be overemphasised or underrated. In the long-run, they did not represent a mere loss or gain of territory but had serious political, economic, social, and cultural overtones.

Although it was true that Buganda Kingdom had in the past gained its size at the expense of Bunyoro Kingdom through war, this particular war in which it gained the Lost Counties was different. It was not even a genuine conflict between Buganda and Bunyoro. The past wars between the two kingdoms were purely indigenous where they fought each other and at the end of it territory borders were redrawn and other war bounty changed hands. The circumstances of this war were completely unprecedented. In this war, Britain, a colonising power foreign to both kingdoms and from outside Africa—having duped Buganda to surrender to colonialism dressed up as protectionism—had turned its sights to the neigbouring Bunyoro Kingdom. Bunyoro had put up a muscular resistance against Britain's machinations. To subjugate it, Britain enlisted the support of Buganda chiefs, and not Mwanga their king whom it had helped dethrone for seeing through its duplicity.

Mwanga himself, being the victim of the treasonous acts of his chiefs, had joined his brother-king, *Omukama* Kabalega, in militarily resisting the colonisation of their kingdoms by the British. It was their misfortune that they were captured in Lango region—where a local chief had sheltered them—and handed over to the British by a Muganda chief. They were exiled to the remote Seychelles, a collection of islands in the Indian Ocean, which Britain had colonised earlier.

While Mwanga and his brother-king Kabalega fought on the side of the resisters, the Buganda chiefs worked as the enablers of colonialism. This not having been the usual war between the two kingdoms to capture territory from each other, left on their own, it is doubtful that Mwanga and Kabalega would have agreed to any surrender of territory from one to the other. It was the treasonous act of the Buganda chiefs against their king that led to the expansion of Buganda and eventually its contraction. In the end, it was under the reign of Chwa, the two-year-old son of Mwanga, in an unprecedented move in Buganda, whom the chiefs had installed as Kabaka to replace his still living father, when, in 1897, the disputed counties were added to Buganda. The addition of these counties to Buganda meant that they formed part of the territory covered by the 1900 Buganda Agreement in which land was distributed to the sitting Buganda chiefs and other notables. It is, therefore, not surprising that the agreement took the form it did by rewarding the chiefs so generously with land.

Buganda Kingdom may not have had a deliberate policy to assimilate the Banyoro into Buganda, but all major practical moves pointed to that. Buganda chiefs were appointed to administer the two counties. The Luganda language became the new language of administration and school instruction, which the Banyoro had to learn. The new land owners extracted taxes from the Banyoro in form of *busuulu*. In order to gain access to certain amenities, many Banyoro were forced or found it profitable to change their Kinyoro names and to adopt Kiganda names and cultural mores. All those things were again, both emotional and material, to one group and a loss to another. Those who gained from the situation were not willing to forego their gain and those who lost were insisting on having their loss reversed. That made the Lost Counties a hot-button issue up to the holding of the 1964 referendum to resolve their placement.

It is one of those strange twists of history that for the first time, on this occasion, Buganda gained territory from a war not endorsed by its king and in which he had actively fought on the side of the losing kingdom. It is also the ultimate irony of history that Mutesa would risk his throne and indeed kingdom over territory, calling it spoils of war as he did, acquired from Bunyoro in a fake war, which his grandfather, Mwanga, would in all probability not have demanded, taken, and kept given those circumstances. It is also ironical that the last expansion of Buganda was the result of the chiefs' betrayal of their king. The Lost Counties were not acquired from Bunyoro under the universally recognised Right of Conquest.

That territory lost and acquired in unprecedented circumstances and came to be known as the Lost Counties came to haunt Buganda and Uganda for years. It nearly caused a breakup of the young nation even before it learnt to walk. So far as Buganda was concerned, the Lost Counties were a gift which nearly caused the destruction of the recipient forever.

The power struggle within UPC was, therefore, the opportunistic cause of the Crisis in the sense that it rode on the back of the more fundamental quarrel between the Uganda Central Government represented by the person of Milton Obote, the prime minister, and the kingdom of Buganda, represented by the person of Edward Mutesa, the Kabaka of Buganda and president of Uganda, over the placement of the Lost Counties.

In the months leading to the 2016 presidential and general elections in Uganda, rumour was rife, and a perception was gained in some political circles that Amama Mbabazi, the then secretary general of National Resistance Movement (NRM), the ruling party, was entertaining a desire to assume the chairmanship of that party. Consequently, to thwart the realisation of that ambition, his opponents within the party took to manoeuvring him out of his political base: the position of secretary general. Political pundits, amateur and experts alike, opined that the situation was reminiscent of the 1964 power struggle within UPC and, thus reasoned that it might lead to the re-enactment of the same result of facilitating a major convulsion in government and in the country as happened in 1966.

Those who hold the view that it was the power struggle within UPC that caused the 1966 Crisis thought at the time that the wrangles within the NRM in 2015-2016 vindicated that argument. As it happened, the NRM power struggle did not lead to a crisis in government. But the two struggles were quite not comparable. Apart from the fact that the NRM secretary general, Amama Mbabazi, and the NRM chairman, Yoweri Museveni, had ceased to get along, just like the UPC secretary general, Grace Ibingira, and that party president, Milton Obote, had, there was no justification for drawing parallels between the two struggles.

To begin with, the struggle between Ibingira and Obote was ideological, with Ibingira being capitalist-orientated and Obote leaning towards socialism. The hegemonic or superpowers—capitalist America and communist Soviet Union—deeming it too dangerous to fight each other directly, had devised a practice of pitting the leaders of the newly independent nations, one against the other, fighting proxy wars over ideologies they hardly understood or would not have cared for if they did. These superpowers took an interest in the struggle on either side of the two protagonists. On the other hand, the struggle between Amama Mbabazi and Yoweri Museveni had no ideological or political philosophy content whatsoever. There were no ideological camps involved on either side, in my view. Each of these two individuals just wanted power for himself and for its own sake, with Amama Mbabazi thinking that having waited long enough, it was his turn to take the driving seat of the party and, thus, occupy the presidency of the country.

Secondly, within UPC, if Ibingira had succeeded in having Obote voted out as leader and getting himself elected in his place, he would immediately have become the prime minister in accordance with Westminster norms. With NRM, Mbabazi was contesting for nomination as the party presidential candidate. It would, therefore, be stretching matters a bit to liken the two struggles by suggesting that the one between Mbabazi and Museveni could have led to a 1966-like crisis because, in the first place, the Obote-Ibingira contest did not cause the Crisis. But let that not unduly detain us.

Despite Mutesa's protests to the contrary, a close reading of his writing reveals the true basis of his quarrel to have been with the man "who was determined to destroy my kingdom" (Mutesa, 1967, p. 188). Add: "by dismembering it." And he was talking about the Lost Counties, not Ibingira's place in UPC! Certainly, in embarking on the project to remove Obote, Mutesa did not risk his own position as Kabaka and the existence of his kingdom solely to make Ibingira president of UPC and prime minister of Uganda.

Lwanga-Lunyiigo (2007) devotes a full chapter on the Lost Counties in his book, *The Struggle for Land in Buganda 1888-2005*. He appears to regard the issue of the Lost Counties as central to the Crisis and the post-independence history of Uganda. He reports that a proposal had been made in the 1930s to offer Buganda the Kagera River as her south-western boundary in compensation for the return of Mubende District (which partly comprised Buyaga and Bugangazzi) to Bunyoro. In his view, if that proposal had been followed up, it would have solved the Lost Counties problem. Lwanga-Lunyiigo concludes:

> If it [the proposal] had been [effected] it would have been very good for Buganda, Bunyoro, and Uganda as a whole, because we would have been spared the

pains of the early 1960s, of the transfer of Bugangaizi and Buyaga counties to Bunyoro, a transfer that created a big rift between Buganda and Bunyoro and threatened the stability of the newly independent Uganda. (p. 102)

Postlethwaite in Lwanga-Lunyiigo (2007, p. 100) admits that, "The inclusion of this area ("the Lost Counties") in the Buganda Kingdom is considered by many to have been one of the greatest blunders we (British) committed in the past. . ." Postlethwaite was the district commissioner of Bunyoro between August 1927 and July 1928. Bunyoro took the transfer of the Lost Counties to Buganda as a punishment imposed on Omukama Kabalega and the people of Bunyoro-Kitara for having instigated a war against British invaders. It was at the same time a reward to Buganda for collaborating with the British (Barungi, 2011).

To Buganda, the demand for the Lost Counties was a provocative and uncalled-for reawakening of an issue that had long gone to bed. But Bunyoro had never forgotten them. It had never let the world forget that it had not forgotten them. It had never stopped claiming them. On the other hand, Buganda regarded their gain as legitimate war spoils. "To the victor, we had thought, the spoils...." Mutesa (1967, p. 165) wrote reflecting Buganda's attitude at the London independence conferences when the matter came up.

Whether one is considering Obote's relations with Mutesa or with Ibingira, the end of 1964, after the referendum over the Lost Counties, was the turning point. In many ways with regard to the relations of those three personalities, one can talk of their stance "before and after the referendum," as will be shown.

The power struggle within UPC facilitated the conspiracy between Ibingira and Mutesa. It enabled Mutesa and Ibingira to identify each other as allies in their respective struggles against

Obote. Without any doubt, acting alone, Mutesa would have found it harder to confront Obote and it would probably have taken longer, if ever, to bring together the conditions which brought about the clashes, both political and military, that occurred in 1966.

Mutesa's grievances against Obote, linked directly to the Lost Counties, his risks in case the plot to remove Obote failed, and indeed his loss when it did fail, were of far greater magnitude than those of Ibingira linked to the power struggle would probably have been. To argue that the intra-UPC power struggle was the cause of the Crisis is to reduce to near oblivion the role of Sir Edward Mutesa in the Crisis. And that cannot be the case.

Let us consider a sample of the defining events of the Crisis and ask a few questions. As will be seen later: Did the people of Buganda dig up the culverts in the roads; cut trees to block highways; attack police stations in Buganda because Ibingira and Obote were competing for UPC leadership? Did the Baganda World War II veterans troop into Lubiri and risk their lives because they supported and wanted to defend Ibingira or Obote against the other? Why was there no violence and shedding of blood in the strongholds of UPC which were in fact outside Buganda? The violence in Buganda and, therefore, the demonstration of the Crisis arose out of the outcome of the referendum in the Lost Counties in which the residents chose to return to Bunyoro Kingdom to the chagrin of Buganda Kingdom and its king.

It is also true that Ibingira and four other UPC cabinet colleagues, were the immediate victims of the Crisis, having been locked up for allegedly attempting a coup against the government in which they served. To that extent, it can be conceded that the power struggle within UPC was one of the causes of the Crisis but not its fundamental or root cause. But to argue that the Lost Counties were the cause of the Crisis is not to say that there were no supplementary causes, as is demonstrated herein. But those merely fuelled an already simmering crisis.

Playing the devil's advocate aside, we are convinced that independent of each other, the power struggle within UPC and the result of the referendum on the Lost Counties could not have sparked off the 1966 political crisis. That has given some commentators a false belief that they can confidently and randomly pick either of them as the cause of the Crisis.

The outcome of the 1964 UPC delegates' conference, which started off the plots to remove Obote from UPC leadership, combined with Buganda's response to the referendum held later that same year, set in motion the train of the events ending in the commotion in the Lubiri in May 1966.

Be that as it may, to avoid diversionary and unnecessary debate, we submit that for the purposes of this work, it does not matter whether the Lost Counties were the single cause or just one of several causes of the Crisis. The weight of the part each played is a matter of individual opinion which should, of course, be supported by evidence. That they played any part at all should be reason enough to justify their examination in these pages. That is the basis that informs this work and on which we intend to proceed.

Chapter 2

LANCASTER HOUSE GRAND SETTLEMENT

The most overt preparation by the colonial power for Uganda's independence was the 1955 agreement which made it possible for Kabaka Edward Mutesa to return from deportation in Britain. The preparations went into higher gear in early 1961 when representatives of all existing districts, political parties, together with Buganda, Bunyoro, Ankore, Tooro, and the Territory of Busoga were invited to London by Britain to discuss the future form of government of Uganda.

At the two London conferences prior to Uganda's independence—the first held from 18 September to 9 October 1961 and known as the Lancaster House Conference and the second held from 12 June to 30 June 1962, and commonly referred to as the Marlborough House Conference—at which the terms under which Uganda would become an independent, sovereign state were agreed upon, the issue of the counties which had been transferred from Bunyoro to Buganda by the colonial powers in 1897 came up. Whereas, to Buganda, the main issue at these conferences was the relationship between Buganda and the rest of Uganda, to Bunyoro, the *Lost Counties* were the main issue on whose resolution acceptance of independence by Bunyoro rotated.

Bunyoro wanted them reinstated and insisted that the issue be resolved before Uganda was granted independence.

Buganda wanted them to remain part of Buganda and regarded the matter as non-negotiable.

A year after going into exile in London, Kabaka Mutesa of Buganda, who did not sit at the negotiation table but stayed in the background for consultation by the Buganda delegation during the negotiations, gave significant insights into what happened during that conference. He writes:

> The issue of the lost counties suddenly returned to cause trouble. They had been a problem ever since 1897. Formerly, they had belonged to the Banyoro, and as in so far as they were inhabited were still largely inhabited by Banyoro. Their position as part of Buganda had been confirmed in the 1900 Agreement. From time to time ever since, there had been agitation for us to return them, and the British had set up three commissions, which in turn failed to reach a definite conclusion. As land and our traditional enemy were involved, naturally the Baganda felt passionately. . . Emotion was still so high on both sides that there was no real chance of a solution; but it did seem possible that it might break up the Conference. . . ..
>
> There was a stage when it was clear we had little to gain and he (Kintu, the Buganda Katikkiro who headed the Buganda delegation to the conference) wished to boycott further talks. [In the end] It was agreed that there should be a referendum in not less than three years (of Uganda attaining Independence), if the Prime Minister wished it. The Banyoro were not pleased. We (the Baganda) were not pleased. Obote, who had wanted the difficulty settled without involving him, was not pleased. It was the best that could be done, and with the problem yet again deferred [Emphasis added] we could go on to other topics. (Mutesa, 1967, pp. 165-166)

Prime Minister Obote wanted Uganda to gain independence as one united nation (a statement consciously repeated in this work in order to emphasise what guided Obote's politics at that time) and, for reasons we need not go into here, it is not beyond credibility that a significant section of the British administration was anxious to rid themselves of their colonial responsibility as soon as possible. Hence, the compromise that made independence possible at the time it came. It was resolved that the place of the Lost Counties would be determined after independence by the people of those counties through a referendum. It was a major concession on the part of the Bunyoro leadership to agree to confine the referendum to only the two counties of Buyaga and Bugangazzi thereby implicitly abandoning its long-standing claim to four other counties of Buwekula, Singo, Bulemezi and Buluuli. That was, in our view, one of Bunyoro's greatest contributions to breaking the independence stalemate. However, that compromise had within it the seed of a future contest which the parties involved had no premonition of.

Since so much of this work revolves around that compromise, it is useful to set out early the relevant law in which it was captured. Section 26 of The Uganda (Independence) Order-in-Council, 1962 provides:

> 26. (1) In order to ascertain the wishes of the inhabitants of the county of Buyaga and of the county of Bugangazzi as to the territory of Uganda in which each of those counties should be included a referendum shall be held in accordance with the following provisions:
>
> > (a) the referendum shall take place on such date, not being earlier than 9th October 1964, as the National Assembly may, by resolution, appoint;

(b) the persons entitled to vote in the referendum in a county shall be the persons entitled to vote in any constituency established in that county under section 46 of the Constitution of Uganda;

(c) the questions submitted to a voter in the referendum in a county shall be such as to ascertain whether the voter wishes the county:
   i. to form part of the Kingdom of Buganda; or
   ii. to form part of the Kingdom of Bunyoro; or
   iii. to be established as a separate District of Uganda;

(d) Subject to the foregoing provisions of this sub-section, the referendum shall be organised and conducted in such manner as Parliament may prescribe.

Sub-section (2) provided for enacting a law to alter the boundaries of the territories in case the voters cast their votes in favour of the county forming part of the kingdom of Bunyoro or in favour of the county being established as a separate district of Uganda in order to give effect to the vote of that majority.

With that postponement of the resolution of the disputed counties, the emerging leaders of independent Uganda, Obote as prime minister and, later, Mutesa as president, grabbed the poisoned chalice they were handed by the departing British. Little did they know that it was destined to destroy both of them and hobble the country they were about to take over for years to come. Within ten years of taking the instruments of power, both men had lost office acrimoniously. In the end, both men lived the last of their lives in political exile, feeding on the bounty of others, and brooding over visions of glory gone by. And Uganda has never known true unity and stability.

For leaving the problem of the Lost Counties unresolved, it is tempting to conclude, given its track elsewhere, that the departing British were playing according to their well-practised script. For that was exactly what they had done in India where, after administering it for 300 years and aware of the age-old antagonism between Hindus and Muslims, they beat a hasty retreat in 1947. That was after a shabby partition of that territory into Pakistan, consisting of East Pakistan (today another independent state called Bangladesh) and West Pakistan (largely for Muslims), with India (dominantly for Hindus) geographically lying between them. Ever since the partition and the departure of Britain, the history of India and Pakistan has been that of wars and tension between the two nations over the territory of Kashmir which lies along their common border.

Another example: The British were aware of the conflict between the Greek and the Turkish communities of the island of Cyprus. Yet, they granted it independence without resolving their differences first. It took the United Nations years to establish an uneasy peace between the two communities. Cameroon and Nigeria, Ghana, Togo and, most prominent, Palestine in 1947 are other examples of countries Britain left with disputed boundaries.

However, in the case of Uganda, the story was different. It is not accurate to say that Britain simply walked away. Britain did not only recognise that there was a bitter dispute between the kingdom of Buganda and the kingdom of Bunyoro over six counties, collectively called "the Lost Counties," along their boundary, but attempted to resolve it before its departure. It had long grappled with the problem, which was its creation in the first place, and, unable to resolve it as it feared imposing a solution, it had placed it in the 'Too Hard' tray in the hope it would go away. It did not. As Uganda was cruising towards independence, the issue of the Lost Counties raised its head once again and threatened to derail the process.

In the dying months of its rule in Uganda, the British government mounted a last-minute effort to resolve the issue by setting up a commission and appointed Lord Molson to chair it, to advise on the difficult dispute between the kingdoms of Buganda and Bunyoro over the Lost Counties. The commission, in its report, recommended that the government exercise either of the following:

(a) The transfer of the two counties of Buyaga and Bugangazzi (in which the Banyoro were in a large majority) from Buganda to Bunyoro (the Omukama of Bunyoro having conceded to the other four counties remaining in Buganda), "if the two Kingdoms could be brought to agree to it".

(b) The holding of a referendum by the independent Uganda government in the two counties for the residents there to determine whether to remain in Buganda or return to Bunyoro, after independence since there was not enough time for the British Government to conduct it before.

In the event, Buganda was adamant that there should be no transfer of territory. The British government opted for the holding of a referendum in which the residents were to choose either: (1) to stay in Buganda; (2) to return to Bunyoro, or (3) to form a separate district independent of either kingdom.

Against that background, only the most optimistic person would have hoped that the matter of the Lost Counties would end happily. The cohesion of the new nation-state was to be severely tested by the Lost Counties.

Chapter 3

UPC/KY COALITION GOVERNMENT

In April 1962, following the conclusion of the Lancaster Conference which settled the Constitution under which independent Uganda would be governed, parliamentary general elections were held. As to the composition of the new Parliament, Section 37 of the Constitution provided that:

> 37. There shall be a Parliament of Uganda, which shall consist of the President and a National Assembly.

The composition of the National Assembly was, as per Section 38 of the Constitution, as follows:

> 38. (1) The National Assembly shall consist of:
>   (a) eighty-two elected members; and
>   (b) such number of specially elected members, not exceeding nine, as Parliament may prescribe.

However, special provision was made for the election of members of the National Assembly from Buganda. Whereas members from the rest of the country were to be directly elected to represent constituencies as delimited by the National Electoral Commission, those from Buganda were to be elected by an electoral college consisting of the sixty-eight directly elected members of the Buganda Lukiiko—for this purpose referred to as the Legislative Assembly of the Kingdom of

Buganda—and allotted to the constituencies within Buganda delimited by the National Electoral Commission.

With further regard to the members of the National Assembly from Buganda, Section 43 of the Constitution provided:

> 43. (1) of the elected members of the National Assembly, three members shall be elected within Kampala and twenty-one members (hereinafter in this section called "the twenty-one members") shall be elected within the Kingdom of Buganda, exclusive of Kampala.

Part of Schedule 6 to the Constitution laid out the procedure for conducting the election of the twenty-one members by the Legislative Assembly of the Kingdom of Buganda.

The meaning and import of the language above was that the twenty-one members of the National Assembly from Buganda were elected by the directly elected members of the Lukiiko to represent constituencies within Buganda as were to be allotted to them. The people of those constituencies did not directly elect their representatives and probably did not even know who they were. Our research reveals that Obote and UPC did not want Buganda's representatives in Parliament to be indirectly elected but, in the spirit of the alliance, agreed to it so long as the electors themselves, that is the members of the Lukiiko, were elected.

Origin and objective of Kabaka Yekka (KY)

Let us have a brief comment on the origin and objective of *Kabaka Yekka* (KY). The name *Kabaka Yekka* owes its origin to the people of Buganda's apparent hatred of political parties. Around 1961, when political parties were canvassing for political support and recruiting members, a person at a rally in Katwe, a suburb of Kampala, shouted, *"Ffe tetwagala kufugibwa bibiina. Twagala Kabaka yekka!"*; translated as, "We do not want to be ruled by political parties. We want Kabaka only!" Ironically, *Kabaka Yekka* thus became the name and slogan of this political organisation.

As independence came into sight, there were three significant institutional political players in the Ugandan field. Two of them, UPC and DP were political parties in the conventional meaning: they were national in character and coverage, with a branch network and leadership, a constitution and a written manifesto stipulating their objectives. A third, namely KY, was not a political party in the strict sense of the word. It was a movement that was formed by the Mengo establishment to fend off the introduction, formation and consolidation of political parties in Buganda in order to preserve the status quo. It was regional in outlook; its interests being confined to Buganda. It was so fused with the Buganda civil service that the two could not be told apart. For that and other reasons, DP had tried to block its participation in the 1962 general elections to no avail. However, for this work, and for ease of reference, KY is regarded as a political party.

For all its shortcomings, in its hey days, Kabaka Yekka was the only political party whose name gained some fame as a form of greeting among its supporters. It went like this: "One person called out 'Kabaka!' and the other responded with 'Yekka!' and both stuck a forefinger in the air." (Barbara Kimenye in her unpublished book titled *Tales from Mutesa's Palace* serialised in *The Daily Monitor* newspaper starting from 2015).

1962 Elections

The three major political parties at the time which participated in those elections were: UPC, DP, and KY. In Buganda, all the elected members of the Lukiiko, except three, belonged to KY.

This made it easy for the Lukiiko, constituting itself into an electoral college, to elect only KY members for the twenty-one members to represent Buganda in the National Assembly. At the end of the counting of the votes, UPC, the political party led by Milton Obote, had garnered 37 seats; DP, led by Benedicto Kiwanuka, had 24 seats (all elected from outside Buganda), and the Buganda-based KY had 20 seats, the twenty-first going to UPC's Kalule Settala through negotiation between Obote and Mutesa. Consequently, no political party or organisation had obtained enough seats to enable it to singly and independently form a government.

It was a hung Parliament and as such only a coalition of two or more parties could make the formation of a government possible. Consequently, it was the block 21 seats of KY from Buganda, combined with UPC's seats obtained from outside Buganda, which enabled UPC to secure the majority of seats to form a coalition government as the senior partner with Obote as prime minister. As the Constitution permitted, UPC and KY, as coalition partners, gained an additional six, and three seats, respectively, after they had distributed among themselves the nine specially elected member seats. In the end, therefore, UPC had 43 seats, KY had 24, making a majority of 67 for the UPC/KY coalition. So, when Parliament commenced business, DP, which had 24 seats, formed the opposition. That was the arrangement and the relative parliamentary numerical strengths of the political parties in Uganda at independence. Whether there was more to that alliance is a subject we shall return to later when discussing the role of the alliance in the Crisis.

Kabaka Mutesa becomes President Mutesa: The Duelling Roles

When independence was granted, as a temporary arrangement, the governor stayed on as head of state with the designation of governor-general. There was an understanding that within a year, he would be replaced with one of the traditional rulers elected for a term of five years. Like so many things in Uganda's chequered history, the import of this agreement was interpreted differently depending on the side of the question one is on.

Regarding his nomination for election to the post of president, Kabaka Mutesa wrote:

> ... there was little choice either for Obote or me. He was not in a position to snub the Baganda, who would have been enraged if any other ruler were chosen, as the new President would have precedence over the Kabaka even in Buganda. Similarly, it was difficult for me to refuse. (Mutesa, 1967, p. 172)

For those reasons, to the Kabaka and the traditional nationalist Baganda, the election of Mutesa was not only inevitable but any alternative was unthinkable. They could imagine no alternative. Fate did not allow us to see how the protocol issue of precedence would have been handled if, after the expiry of Mutesa's five-year term, a ruler from outside Buganda were elected president.

Following the restoration of the kabakaship as a cultural institution in Buganda in 1993 within the Republic of Uganda with an executive president elected through universal suffrage, that question has been answered. Since 1996, Buganda has consistently overwhelmingly given its vote to a candidate from outside Buganda in preference to Baganda candidates. Why? Is it a case of a profit without honour? It appears to be more the case that the Baganda are subconsciously uncomfortable, for reasons of culture and protocol within Buganda, with a Muganda president. They probably see such an aspiring leader as an interloper, a competitor for the glory and power of their beloved Kabaka.

This innocent or subconscious confusion among many Baganda between Buganda and Uganda in elective politics has bedevilled their decisions at election time for a long time. For instance, a colleague told me that back in 1962, when, as a youth canvassing for votes for DP deep in Masaka District in Buganda Kingdom, his grandmother asked him, *"Naye omukopi ayagala atya okuba kabaka?* (But how can a commoner aspire to be a king?)" By "a commoner," the grandmother meant Benedicto Kiwanuka, the leader of DP who would have become prime minister of Uganda if his party had won the election. She genuinely thought that Kiwanuka was campaigning to become kabaka of Buganda, something unthinkable for a Muganda.

Despite the passage of time and assumed heightened political enlightenment and awareness, a non-Muganda president is easier to accept by the Baganda because he is not in apparent competition for the limelight and prestige with their Kabaka, the first citizen of Buganda, as a Muganda president would presumably be. In that regard, for instance, an invitation of the Kabaka to state house by the president of Uganda for a business meeting would more likely be twisted by some Baganda as "a summon" if made by a Muganda president than if a non-Muganda had made it. As will be shown later, whether or not it was made, that was one of the allegations which were made against Benedicto Kiwanuka, a Muganda prime minister.

Since the restoration of the Buganda Kingdom, the Kabaka has made a couple of visits to state house, the official residence of the president of Uganda who happens to be a non-Muganda. There were no murmurs over those visits from within either Buganda or outside Buganda. I have little doubt in my mind that if similar visits had been made while the occupant of state house was a Muganda, voices would have been raised from outside Buganda expressing fears of the rise of Buganda nationalism designed to load it over the rest.

Although the "Buganda factor" (thanks to Phares Mutibwa for the expression) is a calculation every rising Ugandan politician has to go into, for a Muganda politician walking on eggshells is the easier task than accommodating it.

A non-Muganda president is sub-consciously, but erroneously, seen by Baganda as an innocent foreign visiting potentate in Buganda. He poses no risk of a cultural clash between him and their Kabaka and any appearance of a clash will be seen merely as a benign *faux pas* born out of innocent ignorance and not an abominable insult.

The point of view that the Baganda are shy about voting for a Muganda candidate for president is not in any way countered by the fact that during the 1980 general elections, Buganda overwhelmingly voted for DP led by Paul Ssemogerere, a Muganda, well-knowing that he would have become president of Uganda if he had won overall. It should be remembered that in 1980 the kabakaship had not yet been restored and, therefore, the question of precedence in Buganda between president and Kabaka, if Ssemogerere had won, would not have arisen. That may be why, since the restoration of the Buganda Kingdom, no Muganda presidential candidate—not even Ssemwogere who stood again in 1996—has won a majority of votes in Buganda except Robert Kyagulanyi in the 2021 presidential elections.

As to what would have happened after five years, on his part, Obote adopted the attitude of a pragmatic politician: when we reach that bridge, he must have reasoned, we shall decide how to cross it. The bridge he had to cross was the one before him, not one he might or might not reach along the way.

While the Mengo establishment saw the election of Mutesa from the perspective of prestige of their Kabaka, other Ugandans saw the issue of the election of the first president from an entirely different perspective. Towards the celebration of the first independence anniversary of Uganda, the nation unanimously wanted a Ugandan to replace the British governor-general as the head of state. The majority of the regions did not have kings and were against the idea of any of the few kings becoming president simply because he was a king. The Baganda naturally did not want any other king or a commoner to occupy that position because, according to them, no one was above their king and, therefore, only their king qualified to occupy the top position.

Obote was interested in a candidate who would unite Uganda and appealed to the UPC members of Parliament to consider Mutesa who would look beyond the Buganda Government to the Central Government; hence, have a more united country. Parliament, thus, elected the Kabaka as the first constitutional president of Uganda (Mpambara, 1967).

The election of the Kabaka of Buganda to the presidency of Uganda produced such interesting responses from the communities which did not have traditional leaders—the "republican districts" as they called themselves—that I think it is worth a little digression. It brought it home to them that, henceforth, the election to the office of president and head of state was to be drawn from a pool of constitutional heads. They suddenly became aware of the full implications of Section 36 (1) of the Constitution which provided, in part:

> ... the President and the Vice President shall be elected in accordance with such procedure as may be prescribed by Parliament from among the Rulers of the Federal States and the constitutional heads of the Districts by the

members of the National Assembly for a term of five years.

Therefore, those communities which were neither part of the federal states nor were led by constitutional heads would have no chance of having a person from among them becoming Ugandan president. With that realisation, in order not to be left out of the presidential race, those communities hastened to create paramount chiefs of their own by electing one of the most prominent from among their number to that position. That would enable them to have a candidate of their own when the position for president of Uganda next became vacant. Consequently, we had the election of the following: Yekosefati Engur as *Won Nyaci* of Lango District, John Bikangaga as *Rutakirwa* of Kigezi District, Wasukulu as *Senkulu* of Bukedi District, Mungoma as *Omukhuuka* of Bugisu District, Chemonges as *Kingoo* of Sebei District, and Phillip Adonga as *Laloyo Maber* of Acholi District.

It is a mark of how seriously some communities took the newly created positions or alien the whole concept was to them that they chose curious title names for their heads. For instance, the people of Lango chose for their paramount chief the name, *Won Nyaci*, which means "he who parts his hair." It reflected the preferred hairstyle of the person designated to be the first holder of that title! As for the Acholi, even though they have the word *rwot* for king, they chose for their titular head the phrase *Laloyo Maber* which simply means "a good administrator" or more plainly, "a good person."

Naturally, the majority of the UPC members of Parliament had preferred William Wilberforce Nadiope, the paramount chief of Busoga Territory, who, being the vice president of their party, was one of their own, to be the first president of Uganda. Expecting the support of all UPC members for the position,

Nadiope did not take kindly to the fact that it was Obote, the UPC president, who railroaded the members to vote for the Kabaka of Buganda. Mutesa (1967) reports that Nadiope created a momentary scene in the chamber of Parliament, where the election was held, when he realised that he was not going to be elected. To placate him, they elected him vice president of Uganda.

Political Dirty Tricks Begin

Obote's detractors have asserted that the election of Mutesa as president of Uganda was a trap that was laid by Obote, to easily overthrow Mutesa later. They are not averse to *malquoting*, if a word may be coined. A *malquotation* is a word or words not uttered but concocted and maliciously attributed to someone in order to bring ill-will among a section of people who would feel offended if the words were true. The Baganda have an expression for it: *okuwanda ebigambo mu kamwa*, translated as spitting of words in another's mouth, and meaning, to make someone a victim of a deliberate falsehood or misrepresentation.

A *malquotation* includes words actually uttered by the person to whom they are attributed but were plucked from the context in which they used them, and applied without the context being given, which gives offence. A *malquotation* is to an individual what hate speech is to a group or a class of people. It besmirches a reputation without cause, the people who create it without providing evidence as to where, when, in whose presence, and in which context the words were uttered. And yet most often, context is everything.

Removed from their proper context, many statements can be made to sound offensive. Obote is *malquoted* as having said, "When I saw him lift the Bible (to take the oath of office as president of Uganda), I knew I had got him." That was meant to convey a sense that Obote's role in getting Mutesa elected president of Uganda was an ill-intentioned, pre-meditated and cleverly-laid trap for Mutesa to fall into and destroy himself. That may rank among the most devious and mischievous *malquotations* since the beginning of the French Revolution. Queen Marie Antoinette of France was said to have asked those who had come to report to her that the poor and hungry people were rioting in the streets of Paris because they had no bread, "If they have no bread, why don't you give them cake?" The spread of that *malquotation* to depict the queen as uncaring and out of touch with the lives of the ordinary Parisian—If they could not afford the price of cheaper bread, how could they afford the more expensive cake?—further enraged and emboldened the anger of the hungry and angry people who were demonstrating against the luxurious life of the monarchy. The queen lost her head to the guillotine before the reign of terror was over.

Malquotations have been an effective dirty political trick in Uganda, especially against both Milton Obote and Benedicto Kiwanuka, the one-time leader of DP. An even more pernicious *malquotation* so often recycled that, to some people, it has assumed the status of gospel truth, is that Obote said that "A good Muganda is a dead Muganda," as proof of how much he hated Baganda. That is attributed to a man whose wife, Miria Nakitto Kalule, was a Muganda and whose children are, therefore, half-Baganda.

This writer was informed by the late Samwiri Mugwisa, who was Obote's minister for agriculture in the second Obote administration, and a Muganda himself, that Obote had indeed uttered those words but in the form of a question and within a particular context. Seeing how people trooped to a Muganda colleague's house at his passing on, and heaping praises on him, after they had ignored him during his sickness, Obote had asked, "Is a good Muganda a dead Muganda?" Obote's question has since been turned by his detractors into a statement and the context ignored.

More was to follow later after Obote had been overthrown. One of the dirty tricks deployed in the 1970s by those who were fighting for the removal of Idi Amin, then president of Uganda, was to foment hatred against him by tricking him into carrying out extra-judicial killings of innocent people he had been misled into perceiving as his enemies actively fighting for his removal.

According to Timothy Kalyegira, the sentence "A good Muganda is a dead Muganda" attributed to Obote first appeared in print in 1977. In that year, a document titled "Obote's War Call to Langis and Acholis" was found by Amin's intelligence in one of the crates of firearms addressed, and deliberately planned to be found by Amin's intelligence, to Archbishop Janan Luwum, an Acholi cleric. In that document, a call was being made to the "Langis" and "Acholis" to rise against the Amin regime. It was also in the same document that the statement "A good Muganda is a dead Muganda" was included. The document was made to appear to have been written by, with or for Obote. It had two purposes: first to incense Amin into going after the Langi and Acholi and thereby besmirch his reputation or, alternatively, so that they may in turn begin actively fighting him and, second, to alienate the Baganda against Obote so that they would never be supportive of any cause espoused by him, including the ousting of Amin.

In his article, Kalyegira methodically analyses the "letter." He dissects the language of the document and Obote's usual writing and debunks the idea of Obote having had a hand in writing the document found in the cache of arms sent to the archbishop. First, Obote being a native Lango speaker could not have made the grammatical error of referring to the people of Lango and Acholi as Langis and Acholis, respectively. Secondly, the document called on "the masses." Obote always spoke of "the people of Uganda." The document refers to "the movement"; Obote's practice was to refer to his party as "the Congress" and see the people of Uganda as one and indivisible.

He reached the conclusion, correctly in my view, that the "letter" could not have been written by Obote, with Obote or for Obote. In short, Kalyegira all but names the true author of the document. Kalyegira's article left no one deceived, who had been following Uganda politics for the last half century. Besides, being the political strategist that he was, it is difficult to conceive Obote as exposing the Langi and Acholi to the wrath of Amin while at the same time alienating the Baganda from his cause.

It is interesting to see how strained proof of Obote's hatred of Baganda can be. There are those who argue that the fact that they never heard him speak Luganda in public was clear proof that he hated Baganda. When it is pointed out that neither did he speak his mother tongue while addressing the public in his official capacity even in Lango, his native district, nor for that matter any other language elsewhere, they change the subject. Given that there are quite many languages spoken in Uganda, and he could not speak them all, Obote chose the better course to stick solely to English while communicating officially, no matter where he was.

This particular dirty trick succeeded beyond its creator's expectations, although in some cases, probably in the way that was intended. In some way, this marked the turning point in the struggle to remove Amin from power. It led to the execution of Archbishop Janan Luwum, and they have found a place for his soul in the noble army of martyrs and saints. The world realised that Idi Amin and his regime had become incorrigibly ruthless and brutal. Many men among the Acholi community, fearing further reprisals, flocked into exile and formed the bulk of the soldiers that was joined by the Tanzanian army which, in 1979, freed Uganda from the clutches of Amin's rule.

Obote's detractors turned the sentence "A good Muganda is a dead Muganda" into a cottage industry to politically damage him, and by extension, the UPC brand, in Buganda. But there is an inquiry that has never been made: assuming a Muganda president had supposedly asked that question. Would it have been flipped over, turned into a statement and tied around his neck as an albatross to sink him politically in the same manner? Probably not.

The United States of America might provide us with an answer. There is the *n-word*. While Blacks routinely refer to each other as *nigger*, and nothing happens, if a White calls a Black a nigger, a whole city might go on fire. It is a matter of tribal taboos. In America, it is said that there are jokes Whites are not supposed to tell. Likewise, in Uganda, there are certain things one is not supposed to say about a tribe they do not belong to. Obote had unknowingly breached that taboo. At the end of it all, it boils down to not what you say but who you are to say it.

The Baganda are well-accomplished and their language seems quite rich in creating *malquotations*. Benedicto Kiwanuka, president general of DP at the time, was the victim of *malquotations* long before Milton Obote. While he was serving as prime minister, word was spread around that he, Kiwanuka, had said, *"Kabaka bw'aba alina ekimuluma, ajje nkimumalire"*; meaning, "If the Kabaka has any burning issue bothering him, let him come to me so I can solve it."

Kimenye's version of what Kiwanuka said sounds eminently more credible by far. She not only succinctly lays out the context within which Kiwanuka's words were said but also what motivated those who fabricated the *malquotation* as well as its effect. She says:

> As the general election for the national government which would be in power at the time of independence approached, Mengo was in the mood to do anything to remove the Democratic Party and Ben Kiwanuka. Ben had been guilty of a flippant remark, "I'll go up to Mengo and see what's bothering him," in reply to a reporter asking how he intended to deal with the Kabaka's insistence on special status for Buganda in an independent Uganda. From then on, his name was murred in the palace. (Kimenye, 2015, p. 16)

In Ugandan society, a *malquotation* can also take the form of conduct, physical appearance or a non-verbal act. When non-verbal, a *malquotation* is referred to as *okusibako amatu g'embuzi okuliisa engo,* translated as fixing the ears of a goat on someone in order to make him prey to the leopard. (Apparently, goats are the favourite prey for leopards). Thus, during the same period as he was serving as chief minister, and the run-up to the 1962 general elections, word was spread in Buganda that Kiwanuka *yakongoodde Olubiri. Okukongoola* is, in Buganda, a children's gesture of contempt to another. The aggressor points their half-clenched fist towards the one they intend to ridicule as they simultaneously bite their upper lip while exposing their lower jaw teeth and making guttural sounds.

This rude and provocative gesture remains the trigger of many a fight in the villages and it is still practised. Without specifying his vantage point, it was said that Kiwanuka contemptuously gestured *(yakongoola)* at the Lubiri. Even with a made-up outlandish childish insult such as that, it was that easy back then to fool Baganda and enough to make Kiwanuka immensely unpopular for a time, and lose an election. Indeed, myths are more potent than facts.

No matter how preposterous the *malquotation*, there will always be some people that will believe it. It is his misfortune that in the case of Obote, the *malquotations* attributed to him have been passed from one generation to another in Buganda and have assumed the status of gospel truth. And no matter how low it may sound, there are some people, hankering for lowness, who will believe it. So, some dirt has stuck on Obote, with the resultant loss of political capital in the region.

Joseph Goebbels, Hitler's minister for information (propaganda) in Nazi Germany, taught the world that if you have to tell a lie make it really big if it is to be believed. The huge *malquotations* against Kiwanuka, a subject of the Kabaka and Buganda, gained currency and cost him dearly, politically. In monarchical societies, and particularly in Buganda, it is an aberration for a subject, however highly placed in office, to invite the Kabaka to give him (the Kabaka) advice. Having accused him of inviting the Kabaka to solve his problems, they went ahead to dub him *Ssenkagale wa DP*—the arrogant or pompous leader of DP.

The title *Ssenkagale wa DP* dates from 1961-1962 when Kiwanuka was head of DP and chief minister. Today, it is taken as the unofficial but popular title for the leader of DP but it was not originally coined as a term of affection. When first used with reference to Ben Kiwanuka, the word *Ssenkagale*, used on its own, then meant "One full of himself," which is derogatory. But today, *Ssenkagale wa DP* means "the bulwark of DP", which is a mark of esteem. Such are the vagaries of language. Like that of Marie Antoinette, *malquotations* against Obote and Kiwanuka have proved difficult, if not impossible, to dispel because they tend to appeal to the dark side of our nature to depict those higher up in status and position than ourselves as deeply flawed.

Most times, those maligned remained silent hoping that the lies will come to pass and that the right-thinking members of society will see them for what they are and ignore them. Unfortunately, that is not how people respond to lies. Silence is taken to mean admission. Golooba-Mutebi puts it very well. About an analogous situation; he writes:

> The speed with which these views emerge and develop, and the tenacity with which they are held on to, could easily constitute the subject of a major inquiry into how people get to know what they claim they know or whether they actually know what they believe they know. (Golooba-Mutebi, 2016)

The "I knew I had got him" *malquotation* attributed to Obote is refuted by Mutesa. Let him speak for himself. He wrote, "If my becoming President was not really a mark of friendship on the part of Obote, nor was it the trap that others have suggested" (Mutesa, 1967, p. 174).

If Mutesa says he accepted the office of president with his eyes wide open, who else would dare say he was hoodwinked into it? This was not even a case of strangers crying louder than the bereaved. It was a case of strangers wailing for a phantom victim. On this score, Mutesa was certainly more charitable towards his nemesis than his own sympathisers.

That is not to say that Mutesa received no counsel against taking up the position of president. Kasozi (1996) writes that Prince Badru Kakungulu, a cousin of Mutesa's grandfather, together with Sir Charles Gasyonga, omugabe of Ankore, and Sir George Rukidi, omukama of Tooro, had personally paid Mutesa a visit to discourage him from accepting to be made the president of Uganda. Omukama of Tooro is reported to have prophetically said:

> You are being proposed as the first President of Uganda. Don't you think this will put you in an awkward position and is likely to jeopardize not only your position but ours as well? I would strongly feel, we consolidate our kingdoms and leave the Bakopi (non-royals/commoners) with their politics in the central government. (Kasozi, 1996, p. 147)

It is said that after the visit, Mutesa remonstrated with his grandfather (grandfather's brother, in English terms), Prince Badru Kakungulu, for ganging up with the other kings to block his becoming president. Mutesa decided to ignore the advice of his brother-kings and pursued the presidency of Uganda, which he achieved. It was a decision that would come back to haunt him.

On this particular occasion, Mutesa lived up to the character of his ancestor, Kabaka Kayemba *Nantabulirirwa*, the 17th Kabaka of Buganda. According to legend, Kayemba was advised against using a clay boat to row across the lake but he refused. And the inevitable happened. He never returned to the shore. His posthumous nickname became *Nantabulirirwa*, "the Inadvisable", which is interpreted as the headstrong one who brushes aside sound advice to his harm. In full, the saying goes, *Kayemba Nantabulirirwa yasabala bwa bbumba:* Kayemba who never heeded advice rowed a clay boat. The story goes that Kabaka Kayemba having ordered the making of a clay boat, insisted on rowing it across a water way, against the advice of his boat builders. The expression is used to caution a person against embarking on an act of self-harm by being too obstinate.

Kabaka Mutesa Collides with President Mutesa

President Mutesa reported on duty on 9 October 1963, the first anniversary of Uganda's Independence and moved into the state lodge, at Entebbe, formerly occupied by the governor-general, and later named state house. It was not long before his mettle was tested. The matter that had been deferred during the independence negotiations could no longer be put off. In fulfilment of what had been agreed upon during the independence negotiations and incorporated into The Uganda (Independence) Order-in-Council 1962, Parliament passed a bill, The Referendum (Buyaga and Bugangazzi) Bill, calling for the holding of a referendum in Buyaga and Bugangazzi counties for the people in those counties to decide whether to remain as part of Buganda or to return to Bunyoro. It was taken by the clerk to Parliament to the president for signature as the law required and as had been the norm with previous bills. Precisely, Article 56 of the Constitution provided:

> 56 (1) The power of Parliament to make laws shall be exercised by the National Assembly and assented to by the President.
>
> (2) When a bill passed by the National Assembly is presented to the President for assent, he shall signify that he assents to the bill.
>
> (3) . . . a bill shall not become law until it has been duly passed and assented to in accordance with this Constitution.

President Mutesa examined the bill closely. He remembered that the Independence Order-in-Council provided that only those people who were living in the counties and were registered to vote in those counties in the 1962 elections were eligible to vote in this referendum.

Shortly after Uganda attained independence, Kabaka Mutesa, plainly in anticipation of the referendum, under a programme that was termed *Ndaiga Development Scheme*, had enticed many Baganda, especially the ex-servicemen of World War II, to settle in the counties which were subject to the referendum. He had hoped to influence the outcome of the referendum by the new settlers voting to stay in Buganda and, according to him, to use them as some kind of reserve force "when it came to a showdown" (Mutesa, 1967, p. 169). Did this imply that he anticipated violence to occur, if not within the Lost Counties but probably between Buganda and the Central Government and was readying for it? He did not elaborate but a strong hint is certainly given that violence was not ruled out.

President Mutesa perused the bill more carefully and drew the conclusion:

> Nobody who had settled after 1962 was to be allowed a vote, so the recent Baganda settlers who are developing the land are allowed no say in its future... Under these circumstances, it is certain the vote will favour Bunyoro ... (Mutesa, 1967, p. 180)

Mutesa may be assumed to have been aware of, and to have recalled, the speech of Lord Molson during the date on the Uganda Independence Bill in which he observed:

> It is ... arguable that it is desirable that there should be a referendum in those two counties in order to ascertain what I think is already obvious – namely that they (the Banyoro) wish to be returned to the Kingdom of Bunyoro. ("1962: How Buganda Tested Ugandan, British Politicians", 2018)

It may not have been lost on him, although it was a pure coincidence, that the clerk to Parliament, whose duty it was to deliver the bill to the president for his assent, and who was sitting before him waiting for him to sign was Baganchwera Ignatius Barungi, a subject of Bunyoro Kingdom.

President Mutesa recalled the thoughts which had gone through his mind when, as Kabaka Mutesa, he was approached and requested to accept the position of president of Uganda. "The only factor which caused me to hesitate was wondering whether there would be conflict between my duty as President and my duty as Kabaka. I decided that I could separate the roles..." (Mutesa, 1967, p. 172). After an awkward silence, the president spoke to the clerk who was waiting for his signature and, rather despondently, said that he needed to first consult a couple of people. The president put the bill aside and the clerk left without a signed copy.

Here was before him a bill which the law required him to sign as President Mutesa to authorise the holding of a referendum which could result in a part of Kabaka Mutesa's kingdom being parcelled off. The moment of truth had arrived. The problem could no longer be deferred but had to be resolved now. Mutesa was a deeply conflicted person. Where did President Mutesa's allegiance lie? In his oath of office, he had sworn to obey the laws of Uganda. He agonised whether he should fulfil his duty as president and betray that of Kabaka to preserve the Buganda Kingdom by effectively signing away Buganda territory or defend his kingdom as Kabaka and thereby breach his oath as president of Uganda. He decided that on this occasion, his duty as Kabaka superseded his duty as president. He declined to sign the bill. But the same Constitution provided that if the president declined to sign a bill, the prime minister could sign it into law. And that is what Obote did.

For purposes of clarity and ease of reference as to the legal authority under which Prime Minister Obote did so, the provisions of Article 67 (2) (a) and (b) of the 1962 Constitution of Uganda are set out:

(a) where the President is required by this Constitution to do any act in accordance with the advice of any person or authority and the Prime Minister is satisfied that the President has neglected or declined to do so, the Prime Minister may inform the President that it is the intention of the Prime Minister to do the act himself after the expiration of a period to be specified by the Prime Minister, and if at the expiration of that period the President has not done that act the Prime Minister may do that act himself;

(b) an act done by the Prime Minister in pursuance of paragraph (a) of this proviso shall be deemed to have been done by the President and to be his act;

And the referendum went ahead in November 1964 on the strength of the prime minister's signature.

When the polls closed and the votes were counted, the results were announced as follows:

County	Transfer to Bunyoro	Remain in Buganda	Form separate district
Buyaga	8,327	1,289	50
Bugangazzi	3,275	2,253	62

Another bill was passed soon thereafter, the Transfer Bill, this one to put into effect the results of the referendum by transferring the jurisdiction of the two counties from Buganda to Bunyoro and to alter the boundaries between the two kingdoms. That bill stated that with effect from 1st January 1965:

1. The territory of the Kingdom of Buganda shall comprise those counties of the Kingdom of Buganda that on the 8th day of October 1962, were comprised in that territory, **excluding the county of Buyaga and the county of Bugangazzi.**
2. The territory of the Kingdom of Bunyoro shall comprise the counties of the Kingdom of Bunyoro which on the 8th day of October 1962, were comprised in that Kingdom, **with the addition of the county of Buyaga and the county of Bugangazzi.** [Emphasis added]. (Art. 3 of The Constitution of Uganda, Chapter 1 Laws of Uganda, 1962)

As the law required, it was taken to President Mutesa for signature to signify his consent. This was another heart-wrenching moment for him. To sign the Transfer Bill would have been like signing to be amputated (Nsubuga, 2013).

President Mutesa remembered the time, energy, and treasure he had invested in the Ndaiga Development Scheme. He could see in his mind's eye the thousands of men and women who, believing in him, had sold their property elsewhere in Buganda to follow him in Ndaiga. They were about to be left in "a foreign land" where he had lured them to. They pleaded with him not to leave them in foreign hands.

Their plea touched Mutesa deeply. At this juncture, he was a man driven by torn loyalties. Not being sure where, as between his role as Kabaka of Buganda president of Uganda, his allegiance fell, Mutesa let the transfer instrument lie, as he had done the referendum bill.

President Mutesa Confronts Prime Minister Obote

Once again, it was Prime Minister Obote who faced the agony of having to sign an instrument relating to the Lost Counties.

Regarding the compromise that provided for a referendum, Kabaka Mutesa had observed that it had not pleased Obote because he had wished the matter of the Lost Counties would be resolved without involving him. Whoever was responsible for it did not grant Obote his wish. The cup he had hoped would pass him was in his hands. One more time, Prime Minister Obote exercised the powers conferred upon him by Article 67 (2) (a) and (b) of the Constitution laid out above and signed into law a bill President Mutesa had declined to assent to.

Had Obote made a promise to the Kabaka of Buganda to scuttle the referendum and promised the opposite undertaking to omukama of Bunyoro? We have found no credible evidence from a disinterested party to support that possibility. Indeed, if there had been such an agreement, Mutesa would have said so in his book. Would Obote fulfil his constitutional duty as prime minister and sign the bill, the president having declined to do so, and incur the wrath of Kabaka Mutesa and the Baganda, or let it lapse and incur the wrath of the Banyoro and other communities? That is the question he had to deal with. Had the president tried to prevail on him not to initiate the referendum? Kasendwa-Ddumba, an intelligence officer at the time and later chief of intelligence in Obote's second government, states categorically in his September 2005 (revised in 2020) unpublished letter to The Uganda Human Rights Commission (UHRC) that, "The rift between the two sides (Mengo and Obote) grew wider when Mengo failed to persuade Obote to disregard the constitutional provision for a referendum to resolve the issue of the counties Bunyoro claimed had been lost to Buganda" (Kasendwa-Ddumba, 2020, p. 33).

The act of Mutesa's refusal to sign the referendum instruments as president and thereby compelling Obote to sign them as prime minister, constituted at once a collision of

Kabaka Mutesa and President Mutesa, on the one hand, and a confrontation between President Mutesa and Prime Minister Obote, on the other.

Upon signing the transfer bill into law, the prime minister heaved a sigh of self-satisfied relief and smiled, thinking that he had helped settle a long-standing dispute. However, he had smiled too soon. For with that stroke of the pen, his troubles had just started. But the good tidings came first. Those, not least the people of Bunyoro, who had feared that because of the UPC-KY alliance Obote would be in Buganda's pocket and block the referendum, were pleasantly surprised when he did not stand in its way.

Omukama of Bunyoro sent the prime minister a congratulatory message over what he was probably now referring as "the recovered counties." Apart from Buganda, the rest of Uganda saw the prime minister as having solved the nagging problem that had embittered the relationship between Buganda and Bunyoro for the preceding sixty years. Such a relief as Obote felt from the comforting messages he had received turned out to be short-lived. Little did he know that this was the turning point in his personal and Uganda's fortunes. The country was in tranquillity, but it was an eerie tranquillity, the kind of calm that typically precedes a storm that would change everything.

The settlement of one problem between two nations had given rise to an even greater problem, which threatened the very existence of the state of Uganda.

Chapter 4

"STRATEGIES" TO RETAIN THE LOST COUNTIES

Mengo's "Strategy"
It would be a mistake to assume that Mengo was too naïve to do anything to retain the Lost Counties. They did not sit back and watch them go but devised some schemes before the referendum. Buganda also mistakenly relied, on some assumptions for retaining them.

The two-pronged strategy that Buganda adopted can be deciphered from Mengo's activities in the two years following independence and one sentence in Mutesa's book. He wrote: "It was agreed that there would be a referendum *in not less than three years if the Prime Minister wished it*" [Emphasis added] (Mutesa, 1967, p. 165). The plan appears to have been: first, scuttle the referendum by frightening Prime Minster Obote into not calling it, and second, buy time after independence within which to make it possible to influence the electorate by: (a) introducing sweetener projects in the area so as to make it attractive for the Banyoro residents in the Lost Counties to vote to stay in Buganda, and (b) locating new settlers in the two counties from elsewhere in Buganda who would vote in favour of staying in Buganda.

How did Mutesa hope to scuttle the referendum? Lwanga-Lunyiigo (2007) says:

> Kabaka Muteesa gives the referendum a twist.... In section 26 of the Independence Order-in-Council, the wishes of the Prime Minister do not appear. Kabaka Muteesa was implying that the referendum, if it took place at all, would be blamed on Obote. (p. 107)

There were actually two "twists" in that one sentence which probably laid out Buganda's "strategy" to retain the Lost Counties. Where was the strategy in *"if the Prime Minister wished it"*? Well, lest the prime minister had forgotten, his government was an alliance between his party, UPC, and KY, the exclusively Buganda movement. The prime minister was not expected to do anything that was, or thought to be, prejudicial to the interests of Buganda or else.... And, since the holding of a referendum in the Lost Counties was potentially prejudicial to Buganda's interests, it was assumed that Obote had a political obligation to evade it or could be threatened into doing so. Thus, the *"if the Prime Minister wished it"* twist assumed on the part of Mutesa carried both a promise and a threat; the promise of continued good relations, if Obote scuttled the referendum, and the threat of political retribution, if he went ahead with it, with undesirable consequences for Buganda.

The second strategy lay in the second "twist." The Uganda (Independence) Order-in-Council talked of the referendum being held "on such date, not being earlier than 9th October 1964, as the National Assembly may, by resolution, appoint." It did not say "in not less than three years," as Mutesa stated. It was another twist or inaccuracy. Mutesa, therefore, implied that Obote, by holding the referendum in November 1964, two years after independence, called it ahead of schedule and in bad faith in order to deny Mengo time to position itself better to win it.

Had Kabaka Mutesa's interpretation of "not less than three years" been correct, a completely different timetable with regard to the referendum would have come into play. It would not have had to be held when it was, two years after independence, as it was. It would have meant any time after three years, which is open-ended and could have been translated, so far as Buganda was concerned, as call the referendum as and when we are ready.

Mutesa's formulation was aiming at having a fudge; that is, deliberately leaving things obscure in order to buy time in the hope that the problem will eventually solve itself. In Mutesa's calculation, time would have changed the situation on the ground, for soon after independence, the Buganda Government launched the Ndaiga Development Scheme whose stated aim was to raise the living standards of the people in the two counties. At the same time, under that scheme, Baganda ex-servicemen from other parts of Buganda Kingdom, were encouraged to acquire land and settle in the two counties.

Mengo had hoped that by introducing development projects in the area, the Banyoro would be induced to vote to stay in Buganda while the new migrants would out-vote those Banyoro who did not want the counties to remain part of Buganda. In Mutesa's own words:

> I hoped to develop the area, persuade many Baganda to live there and, by bringing roads and schools and better prices for their crops, persuade the inhabitants (read Banyoro) that life as part of Buganda was tolerable—even pleasant... I still feel that my plan could have led to a peaceful and prosperous solution if I had had the support of the Prime Minister. (Mutesa, 1967, p. 169)

Lwanga-Lunyiigo (2007) thinks that, as far as attracting the Banyoro to vote to remain part of Buganda was concerned, the Ndaiga Development Scheme came sixty years too late. As for the expected new voters, the law stipulated that only those who had registered to vote in the area during the previous general elections of April 1962 were eligible to vote in the referendum. So, the ex-servicemen and other new settlers had no vote.

In the end, the referendum was held as it was constitutionally permissible both as an activity and as to its timing. Buganda's strategy to retain the Lost Counties had been based on a deliberate misunderstanding of the Uganda (Independence) Order-In-Council and a miscalculation of what the prime minister would do or not do.

Although Mutesa's version as to when to hold it was not correct, the referendum did not have to be held when it was in November 1964. The Order-In-Council simply prohibited the holding of the referendum before 9 October 1964. How long thereafter it could be held was not specified. Mutesa would have preferred that time to be elongated as much as possible in order for the conditions on the ground to change in Buganda's favour. Obote called the referendum almost as early as the law permitted. Whether by design or default, the possibility of a change of attitude by the Banyoro living in those counties in favour of staying as part of Buganda had been forestalled.

Given that Obote was the leader of a political party, whose members could bring pressure to bear on him, how much of a free hand politically Obote had in determining the referendum date is difficult to tell. What was beyond the discretion of either man was who was eligible to vote in the referendum. Mutesa's scheme to introduce new voters was obviously a non-starter. It is worth repeating, though, that Mutesa himself pointed out that this was an exercise that Obote had not looked forward to and did not particularly relish.

Did Mutesa believe what he wrote about the date of the referendum and the prime minister's role in it? Or was it just a "twist" as Lwanga-Lunyiigo (2007) delicately termed it? The three years he talked about was probably the period in his estimation it would have taken the Ndaiga Development Scheme to bear fruit in order to achieve the desired end. In my view, no over-reliance should be placed on this part of his writing. For it should be remembered that he was writing his autobiography a year after losing his throne. The urge to justify his actions and to cast blame on others for what had gone wrong regarding the referendum during his reign was strong. Could Mengo have gone about retaining the counties differently and better?

The Better Strategy

Having conceded to the holding of a referendum to determine where the Lost Counties would fall, Mengo should have interested itself in the three questions which were going to settle the issue: Who was to vote in the referendum? When would the referendum be held? Which number of votes would decide the issue?

The better strategy for Mengo would have been to have all those questions resolved during the Lancaster Conference for two reasons. First, Britain, which had "a special relationship" with Buganda and which was responsible for putting it in the disastrous possession of the contested counties, would have been more inclined to lean towards Buganda's demands. Second, Obote and UPC, in pursuit of an alliance which was yet to be fully consummated, would have supported Buganda's position. It is not known whether Mengo tried at all or just failed to convince the conference.

As to who was to vote, as we came to learn, Mengo would have preferred all the people residing in the counties at the time of the referendum. Hence, the Ndaiga Project of transporting would-be voters to the two counties before the referendum was a futile exercise as the constitutionally agreed position was that only those who voted from the counties in 1962 would participate in the referendum. Was the Ndaiga Project an afterthought, a misunderstanding of the agreement, or an attempt to get what Mengo had failed to gain from the negotiating table?

The date when to conduct the referendum was also crucial. It should have been Mengo's strategic objective to convince the conference to accept its preferred timeframe of "not less than three years" for the reasons Mutesa states.

What would have been of even greater importance if they had negotiated well was the question of the number of votes required to change the existing status of the counties. Call it the pass mark. This would have been Mengo's strongest position. It is not unusual for the law to provide that approval of certain decisions require numbers greater than a simple majority—a super majority, as it were. For example, in Uganda today, to change an entrenched article of the Constitution by Parliament, a two-thirds majority of votes by members is required. Still in Uganda, the president of the country is duly elected only if they garner at least 50 percent of the votes cast plus one vote. Yet, in other countries, all that is required is a simple majority.

With a referendum which had the potential to change the status quo in the two counties, it would have been reasonable for Buganda to demand a number bigger than a simple majority to change that status. As the numbers from Bugangazzi showed, at 3,275 votes in favour of Bunyoro, as against 2,253 votes in favour of Buganda, the vote was not overwhelmingly in Bunyoro's favour. The way it was framed, even with a majority of one vote, the counties would have reverted to Bunyoro. With the requirement for a high super majority,

Bugangazzi might have remained in Buganda. But the time to make that demand should have been during the independence negotiations. Who knows, with Obote's support, the demand would have succeeded as others did.

If they did not, we cannot blame the Baganda negotiators of the time that they did not advance a condition which would have enhanced Buganda's chances of retaining the counties. It would be years before a view emerged that to bring legitimacy to a referendum, a simple majority should not always be sufficient to change a *status quo*. In certain circumstances, to legitimise a referendum, the majority should constitute at least a given percentage of the electorate and win by a certain percentage. In his article on referenda, in the *Guardian* newspaper, Ian Jack (2018) argues that Britain would not have experienced the problems it went through with regard to Brexit if the idea introduced by George Cunningham regarding the legitimacy of a referendum had been followed.

In 1978, the British Labour government introduced a bill in Parliament to provide for the conducting of a referendum in Scotland to permit the people to determine the devolution of power to Scotland through setting up of a Scottish Assembly. George Cunningham introduced an amendment to that bill, which made it a requirement that, to consider the devolution as having been approved by the people of Scotland, at least 40 percent of the Scottish electorate must have participated in that election. As a result of that amendment, the devolution failed because, although the majority voted in favour, the turnout was not high enough to meet the 40 percent threshold.

Abstaining from voting is in itself a form of making a choice and expressing an opinion regarding the issue at hand and should be considered. The legitimacy of modern-day referenda can be enhanced by the law requiring not only the participation of a minimum percentage of the electorate but also setting a threshold (pass mark) higher than a simple majority to determine an issue one way or another.

The referendum on the Lost Counties only required a simple majority because the above idea came after its time and that was part of Buganda's undoing.

Chapter 5

PARTING OF PATHS

From Mutesa's viewpoint, the main trigger of the quarrel that caused the parting of ways between him and Obote was the perceived refusal by Obote to quash the referendum over the Lost Counties. Mutesa believed that Obote wilfully went ahead to hold the referendum even though he should and could have avoided it. At least he could have delayed it so as to give Buganda a chance to better position itself. Obote could not frustrate the referendum because it was a constitutional requirement and the foundational compromise which enabled Bunyoro and Buganda to agree to independence.

Kabaka Mutesa and the Mengo establishment felt betrayed by Prime Minister Obote when he initiated the referendum bills and also went ahead to sign them when the President Mutesa refused to do so. There are two reasons why they felt so. On his part, Kabaka Mutesa had understood that the implementation of the resolutions requiring the referendum depended on the wishes of the prime minister. If the prime minister did not wish it, there would be no referendum. And he expected to persuade the prime minister not to wish it. Curiously, Kabaka Mutesa expected the putting into effect of a formal constitutional requirement to depend on the wishes of Obote as an individual.

Was there a secret promise made but not kept? Did Mutesa and Obote have a private "gentleman's agreement" to subvert a public agreement embedded in law? Lwanga-Lunyiigo (2007) seems to doubt the sincerity of Mutesa's "understanding" that the holding of the referendum depended on Obote's wish. He writes, "In section 26 of the Independence Order-in-Council, the wishes of the Prime Minister do not appear. Kabaka Muteesa was implying that the referendum, if it took place at all, would be blamed on Obote!" (p. 107). As has already been shown, President Mutesa had been under the erroneous impression that Obote, being indebted to him, as Kabaka, for his position as prime minister, would not carry out his duty, if there was a possibility of the result clashing with Buganda's interests.

It will be recalled that the first post-independence government was a coalition between Obote's UPC and Mutesa's KY. As political partners, Kabaka Mutesa thought Prime Minister Obote owed it to him not to do anything that was contrary to his or Buganda's interests. When he perceived Obote as having done so, he felt betrayed. In exchange for the support that made Obote prime minister, Kabaka Mutesa had thought that Obote had issued him with a cheque promising that no referendum would be held; but when that cheque was presented, it was returned unpaid.

The fallout from the referendum hit Mikaeri Kintu almost immediately after the results were announced. He, under whose watch as Katikkiro the resolution on the Lost Counties was concluded; he who had negotiated the Uganda Constitution on behalf of Buganda; he who and had assured the Buganda Lukiiko that the counties would remain part of Buganda, was forced to resign his office after escaping being lynched by a mob of Baganda youth. People stoned vehicles and torched government premises; they cut trees to block roads in various parts of Buganda.

Immediately after the announcement of the referendum results, the Baganda youth burned the property of some

Banyoro living in Buganda. Not to be outdone by their Baganda compatriots, the Banyoro youth set ablaze the property of Baganda living in Buyaga and Bugangazzi, the counties where the majority of the residents had just voted to return to Bunyoro. Even though these incidents soon died down, the referendum had started a chain reaction which proved difficult to stop.

The animosity aroused by the referendum against Obote among the Baganda traditionalists galvanised Ibingira's ambition to lead UPC and, thereby, become prime minister. With Kakonge out of the way, it also provided an opportunity to begin plotting to displace Obote from party leadership. If he could successfully tap into Buganda's dissatisfaction with Obote over the referendum, Ibingira began thinking, nay, he became convinced, that the attainment of his ambition was within reach.

To President Mutesa, the holding of the referendum caused loss of trust and removed any doubt that he might have had that it was still possible for Obote to protect Buganda's interests regardless. It marked the point he began looking elsewhere and for other means to safeguard those interests. It was the point of no return. The holding of the referendum clearly opened a new chapter in the relations among those three personalities. It is most likely to have been the basis of the partnership between Ibingira, the secretary general of UPC, and Mutesa, the president of Uganda and Kabaka of Buganda.

Despite the relative quiet through 1965, from the time of the referendum on, deep mutual suspicion, if not actual animosity, developed between the president and the prime minister. The two met less and less frequently and eventually only communicated by letter.

Chapter 6

SECONDARY FACTORS AND EPISODES THAT STOKED THE CRISIS

A big mahogany tree may be felled by the heavy and hard strokes of an axe. But the soft nibbling of the tiny termites can also bring it down. We equally believe that the 1966 rupture in the history of independent Uganda was brought about by the momentous plots and intrigues captured in newspaper headlines, commissions, and investigations, as no less by the corroding effect of lack of political courage and clear definition and understanding of official roles, misconceptions, personal likes and dislikes, perceived slights, attitudes, simple miscalculations, influence of different backgrounds, ideological orientation and experience of the main protagonists that went unnoticed and unreported. We call them the secondary or indirect causes (although this self-taught historian would have preferred to refer to them as "opportunistic causes"), but the professional historians call them the underlying causes.

They are secondary in the sense that each on its own could not have caused the Crisis, but in combination with the main cause, may have helped to bring it about. Some of them get a mention in these pages because, according to popular analysis, in one way or another, they were part of the cocktail that brought about the Crisis. It should be noted, however, that they are not placed here in rank of the influence they exerted, if any, but rather randomly.

Some of those indirect causes, such as Mutesa's request to the prime minister for the military band to play at his birthday celebrations at his Mengo Palace—which was denied—were weighty and others less so. One would be tempted to ask why, in the first place, it should have been the prime minister's responsibility to approve the military band to play at that function. But such were the times. Many of the so-called indirect causes, some of which we would rather refer to as mere irritants, have been hovering around people's minds for a long time. Most of them are set out here, if only to dismiss some of them.

Inherited Complicated and Difficult Situation

One scholar, in particular, believes that Uganda was not sufficiently prepared for independence. Wrigley, in his contribution to the anthology *Uganda Now: Between Decay and Development*, writes:

> ... I have come to believe that nothing in Britain's dealings with Africa did her less credit than the haste and manner of her departure. Another decade at least of colonial rule, devoted to the serious planning of workable political structures, would have given the launch a better chance of success. But the British—not those on the ground but their masters in London—were anxious to be gone, and so they simply took the existing administrative units and turned them into states, handing the African people a government framework and telling them to build themselves a nation around it. The chance that this could be done without blood and tears were slender everywhere, but nowhere more slender than Uganda, where the basic structural defect, the size and solidity of Buganda, had

been plastered over but not properly repaired. (Wrigley, 1988, pp. 32-33)

If more than fifty years after being handed the instruments of independence Ugandans are still struggling to find a formula under which to live with each other in peace, harmony and prosperity, what was the situation like immediately after independence?

Power Struggle within UPC

Serious commentators who do not consider the Lost Counties as the cause of the 1966 Crisis are broadly divided between those who regard the power struggle within UPC and those who take the UPC/KY alliance as its cause. Having sufficiently covered in Chapter 1 why the power struggle, although important, was not the cause of the Crisis, it is not necessary to re-state the argument. It is, therefore, placed here to provide a fuller catalogue of the secondary causes of the Crisis for ease of reference but not to expound on it further.

Political Alliances

Let us have a word about the role alliances have played in Uganda's political history before possible combinations and the supreme alliance—UPC/KY Alliance—are critically examined. But first, what is the meaning of alliance? The *Concise Dictionary of Current English* defines an alliance, in part, as "joining in pursuit of common interests." With that definition, an alliance must pass the mutuality of interests' test in order to qualify as such.

An alliance is an arrangement whereby two or more organisations agree to combine their separate resources, whether financial, military or human, in order to gain the strength necessary to form a government or overcome a common enemy. When the project succeeds, the parties form a coalition government in which power is shared in proportion to their relative strengths, numerical or otherwise, and in the case of international war, decide how to deal with the defeated enemy state.

In internal politics, as opposed to the pooling of resources by the parties, an alliance may involve the making of mutual concessions or forbearance. The UPC/KY Alliance, for instance, was made possible by both pooling human resources in terms of members of Parliament and mutual concessions. An alliance also requires each partner to weigh which of his/her interests to pursue and which to forego for the greater good.

The different parties to an alliance make a bargain that will enable them to realise their separate or joint aspirations or forestall their separate or joint fears. In a democracy with a parliamentary system, an alliance is one of the methods groups of individuals employ in order to acquire or exercise political power. Others include: a merger, a government of national unity and, according to Uganda's contribution to political science, a broad-based government.

In an alliance and coalition, each party retains its separate identity. A merger on the other hand, is an arrangement whereby two or more parties form a single new entity under a new name. In Uganda's recent history, the most famous merger was that between Uganda National Congress (UNC) and Uganda People's Union (UPU) to form Uganda People's Congress (UPC). With the formation of UPC, UNC and UPU were no more. But it is not a merger when one party in an alliance or coalition swallows or allows itself to be swallowed up by another. It is an absorption or, in company law terms, a take-over. (In current Uganda political parlance, it is referred to as being swallowed.)

Sometimes, a country may face an existential threat which demands the formation of a government of national unity to deal with it. In such circumstances, all significant political parties and even individuals outside political parties join hands to confront that threat. In 1939 at the outbreak of the World War II, the British Conservative, Liberal and Labour parties, not to mention leaders of trade unions and industry, formed a government of national unity led by Winston Churchill. In 1979, Ugandans belonging to various political parties and groups got together and formed the Uganda National Liberation Front (UNLF) in order to oust President Idi Amin's government. When the crisis is overcome, the coalition usually dissolves, and the parties go their separate ways.

While they were in the bush fighting a war of insurgency against a sitting government, the Popular Resistance Army (PRA), led by Yoweri Museveni, Uganda Freedom Fighters (UFF), led by Yusufu Lule, another outfit called Vumbula, led by Kakooza Mutale and other miscellaneous malcontents, merged their military and political forces to form the National Resistance Army/Movement (NRA/M).

One other alliance, if indeed it warrants being so named at all, is one where the Baganda who fought in the Luwero insurgency on the side of NRA/NRM claimed that they did so with the understanding that Buganda kingship and federal status would be restored if their "alliance" won the war. It won and NRA/NRM largely studiously ignored the latter.

When, in 1986, the NRA succeeded in ousting the military government that had overthrown Obote's government, they incorporated DP and some elements of UPC together with other fighting groups and formed what they called a broad-based government. By the end of the day, the fighting groups had been swallowed up and DP and UPC were struggling to remain alive. A law had been passed prohibiting all political parties — except NRM whose leaders claimed was not a political party — from carrying out activities outside their party headquarters.

To increase their strength in the legislature in order to face off with NRM which was threatening to obliterate them from the political map of Uganda, during the 1996 general elections, UPC and DP formed the first Inter-Party Cooperation (IPC) arrangement and fielded a joint presidential candidate to run against Yoweri Museveni and NRM. Although it came to naught, a further attempt at forming alliance was made in preparation for the 2011 elections. This brought together the Conservative Party (CP), the Forum for Democratic Change (FDC), the Social Democratic Party (SDP), and UPC. The formation of The Democratic Alliance (TDA) to contest in the 2016 elections has been the latest effort, although in the end, the individual opposition parties became fragmented in their commitment.

Clearly, most of Uganda's major political successes, and failures, have been through alliances and coalitions. They have become a normal feature in political calculations. Many pundits actually believe that the post-Museveni government will most likely be a government of national unity, which is a coalition on a grander scale.

Apart from the UNLF alliance, one feature which has characterised all alliances in Uganda is the lack of documentation. Nearly all have not been in writing. It is perplexing why in Uganda agreements of this nature have tended to be verbal despite the literacy levels of the leaders involved. Since most of these agreements are concluded when victory is in sight, maybe they get carried away by the euphoria and asking that the terms be written would cast a shadow of mistrust and doubt about the impending victory and the sharing of the spoils. In any case, after agreeing, probably verbally, to the initial distribution of key ministerial positions, the partners seem to leave everything else to chance. They take a political alliance as a good marriage where each party does what is expected from and of them without reference to any document. Even in marriage, prenuptial agreements have dented that assumed trust that all will be well.

Although literacy is widespread, especially among the so-called political elite, they do not commit themselves in writing when it comes to political matters. This is what being functionally illiterate means: you can write but do not write what you should; you can read but do not read when you should. As a result, when a dispute arises, the politicians resort to, a "We said this. No, we did not. We meant this. No, we did not" scenario and none of the parties can be nailed down to a particular position.

By the time of the second and final Lancaster House Conference, Buganda had apparently implicitly resigned itself to the fact that it was going to be part of independent Uganda and had abandoned its project to go it alone as the sovereign state it was before the 1900 Agreement with the British. It was now determined to focus on ensuring that, under the new arrangement, it did so on the best terms possible for itself and its king.

As independence came into sight, there were three significant political parties or organisations in Uganda. Two of them, UPC and DP, were national in character and coverage. The third organisation, KY, was regional in outlook, its interests being confined to Buganda.

There had been a general election in March 1961 in which 82 seats had to be filled for the National Assembly. In that election, DP won 43 seats and UPC got 35 seats. DP's total of 43 seats included 20 out of the 21 available from Buganda, a region which had boycotted the elections with only 10% of the eligible voters participating. UPC had won one seat out of 21 in Buganda. That meant that, outside Buganda, DP had won 23 seats compared to UPC's 34. It was, therefore, DP's seats from Buganda, coupled with those from the rest of Uganda that had enabled it to get the necessary majority in Parliament and form the first African government in 1961.

Those numbers had taught political actors a clear lesson: if those results were replicated in the next elections and KY agreed to participate in them and were to win all 21 seats from Buganda, no single party or organisation on its own would be able to get enough seats to form a government. As it turned out, in the 1962 elections, UPC got 37 seats, DP 24 and KY 21. Therefore, no single party had got enough seats to form a government on its own. As a result, it was inevitable that the next government would have to be an alliance or a coalition among those three major players. The question was what combination of parties would form that coalition. Clearly, it was KY which, in the words of Viscount Ward of Witley, "hold the balance of power" (1962: How Buganda Tested Ugandan, British Politicians, 2018).

There were three possible formations, and a fourth, although a remote one, for a winning alliance: a DP/KY alliance, a DP/UPC alliance, a UPC/KY alliance, and the improbable combination of all three to form a government of national unity. Let us survey the possible alliances.

DP/KY alliance

By participating in the 1961 elections in Buganda, which Mengo had boycotted because it was still pursuing the possibility of a separate independence or, in addition, it was unwilling to engage in the independence processes before it was sure of Buganda's and its king's position in independent Uganda, DP had defied Mengo and done the unforgivable. In religious terms, it had committed a sacrilege and, politically, treason. That ruled out a DP/KY alliance.

But there must have been more to fuel the fury of Mengo than the DP's mere participation in the election for, in principle, UPC had done exactly the same thing. It, too, had taken part in that election, its secretary general, John Kakonge, winning a seat from Lugazi area within Buganda, but did not incur Mengo's wrath for its action. The reader is invited to make their own assumptions. This antagonism was to have a great bearing on the working combination that ultimately emerged.

DP/UPC alliance

First, those two parties were arch rivals for power. Each wanted power on its own. But more importantly, an alliance between the two would have amounted to courting disaster. I believe the leaders of DP and UPC had enough political sense to not even consider a DP/UPC alliance for it was simply politically unthinkable. It would have torn the country apart instead of uniting it.

The Mengo establishment would have perceived that combination as a conspiracy of the anti- and non-Ganda DPs and UPCs to gang up against Buganda and isolate it politically from the rest of Uganda. That would have spurred Buganda further to demand its separate independence. The possibility of such an alliance did not merit a second look because all parties seemed to realise that its cost to the emerging state would have been too high to bear.

UPC/KY alliance

The difficulties of the above options left the UPC/KY alliance as the only viable combination of political organisations to form a workable government. By default, a combination of those two was inevitable since neither of them wanted to associate with DP. It was the only alliance possible in order to avoid an impasse of the kind that would have meant Uganda remaining under British rule with no independence date on the horizon — a situation which neither the Ugandan politicians nor the British desired.

The fact that there was nothing unusual or sinister about it notwithstanding, the UPC/KY alliance has given a bad name to alliances in Uganda. Today, any political formation that smacks of an alliance is likely to be portrayed, especially by those who stand to be disadvantaged by it, as destined to lead the country to disaster. The alliance is used as a scarecrow frame of reference.

The UPC/KY alliance has often been repeatedly described and referred to as *infamous, unholy, unprincipled* and *a marriage of convenience with one-sided benefits*. Those are words thrown about rather carelessly, in my view. To those who disapprove of the alliance, the political problems Uganda found itself in a few years into independence, and more precisely the 1966 Crisis, are traceable to the alliance. Those are strong sentiments. But what are the facts regarding that alliance? By what criteria should its success or failure be assessed?

To ease that process, given the serious nature of the arrangement, one would have expected it to have been written; but it was verbal. There are hilarious anecdotes regarding the birth of the alliance: who went to whose place, who wore what on what occasion, who knelt and prostrated before whom — all going to demonstrate which party was being courted and which was pliant to deceive and entrap the other. Those anecdotes surrounding the formation of the alliance will not be rehashed here.

Until quite recently, the burning but unanswered question was whether it was an agreement between two individuals, Mutesa and Obote, or it was a treaty between KY and UPC. In one part of a series of autobiographical interviews with *The Daily Monitor* newspaper reported in 2005, Milton Obote cleared the air for the first time. He had this to say:

> The UPC/ KY Alliance was a matter of discussion between Mutesa and me only. Even UPC Central Executive Committee did not discuss it. I used to report just the outcome. UPC and Mengo had a common cause: we both wanted DP government out of office. Our dilemma was how we get rid of DP. In April 1962 elections UPC got 37 seats, DP 24 and KY had 21. (Karamagi, 2005)

If that was how little the top leadership of UPC was allowed to know of the discussions of the alliance, one can imagine how much less the Mengo leaders knew, given that the Kabaka himself, who was under no obligation to anybody, was personally in charge of the negotiations with Obote. The opaqueness is all the greater since the final outcome of their agreement was not reduced to writing.

That long over-due clarification by Obote notwithstanding, future scholars may still want to know: when was the alliance consolidated? When did it come to an end? Was it ended by a single blow or did it dissolve quietly and gradually? Barungi (2011) asserts that the alliance had collapsed by August 1965. It is safe to say that much the same way as its birthday is unknown, no one knows exactly when it died, who or what killed it. But ultimately all that does not matter much.

Secondary Factors and Episodes that Stoked the Crisis

We now know, although from one party, that the alliance was between Sir Edward Mutesa and Milton Obote as individuals, even though dressed up as having been between UPC and KY as institutions. Since its terms were not stipulated, it is not possible to tell with certainty whether it was breached at all, and if so, by which party and to which extent it was breached and how conflicts which arose within it could have been resolved.

In spite of all that, some rough sketches of the alliance can be discerned from secondary sources through noting some activities and the conduct of the parties. Those observations in turn enable us to make a reasonable assessment whether or not the accusations levelled against the alliance as an arrangement and the individual parties to it are justified.

The UPC/KY political alliance was about gaining power or securing a vital interest. It must, therefore, be judged against the aspirations and fears of the parties and how far they were realised or allayed through gaining power. I will take one by one.

We will begin with KY—this being taken to include Buganda as a territory, the Mengo establishment, and Kabaka Mutesa as an individual. KY needed assurances and made demands regarding, first, the powers of Buganda and, second, the position of its Kabaka in an independent Uganda. Without clarity and assurances on those matters, the date of Uganda's independence, nay, independence itself could not be ascertained.

Buganda believed that it was a special entity from the rest of Uganda. It argued that if Britain was going to grant Uganda independence, it should leave Buganda as an independent state, just as it found it at the advent of British protection. Consistent with its position over the years, the Mengo establishment also remained uncomfortable with the setting up and operation of political parties in Buganda.

Up till 1955, Buganda's relationship with Britain, the colonial (or protectorate) power, was governed by the 1900 Agreement. Buganda was by and large a separate entity within Uganda, although, as was shown at the beginning, there were activities, services and institutions which linked it to the rest of Uganda. In 1955, upon Mutesa's return from deportation to Britain following his resistance to merge Uganda into an East African Federation under the Colonial Office, a new covenant (Buganda Agreement, 1955) was entered into between Britain and Buganda whose stated purpose was to guide the new relationship between Britain and Buganda but the effect of which was to make Buganda even more integrated into Uganda.

Buganda Kingdom, like the districts in the rest of Uganda, was meant to elect members to the Legislative Council (Legco), the nascent National Assembly. But when the time came to do so, in 1958, Buganda boycotted them, as it did those of 1961, mainly on the ground that it was not clear what the position of Buganda was going to be in the independent Uganda that was emerging. In October 1960, Buganda declared that it would become an independent state on 31 December of that year. In short, Buganda was showing all signs of pursuing a future separation from Uganda.

On the other hand, Obote/UPC wanted, first, Uganda to gain independence; second, to gain it as soon as possible, and third, to gain it with Uganda as one united country, which included Buganda. Last but not least, Obote/UPC wanted Uganda to gain independence with UPC and Obote obviously at the helm.

Secondary Factors and Episodes that Stoked the Crisis

Did the Alliance deliver what each party bargained for? Did Uganda as a stakeholder gain or lose by the alliance?

In 1962, under the Independence Constitution, Buganda participated in the general elections with the rest of the country and we have the alliance to thank for that. Buganda was accorded full federal status within Uganda, which made it "a state within a state"—with its own Parliament (Lukiiko), judiciary, and police force—unlike the other kingdoms of Bunyoro, Ankore, and Tooro and the Territory of Busoga which were granted a semi-federal status. The rest of the administrative units in the country remained local governments which were to be governed directly by the Central Government.

Yet again, Mutesa did us all a great favour by writing down his views and feelings. He wrote that Obote had been helpful in getting Buganda's demands accepted at the London conferences. It is also on record that Obote alone convinced UPC members to vote Mutesa president of Uganda with precedence over all Ugandans, like the governor he was replacing, which the Baganda craved, in preference to Wilberforce Nadiope as we have seen.

The alliance made it possible for UPC to form a government with Obote as prime minister and head of that government. Buganda's demands having been met with the help of Obote, Uganda moved into independence as one nation. Mutesa (1967) sums up the mutual gains, his and Obote's, from the alliance when he writes, using the royal first-person plural, "Obote was friendly, understood our position and owed his office to our support" (p. 168).

This alliance was also beneficial to the Mengo establishment and UPC in that, by UPC agreeing not to sponsor candidates in Buganda but give KY a free hand in Buganda to tussle it out with hated DP, which it annihilated, party politics in general was kept at bay from the region a little longer, an outcome Mengo desired although it contradicted UPC's pretention to being a national political party. At the same time, it isolated and contained DP, a situation pleasing to both Mengo and UPC. It was also at the joint insistence of Mengo and UPC that fresh elections were held in April 1962, which gave them a chance to actualise their alliance and form a government. Benedicto Kiwanuka and his DP, which were already heading a government following an election held less than a year earlier but which Mengo had boycotted, were overwhelmed by the joint UPC-Mengo force at the Lancaster Conference which demanded that fresh elections be held and which they won.

Again, in the absence of a written agreement, it is not clear whether UPC's not putting up candidates and opening branches in Buganda was meant to be a permanent feature of the UPC-KY relationship or an arrangement meant to last only for that particular political season. The answer determines whether or not there was a breach of an understanding.

Although it later floundered for a variety of reasons, in my opinion, the UPC-KY alliance was a matter of give-and-take founded on benefits at both individual and institutional levels. The alliance, in whatever form it was expressed, was designed to address the concerns of the contracting parties, as they were at the time. It was not designed to solve problems which might emerge in the infinite future. As it has been stated before, the alliance encompassed the irreducible objectives of each party: the special place of Buganda and the position of its Kabaka in an independent Uganda, for KY, and early independence for a united Uganda with UPC leadership at the top, in the case of UPC. The success of the alliance should therefore be measured on the extent to which the separate and collective objectives of the parties were achieved.

Secondary Factors and Episodes that Stoked the Crisis

The calling of the referendum and signing of the laws relating to it by one party without the consent of the other, may have been the beginning of the unravelling of the alliance. But that does not make its creation wrong and its implementation a failure from the very start. No matter how it came into being or ended, in my view, the alliance in itself did not cause or contribute to the Crisis. As for Uganda as a whole, but for the alliance, its independence would have waited a little longer. The alliance was, therefore, a considerable achievement both in formation and performance, until it faded away.

Having set out the benefits of the alliance to the two parties the way I have, it is tempting to leave it at that and dismiss the assertions of its critics with the wave of the hand. But it is only fair to devote some space to investigating the basis of those assertions.

The above discussion has been premised on the fact that the alliance enabled the parties to it to realise their vital separate expectations and to forestall their fears, which each party on its own would not have achieved. If an alliance requires the satisfaction of mutual interests, what were the common interests of UPC and KY? One would need to look very carefully to see any. Their different interests, call them ideological differences, were more glaring by far. At the risk of repetition, a non-exhaustive list of their differences will be laid out.

UPC wanted Uganda to gain independence as one united country. That oneness was the end UPC pursued and the forging of the UPC-KY alliance was the means to that end. KY, representing the Mengo establishment, had up till that time persistently demanded that Buganda be granted independence as the independent country it was before 1900. UPC was republican in orientation; KY was monarchist in outlook. KY wanted the Kabaka of Buganda, and the Buganda Kingdom itself, to enjoy a special position in Uganda. UPC, on the other hand, was perceived as tilting against the occupancy of a public position by a person solely by virtue of their birth. KY conceded to Buganda remaining in Uganda provided it enjoyed a special position as a federal province with almost all features of a sovereign state. UPC decided for greater good that it could live with hereditary leaders and a special position for Buganda. Those were fundamental differences which would justify the critics, not looking at the big picture, in giving the alliance the unsavoury names they did, but that is stuff alliances are made of. It is the big picture that counts in the end.

Indeed, at that point in time, as Lwanga-Lunyiigo (2015) has so ably demonstrated, if inadvertently, UPC had more in common with DP, its arch political rival, than with KY. But a UPC-DP alliance was completely untenable and out of consideration. If we may remind ourselves, it was hard to characterise KY as a political party. It had no constitution, no branch network (the *Gombolola* and *Saza* chiefs, supposedly civil servants acting as its mobilisers' chairmen), and a two-word manifesto: Kabaka Yekka – the King Alone. It is said that DP's protestations that KY was not a qualified political party eligible to participate in a general election fell on deaf colonial ears only too eager to show its back to Uganda and would not entertain any scheme that would cause any further delay.

But UPC and KY had one compelling thing in common and for which the two were prepared to sweep all their ideological differences under the carpet: the desire to edge DP out of power in post-independent Uganda, come the next general election.

In policy contestations within political organisations, there often comes a time when the purists are pitted against the pragmatists within the same party. This was one such time as far as UPC was concerned. John Kakonge, the pragmatist UPC secretary general, reminded the ideological purists who were complaining against the alliance that politics was the game of the possible. For reasons which Mutesa does not go into in any detail but one of which I have hinted at, Mengo could not stand DP.

The mutual desire of UPC and KY to block DP and the unaviability of an alternative political formation were gave birth to the alliance, however one may want to describe it. KY was willing to be courted. UPC was looking for a party to woo. There was only one remotely acceptable suitor and one available party to engage for KY and UPC, respectively. In such circumstances, Obote must not have found it an exacting task but a relatively easier one than would have been expected, to convince Mutesa and the Mengo establishment that the life of Buganda and its king in an independent Uganda would not be the disaster they feared but might even be pleasant. Although it had a few loose ends, the treaty between UPC and KY, or rather between Obote and Mutesa, had been ratified on both sides. So, instead of it being called all those unsavoury names and censuring Obote as one of its architects, the UPC-KY alliance should be more accurately described and known as "the Inevitable Alliance." Above all, it delivered the individual and collective objectives of the partners: DP was eased out of power; UPC acquired power; Obote became prime minister of Uganda; Edward Mutesa became president of Uganda; Buganda Kingdom enjoyed a federal status within Uganda; and Uganda gained independence as one united country. None of those could have been achieved by either party acting alone or, in the circumstances, under any other party combination apart from the UPC-KY alliance.

Since so much of Uganda's post-independence history hinges on this alliance and Obote's role in it, a reverse translation from English to Luganda is for once an absolute necessity for a particular audience. *Wewaawo tekwaali kuseereza ligenda mugga, naye ng'otunuuride eby'obufuzi nga bwebyaali biyimiridde, Obote teyalina kulinya lusozi Gambalagala okupeerereza ab'e Mengo okukiriza KY okutta omukago ne UPC awamu n'okubamatiza nti ekifo kya Kabaka ne Buganda mu Uganda eyawamu byaali bija kuba bya ssanyu na ddembe. Wewawo gwalimu ebiragaya, mukifo ky'okuguvumirira, omukago gwa UPC ne KY gusaana kuyitibwa "Omukago Ogwaali Gutewalika." Okusiinga byonna gwatukiriza ebigendererwa byagwo: DP gwagisuuza obuyinza, UPC yafuna obuyinza, Obote yalya obwa Katikkiro bwa Uganda, Kabaka Mutesa yalya obwa President bwa Uganda, Buganda yafuna federo ne Uganda nefuna obwetwaaze nga egwanga erimu. Kw'ebyo tewaali nakimu kyali kisoboka kutukwaako okujjako nga UPC ne KY bikoze omukago.*

Mutesa and Obote put together an alliance of parties which steered Uganda into independence. The dissenters have used their time to denigrate that arrangement. It should not be too hard, with all the benefit of hindsight, for the dissenters to present their alternative solution to the impasse the framers of the UPC-KY alliance were faced with in order to move the country forward. Instead, what we have heard from that side so far is name calling.

Government of National Unity Composed of DP, UPC, and KY

Given the deep misunderstanding, if not outright animosity, between KY and DP, a government of national unity in which both sat was inconceivable. Apart from the well-known rivalry between DP and UPC for the leadership of Uganda, it would have demanded such goodwill among the three parties as I suspect was not available at the time. It is also doubtful that the British would favour this arrangement since it ran contrary to the British mindset, and possibly express desire, which required a government with an opposition party, the "loyal opposition," which was then considered an essential element of the democracy Britain may have wished to leave behind in Uganda. The absence of support by the British who were driving the process would have doomed it from the start even if someone had had the presence of mind to table it. A government of national unity faced too strong obstacles to materialise.

UPC in Buganda

Interestingly, Mutesa gives the impression that he did not see the Lost Counties as the main cause of his split with Obote. In an apparently charitable spirit, but more likely to disguise his legitimate Buganda nationalism, he writes:

> The lost counties were a difficult issue and I do not blame Obote for not giving me his complete and immediate support. It must be made clear, however, that this was not the cause of the split between us. The quarrel was well known when we gave him our support, and he began to move against us long before it came to a head. (Mutesa, 1967, p. 170)

Mutesa does not elaborate on this but he probably meant Obote's UPC opening up branches in Buganda in 1964 before the referendum was held. He blames Obote, though, for making much of his refusal to sign the Lost Counties Referendum Bill when Obote should have realised that such refusal was inevitable, given "my dual role was delicate" (Mutesa, 1967, p. 174). In any case, Mutesa observed, ". . . if I refused three times to sign a Bill the Prime Minister could sign it himself" (p. 174).

In other words, Mutesa is telling us that the events surrounding the referendum were no big deal, that they were understandable and forgivable. It is also a confession that it was impossible, constitutionally, to block it on his own.

A few pages later, however, Mutesa suddenly changes his mind and writes that by going ahead with the referendum, "Far from uniting the country, Obote had decisively split it... In this case, he purposely antagonised the ablest and richest unit in his country...." (Mutesa, 1967, p. 180).

The above notwithstanding, among other things, Mutesa attributes the split to UPC fielding candidates during the by-election inside Buganda, which they had agreed not to do at the general election. This must have been the equivalent of the concept of "ring-fencing" in today's political parlance; an area is virtually cordoned off for the exclusive use, enjoyment or exercise of power by one person or a category of people. This was complicated, a little confusing and may need some explanation. First, the fact that Kabaka Mutesa would complain about it is an indication that he had gotten himself involved in retail politics, which Archbishop Joseph Kiwanuka and his brother-kings had warned him against.

If it were asked who, from the triumvirate of Mutesa, Obote, and Ibingira, the recruitment of members and opening up of UPC branches in Buganda (which of course precedes the fielding of candidates) favoured and who it hurt, my answer would be: it is a matter of dates—whether it was done before or after the referendum.

The recruitment of UPC members in Buganda must be seen in the broader context of the power struggle within the party and the geopolitics then raging in the world. This was the period of the Cold War when the Western powers and the Eastern powers were competing for influence and allies in

Africa and the so-called Third World generally. Power within a party depends on the support one has within its organs.

Within UPC, there were three ideological groupings: the conservative wing (call it the right wing or the dollar wing, according to the rank and file members) headed by Ibingira, which was also thought to be pro-West and capitalistic in ideological orientation; the Kakonge group (the left wing or the ruble wing), which was deemed to be pro-East and, therefore, communistic; and the Obote wing, which was thought to be the moderate among the three. In reality, support within the party members for each of those individuals, as is largely the case up to today, was attracted not so much by ideological conviction as by personal acquaintance and liking.

After being elected UPC secretary general, Ibingira began to change the face of the UPC secretariat, which is the civil service of the party, dismissing personnel that had been recruited by Kakonge, the previous secretary general, and replacing them with his own. He also embarked on a vigorous recruitment of members in Buganda. His objective was clear. He was looking for people who would be beholden to him and support him in his future battles against Obote.

Since Mutesa was allied with Ibingira, this was not a development that should have caused him (Mutesa) any concern. On the other hand, the person who should have been worried by it should have been Obote whom it placed in an unpleasant dilemma: as head of the party he would have wished to see the party grow and welcome the efforts of his secretary general to that end, but he would not have wished to see growth that was designed to undermine his power within the party.

Sight should not be lost of the fact that this was the time when a number of members from Buganda who had entered

Parliament on the KY ticket had crossed to UPC. Where a member of Parliament is directly elected, when that member changes parties but wishes to remain in politics, he has no alternative but to try to change the political colour of his constituency. He has to recruit members to join his new party and open branches in his constituency who will support him when the next election comes. His old party has no power or control over that. But Buganda's members of Parliament were not directly elected. So, recruiting of UPC members and opening branches in their constituencies was not of immediate advantage to the Buganda MPs. We may take this as another mystery of the game of politics for which there is no need to strain for an explanation.

Buganda politicians were expected to pursue the collective interests of their party and regions, but many were not shy to follow their private ones when their personal political advancement in a wider Uganda demanded. Looking at the broader picture, some politicians from Buganda saw the Mengo establishment, especially after the loss of the referendum, as a power on the wane and UPC as the rising power on which to hitch their political wagon.

Kirunda-Kivejinja's assertion that, "It later transpired that Obote, with his own perspective on the party, appeared to have given an undertaking to Mutesa NEVER TO RECRUIT ANY MUGANDA INTO THE UPC...." (1995, p. 24) seems to be far-fetched and probably a product of his personal biases. His book, *Uganda: The Crisis of Confidence*, is infected by the intense bitterness and venom against the person of Obote and everything he stood for. It is instructive to remember that Kirunda-Kivejinja was one of a group of young members who were expelled from UPC in March 1965 under Obote's watch. Kirunda, who was a full-time employee of the party at the time, neither understood nor forgave Obote's action. And it shows. In any event, keeping UPC out of Buganda would have been a promise Obote would have found difficult to carry out. As Kirunda-Kivejinja himself quotes from a statement from UPC leaders from Buganda:

> ... the name of the party is Uganda People's Congress. If he (Obote) wanted to exclude the Baganda from joining it, he could either change the name of the party and call it the Rest of Uganda People's Congress (Minus Buganda) or should himself abdicate as a declaration of failure to lead and organise a national party. (Kirunda-Kivejinja, 1995, p. 46)

As Mutesa was reproaching Obote for promoting UPC in Buganda, Kirunda-Kivejinja and his group were at the same time remonstrating with him for restraining them from vigorously extending the party into Buganda. Uneasy is the head that wears the crown. The push to introduce UPC into Buganda would in later years give justification to the popular chant at UPC rallies, "UPC everywhere, UPC everybody."

At first glance, one might be baffled to think that Kabaka Mutesa would wish to lock the people of his kingdom into a parochial Kabaka Yekka movement. But this approach was anchored in past attitude and practice. It should be remembered that this was "Buganda where a self-appointed and self-perpetuating oligarchy had ruled the kingdom for half a century" (Karugire, 2010, p. 151). A self-perpetuating oligarchy is like a private members' club to which admission is by invitation and where a member already in recommends a friend to be brought in. And the show goes on. It had blocked party politics from taking root in Buganda by harassing the leaders and supporters of the emerging political parties, obviously for fear of losing its power. They assaulted them verbally and physically upon their person and property. Feeling threatened by the competition for power and the risks that go with party politics and the requirements of accountability that democracy demands, the Mengo establishment had chosen to impose on its people the vicissitudes of courtly favour.

When independence became inevitable and political parties unavoidable, the "self-perpetuating oligarchy" formed, not a political party but a movement called Kabaka Yekka. This movement, despite advancing neither a policy by which to govern nor a philosophy of governance, was strong enough to fend off genuine political party activity in Buganda for some time. The denial of support from what should have been their natural political base may partly explain why, although the founders of the earliest nationwide political parties in Uganda were Baganda—Ignatius Musaazi of Uganda National Congress (UNC), formed in 1952; Joseph Kasolo the founder President General in 1954 was followed by Matayo Mugwanya who was succeeded by Benedicto Kiwanuka, the most prominent of them all within DP in 1958—none of them was able to lead their parties to independence. Apart from going against the engrained aversion against political parties, these party-political leaders were outsiders and not part of the Mengo establishment.

The poignant observations of Barbara Kimenye are instructive. Kimenye, a young English lady, arrived in Uganda via Tanganyika in the mid-1950s, a politically critical and exciting period in Uganda's and Buganda's history. She joined the Buganda civil service and moved in the social circles of the topmost layer of Buganda's society. From the vantage point of an outsider and an insider at the same time, she observed the goings-on in Buganda and indeed Uganda. She tells us:

> ... many Baganda intellectuals were prominent in the formation of political parties and supporting the call for a united independent Uganda. Unfortunately, these progressives were seldom seen at the convivial gatherings in the Old Twekobe (Buganda Parliament Building)... So, the Kabaka was deprived of their opinions and advice, and instead heard only the narrow viewpoints of a blinkered clique. (Kimenye, 2015, p. 17)

The treatment, the near ostracising within Buganda of Baganda intellectuals involved in the formation of political parties has had a psychological effect on the politics of Uganda to this day. It appears that there is a tendency among Baganda of real ability, fearing rejection from their area of origin, to shy away from offering themselves for national elective office, on the one hand, and probably to a lesser extent, a distrust of Baganda politicians among the rest of Ugandans, on the other. For the over fifty years Uganda has been independent, no political leader has emerged from Buganda as an executive head of state through a universal election, but Buganda has supplied a disproportionate number of appointed vice presidents, usually for cynical reasons. President Yusufu Lule, a Muganda, was elected by the National Consultative Council (composed of external groups fighting President Amin) shortly before the fall of Idi Amin's government mainly to ease the progress of the war through what would otherwise have been a hostile Buganda territory. He was dismissed and his government fell after 68 days. President Godfrey Binaisa, another Muganda, was elected by the same body largely to assuage the Baganda who were rioting in the capital city over the sudden and unexplained dismissal of Yusufu Lule. Binaisa's government lasted eleven months. In order to harvest the best available talent, it should be equally unacceptable for one to seek an elective office and be given support as one to be denied support merely because one comes from a particular area or is of a particular ancestry. The same applies to one recoiling from offering oneself for leadership for the similar reasons.

The failure of the Baganda founders of political parties in Uganda to lead their parties to independence may be contrasted with the political leaders in the other English-speaking African countries—Kwame Nkrumah of Ghana with his Convention People's Party (CPP), Julius Nyerere of Tanganyika with his Tanganyika National Union (TANU), Jomo Kenyatta who led Kenya African National Union (KANU), Kenneth Kaunda of Zambia with his United National Independence Party (UNIP) and Hastings Banda of Malawi who led with his Malawi Congress Party (MCP).

In the even broader scheme of things, seeing that the crossings from DP and KY to UPC had rendered UPC very strong, those politicians in Buganda who were opposed to it decided to join in order to fight it and Obote from within (*Tulwanire muli munda*). In fact, Dr Emmanuel Lumu, a cross-over from KY and a pro-Ibingira man, had taken leadership of UPC-Buganda from Mr Godfrey Binaisa, a supporter of Obote and a founding member of UPC. It is against that background that the putting up of UPC branches and sponsoring candidates in by-elections in Buganda should be seen.

That having been said, Mutesa and Obote's attitude to recruitment of new members into UPC in Buganda again depended on the time. Before the referendum, and, therefore, before Ibingira began plotting against him, Obote would have welcomed the recruitment as strengthening his party. On the other hand, it would have raised Mutesa's ire. After the referendum, and after Ibingira had started manoeuvring for his removal from leadership, Obote would have resented recruitment of new members from Buganda as it was designed to weaken him. But on the other hand, Mutesa should have welcomed it since it served his object of removing Obote. Once again, the referendum was the marker in the change of attitudes.

Definition of Roles and Statuses

In 1963, when the conference of Non-Allied Countries was scheduled in Cairo, Egypt, President Mutesa expected that he, and not the prime minister, should represent Uganda. No doubt the president felt snubbed when it was the prime minister who went instead. Yet, it is common knowledge that at conferences of that nature the executive heads of government represent their countries. The president was a ceremonial head of state, not head of government. Mutesa was not satisfied with being a figure-head confined to merely reading speeches prepared for him in Parliament, an exercise he found tedious.

The control of the army was also a bone of contention. Mutesa (1967) complains that he had not been officially informed by the prime minister of the invitation of British troops to put down the mutiny in the Uganda army back in 1964. He also writes that the prime minister's action provided him, as president, with the necessary precedent to "sound out" some foreign leaders if they could send troops to Uganda in 1966 without informing the prime minister. Those were indeed ominous signs of mistrust between the two men.

There had been troop movements within the country through early 1966 of which Mutesa had had no prior notification. Apparently, Obote complained of the same matter. Mutesa (1967) further writes that at one time, after a visit to the president, Colonel Idi Amin had been told by the prime minister never to approach the president without getting his permission and yet the president was Idi Amin's Commander-in-Chief. Mutesa was also not pleased that the prime minister did not submit to him changes in the cabinet for his approval.

For a full year after independence, the governor, now called the governor-general, stayed behind in Uganda as ceremonial head of state. By replacing him as an elected president, Mutesa may have thought that he enjoyed all the powers and perks of the colonial governor he was replacing. Indeed, that could have been the attraction in seeking the position in the first place. If he did so believe, he was mistaken both with regard to the content of the powers and circumstances of the colonial governor vis-à-vis those of the president of Uganda.

On the surface, the president of Uganda had the same powers vis-à-vis the prime minister of Uganda and Parliament as the governor had vis-à-vis the Kabaka of Buganda and the *Lukiiko*. The governor had to approve senior appointments of personnel made by the Kabaka. The president had to be informed of the changes in the cabinet made by the prime minister. The governor had to approve the laws passed by the Lukiiko. The president had to consent to the laws passed by Parliament. That is where the similarity or near similarity stopped. The submission of changes in the cabinet to the president by the prime minister depended on the good behaviour of the prime minister. With regard to laws passed by Parliament, if a law was presented to the president for his consent, a number of times without his doing so, the prime minister could sign it into law. So far as the appointments of personnel by the Kabaka and the Lukiiko passing laws, it should be remembered that the governor carried a big stick to keep both on the straight and narrow. The president had no stick and even the power to consent to the laws was mere tokenism.

Matters were not helped by the respective followers of the two men within the civil service. They exacerbated the situation by virtually fighting over whose portrait, the president's or that of the prime minister's, should hang in their respective public offices. They ought to have known that, conventionally, the world over, it is that of the head of state, ceremonial or executive, that adorns public offices. In the case of Uganda, it should have been that of Sir Edward Mutesa, the president.

These misunderstandings of each other's roles and the conduct that followed, whether deliberate or otherwise, did not generate the good will between leaders so necessary to steer a young nation forward.

Lack of Political Courage and Self-Delusion

Upon his return from the second London Conference at the conclusion of the negotiations of the Independence Constitution, Mikaeri Kintu, the Katikkiro of Buganda, told the people that all Buganda's demands, *Ebyaffe*, had been acceded to, "despite opposition from a few people", implying Benedicto Kiwanuka and his DP. Why did he say that when he knew or ought to have known that the vital issue of the Lost Counties had been deferred to be resolved through a referendum after independence? Three possible answers spring to mind. First, can it be safely said that Kintu genuinely, but mistakenly, believed that all issues had been settled in Buganda's favour? In other words, had he misunderstood the terms of the independence settlement? Second, did he think that because of the KY-UPC alliance, Obote would be prevailed upon not to conduct the referendum since, in Mengo's view, its being held depended on his (Obote's) wish? Third, did he lack sufficient political courage to level with the people of Buganda by telling them the truth about the pending referendum and the uncertainty that was bound to go with it?

The first reason is unconvincing. It is not supported by Mutesa's writing regarding the London negotiations. The second is more credible because Mutesa himself appears to have thought that the holding of the referendum would depend on Prime Minister Obote's wish. At a superficial level, it may appear that Kintu withheld the truth because of lack of political courage; that he told the people what they wanted to hear — that Buganda was going with Uganda into independence on Buganda's terms, that is, as a federal state that retained the Lost Counties which had been part of the Buganda Kingdom "as long as anyone could remember". The actual constitutional provisions were not revealed to the people they led. It was also false to give the impression that the Lost Counties had been part of Buganda from antiquity when there were people in 1962 to whom the years 1897, when Omukama Kabalega was defeated, and 1900 when the counties were formally annexed and added to Buganda were within living memory.

In fairness to Kintu, being the Katikkiro, he could not contradict his Kabaka. Probably Kintu alone on the Buganda delegation had opposed even the discussion of the question of the Lost Counties at the London conferences. He regarded as sacrosanct and beyond discussion Buganda's boundaries which were set under the 1900 Agreement. It was his Kabaka who had prevailed on him to concede subjecting the Lost Counties to a referendum after independence.

Buganda's anger, anguish, disappointment, shock and sense of betrayal over the referendum stemmed from the erroneous assurance they had gotten from their leaders that Buganda had got all its demands (*Ebyaffe*). Lwanga-Lunyiigo

(2007) observes, "The Baganda understood this to mean all things, including the contested counties of Buyaga and Bugangaizi" (pp. 106-107). If Kintu had found a gentle but truthful way of telling the people of Buganda, without at the same time offending his Kabaka, that the issue of the Lost Counties had not been finally resolved but had remained pending a referendum, they would have been psychologically prepared for the outcome. Knowing that an election can go either way, the people would have taken it in better spirit. But because he had not levelled with them, the surprised and shocked Baganda youths tried to lynch him on the announcement of the referendum results and he had to vacate the office of the Katikkiro three days later. In the spirit of a true servant, Kintu decided to cover up for his Kabaka and it eventually cost him his office.

Mengo and Uganda were not lucky in the persons who held the office of Katikkiro during this crucial period when the fallout from the results of the referendum on the Lost Counties was becoming manifest. When the Lukiiko relieved Kintu of the office of Katikkiro following the referendum, J. S. Mayanja-Nkangi was elected in his stead. Before his candidature for the position, he was one of the 21 members of Parliament representing Buganda in Parliament and a member of cabinet of the Uganda government. I believe Mutesa and Obote at this time genuinely tried to avoid the crisis then staring them in the face by shifting of personnel. Abu Mayanja was elected by the Lukiiko to replace Mayanja-Nkangi as a backbench member of Parliament representing Buganda. He was a minister of education in the Buganda Kingdom government at the time. Having been a founder member of UNC, then defunct, from which UPC emerged, he must have been considered a valuable addition to the National Assembly.

The withdrawal and replacement of Mayanja-Nkangi from both positions so he could take up the office of Katikkiro must have involved some consultation between the leaders of the two partner parties to the alliance, Mutesa the president and Obote the prime minister. The prime minister must have thought it beneficial to embed a man of Mayanja-Nkangi's qualifications and exposure in Mengo. Both Mutesa and Obote must have believed that Mayanja-Nkangi, being a youthful 34-year-old with multiple university degrees and who had served as a minister in the Central Government would, for the benefit of the two, have a better understanding of how the two institutions, the Uganda government and Buganda Government, work than the old traditionalists then in charge at Mengo. Something must have gone terribly wrong to disable that well laid plan. To start with, little did Obote know that, ultimately, effectiveness and influence in Mengo did not depend on one's education and overall experience but on one's personal closeness to the Kabaka. Mayanja-Nkangi either never gained that closeness or lost it down the road. To delve into what brought about that closeness or its loss is a different matter altogether and would be an unnecessary digression.

In a *Bukedde* newspaper write-up following his demise in 2017, Mayanja-Nkangi is reported to have related that a few days before the attack on Lubiri, he had received a telephone call from Obote at 11.00 pm inviting him to a meeting. Mayanja-Nkangi had complained that it was late and that he was already sleeping. And, irony of ironies, he had advised Obote that if the matter was grave and urgent, he should put it in writing. If that was indeed what he told Obote, Mayanja-Nkangi's response was beguiling. Politicians at the level of Katikkiro do not "switch" off and go to sleep, at least not when a call from the nation's chief executive comes through, more so at a time when

Secondary Factors and Episodes that Stoked the Crisis

the country is in turmoil. But then, interviews of this nature, like memoirs, tend to be selective and self-serving.

The truth could be that pride may not have permitted Mayanja-Nkangi to admit to Obote that he was of little help at this point and might have made his personal situation even worse by being seen or heard to be in contact with Obote at this time. Mayanja-Nkangi was a man of cautious nature. Unbeknown to Obote, Mayanja-Nkangi was at that time preoccupied with self-preservation in the Mengo government he ostensibly led. He who Mutesa had appointed Katikkiro over objections of the old guard because of his young age and marital status (single) was no longer in control, let alone being within the inner circle of those who were making the decisions in Bulange or Lubiri. The moment a leader in Mengo was perceived as having lost the ear of the Kabaka, his influence in the establishment went out faster than the light of a candle in the wind. At this time, when matters were coming to a head, power had gone out of the hands of the nominal, formal leadership at Mengo to at least three militant *Saza* chiefs whose influence within the palace loomed large.

More worryingly, however, so far as Buganda leaders are concerned, is the high probability that some of them deliberately lied to the people of Buganda long before the Crisis. For example, Lwanga-Lunyiigo, quoting M.S.M. Kiwanuka, writes:

> On 24th August 1962, two months before independence, one of the architects of the UPC-KY alliance, Abu Mayanja, at a rally at the Clock Tower, Kampala told a gullible audience: 'I can assure you that everything will be alright. Do you expect a Government formed by KY and UPC to give away

Buganda's counties to Bunyoro? (Lwanga-Lunyiigo, 2007, p. 107)

Abu Mayanja was a lawyer who had been a member of the Buganda delegation at the London conferences and who could not feign ignorance of the existence or the meaning of Section 26 of the Independence Order-in-Council. The holding of the referendum was mandatory and not discretionary.

With regard to this aspect of the independence settlement, Lwanga-Lunyiigo (2007) concludes: "Buganda leaders had unashamedly deceived the people and seemed to be getting away with it" (p. 107). In my assessment, the Buganda leaders were not that mendacious. They had a plan to keep the Lost Counties within Buganda. Although it was not documented, the contours of that strategy could be discerned as if it were set down in writing, as I have indicated.

Backgrounds and Ideological Orientations

We naturally refer to the background, even the genetics of a man, especially if he is an outstanding personality vested with important responsibility, in explaining or trying to understand his actions. We wonder when he does not conduct himself in accordance with the expected pattern, given his background and hereditary character traits. The personalities, as indeed the state of health of those actors at the time of their making certain decisions, do impact on the events which affect the course of history of their nations.

The peculiar backgrounds of the key actors, Obote and Mutesa, and the value systems they individually subscribed to (ideology) did have some influence on their inter-personal relations, interpretation of happenings, their reaction to them and, consequently, the course of events leading to the 1966 Crisis. Obote and Mutesa were opposites in many respects.

Secondary Factors and Episodes that Stoked the Crisis

Ours is a purely intuitive or common-sense sketch of Mutesa's and Obote's backgrounds but will serve our present purposes. We leave it to future writers to bring forth systematic theories about these characters' personalities and how they were impacted by their backgrounds.

Hardly any Ugandan politician of the time had had to struggle with similar unfavourable circumstances as Obote did. So far as it is possible, Obote was a self-made man, the butt of clumsy ridicule for having been a goatherd by all accounts, a blue-collar workers' trade unionist who had elbowed his way to the premiership of the country. Milton Obote was not born a prince destined to be king, but he pulled himself up by his bootstraps to become a prince in performance among politicians. After he was done with the goat herding phase of his life, he entered the elementary European education system in the schools in his region and eventually joined the far away Busoga College Mwiri in eastern region.

At Mwiri, instead of engaging in cricket, the sport for which the college was renowned, he became a notable debater. It is probably during this period that to his given names of Apollo Obote, he added the name Milton, a statesman and one of the greatest Englishmen of letters, probably after he had read John Milton's epic poem titled *Paradise Lost*.

He then proceeded to Makerere University College, the East African Constituent branch of London University, where he read political science. During his stay at Makerere, Obote is remembered as having acted in Shakespeare's play, *Julius Caesar*, in which he took the leading role as Emperor Julius Caesar, no less. Before completing his studies at Makerere, he was lured with a prospect of joining Khartoum University to read law. It is said that the British government intervened in the matter and the project did not materialise.

Unable or unwilling to return to Makerere, he journeyed to Kenya where he got exposed to the Mau Mau Movement, then at its height, which was fighting to end colonial rule in that territory. He ended up as a trade union leader in a sugar estate in that colony.

Looking for a more enlightened leadership to represent them, in 1957, the Lango elders invited him to return to Uganda to represent the Lango sub-region in the Legislative Council (Legco), Uganda's nascent Parliament. He soon caught the attention of his colleagues as a distinguished debater and performer. He joined the Uganda National Congress (UNC) and upon the dismissal of Ignatius Musaazi, its founder, he was elected its leader. UNC combined with Uganda People's Union (UPU) to form UPC in a new formation which he led. His party participated in the 1961 general elections in Uganda which DP won. He was the leader of the opposition when the initial negotiations for Uganda's independence started in London and prime minister when they ended.

Obote's herding of goats has been a cause of derision by some people in order to belittle him by painting his portrait in unflattering light, yet, it was an activity he engaged in, not as a grown-up vocation of choice but as a child's normal contribution to family chores in his part of the country in his time. And understandably so. Although the times are changing, previously, in every society, and in none more than in African societies, in every era and in every household, there has been a division of labour according to age and gender. Growing up in Masaka where we were raised, as a boy we used to employ our time as bark-cloth textile makers (*omukomazi*). We remember vividly the village "factory" (*ekkomago*) in which we used to forge the tree bark into textile of different textures for different usages and the various sites to which it was shifted over the period we were engaged in that work. Today, our work then might be characterised as child labour.

We also learnt a thing or two about goat herding, for we were ourselves once goatherds. Although the household we grew up in did not keep goats, that of our friends and agemates and immediate neighbours did. So back in the days when, among youngsters, there were no walls between work, play, and study but all were treated alike, we used to accompany our next homestead friends to the grazeland to help them tend their family goats, so long as our home chores were completed.

Goats are the unruliest of domestic animals. They dig in as they are being taken to graze; they dig in as they are being brought back home from grazing. Unlike cattle which keeps together, once in the bush the goats scatter all over the place. They have a great propensity to get lost. Hence, in Luganda they are called *embuzi*, which means that animal which frequently gets lost.

Goat herding inculcates mental habits of extreme alertness and watchfulness, a vital skill in navigating the treacherous paths of the game of politics. Apart from trying to ensure that no goat got lost, we had to keep a close eye on them lest they meandered into people's gardens and ate their crops along the way, either of which would get our friends into trouble. If the goats Obote looked after in Lango region where he grew up behaved no better than those we helped look after in Masaka, he must have had the same experience as we did. Coupled with that of leading trade unionists, it must have prepared him well for the greater leadership he later assumed in the world of politics, his occupation by choice, which involves negotiations, balancing and reconciling various interests.

Mutesa, on the other hand, was an aristocrat, born to be king, and an absolute monarch at heart. He had been invited to become president. He expected it. His people would have demanded it. He lived his life among courtiers who almost regarded him as a deity, if not the Lord of Hosts and, in his later years, especially after his triumphal return from exile in 1955, his subjects worshipped him with an intensity approaching the religious. Since his passing, to this day, many still strive to make a martyr of him to some cause nobody knows which kind. A popular Luganda singer and song-writer has listed, in one of his songs, 72 titles for the Kabaka of Buganda, and still counting. The Kabaka acquires additional titles as and when his subjects get inspiration to create new ones, without any of the old ones being abrogated or dying out. All describe his extraordinary, almost super-human character and prowess. One of those titles is *Nantasobya* – one who never errs. That cannot fail to get to his head, affect his decision-making, influence his would-be advisors and those who implement his decisions.

In Buganda tradition, there was a thin line between cultural norms and laws properly so called. The Kabaka set new norms and abolished existing ones at will. His word was law. Mutesa writes with apparent nostalgia:

> All authority flowed from the Kabaka. Just as he was the personification of the Baganda, so he and his actions were beyond judgement or question. A tradition that would be binding on all others ceased to be a tradition if he said so. The old might mutter and shake their heads at a discreet distance, but it simply was so. It is misleading even to say that if a Kabaka did something it became right, because that implies that people considered and decided that such an action was acceptable. It was more automatic than that. (Mutesa, 1967, p. 31)

Against that background, it is not surprising that Kabaka Mutesa expected "his prime minister", Obote, to foil the referendum on the Lost Counties, if it did not suit him, (the Kabaka), even though it was constitutionally mandatory. But Milton Obote was not "his prime minister" in the same sense that Mikaeri Kintu at Mengo was "his Katikkiro". For constitutional and cultural reasons, but largely political ones, President Mutesa could not make Prime Minister Obote do his bidding the same way Kabaka Mutesa would do with regard to Katikkiro Kintu.

Traditionally, the Katikkiro was the Kabaka's delegate who could be removed from office at his pleasure. Such a Katikkiro had one constituency to mind: the Kabaka. Although in the modern times, as recently as in the 1955 Second Buganda Agreement, had been introduced the notion of an elected Katikkiro by the Lukiiko, old habits die hard. Under that agreement, the Kabaka retained the power to appoint twenty *saza* (county) chiefs, who were ex-official members of the Lukiiko which elected the Katikkiro. He was still able to manipulate it by removing doubtful members and appoint trusted ones—trusted to elect one of his choice and dismiss one who had run out of his sympathy. Kintu had been the beneficiary and victim of that practice. That habit was still very much in vogue as the Crisis was unfolding. One can foretell that the Kabaka's free hand to choose his Katikkiro will be one of the bones of contention between the forces of democracy and tradition in any future constitutional arrangement in Buganda.

Unlike Katikkiro Kintu, Obote, as prime minister, had four groups whose views and concerns counted and he had to consider in making his decisions: his cabinet, the broad UPC membership, the KY movement, which was the partner in the alliance, and the Ugandan public at large.

Universally and from antiquity, telling kings the unvarnished truth has never been encouraged or well-taken and those not careful enough with their words often lose their office and, in the past, sometimes they lost their very lives. In old Europe, a king would employ a person to act as "a fool" or a court jester for the sole purpose of telling him the real truth about his (the king's) activities and manner of rule in such a way that it would be taken as a joke but not as criticism. In Buganda Kingdom, the role of court jester was played by the court musicians. In their songs, they rendered advice and also conveyed unpalatable news to the Kabaka and it was thought to be part of innocent entertainment. And everybody was safe. That is how he would counter the counsel of sycophantic advisors. In the classical story, it took a child to point out that the king, who was taking a stroll in his capital city street was naked. All his courtiers were competing with one another in praise of the fabulous clothes he was wearing. Modern day kings and leaders who wield unbridled power, either in the public or in the private sector, tend to become insulated from some sound, disinterested advice.

Mutesa did not have to watch his back, for, as Kabaka for life, he was safe on his throne. He had no competitors for his position. The only competition around him was among those whose business was to humour him and to anticipate all his desires. He had subjects who loved him with all their hearts regardless, with a love attached to a chain of habits stretching centuries back.

Obote did not enjoy such luck. With no similar cultural advantage to favour him, in his universe as a politician, he had to earn the support and loyalty of the members of his party virtually on a daily basis. His tool of trade was suasion of people. Many of his colleagues regarded him, at best as the first among equals, and at worst, saw themselves as better and an obstacle to their own ambitions. Some were waiting in the wings to replace him as opportunity arose, should he stumble. He had supporters who respected him with their heads as long as they deemed him furthering their interests and could withdraw that support any time, if they saw him as a hindrance to them.

Deep down, Obote did not believe one should get into a position of leadership simply by virtue of their birth. That was why, long after Mutesa had lost office, he would taunt Mutesa that he, Mutesa, did not know that he was president by election and not by birth. Mutesa himself could not help thinking leadership and privilege were the divine rights of a king. Those, among other reasons, made Mutesa more comfortable with Grace Ibingira from the Ankore Kingdom aristocracy than with Milton Obote, a commoner. Obote believed in the use of state resources to uplift the well-being of the common man. He emphasised the unity of all Ugandans regardless of their status, tribe, religion, or region of origin. To Kabaka Mutesa, his territory and people were naturally uppermost in his mind. Two more different men you would never find. Given their inherent differences, it is a great credit to both men, and no less wonder, that Mutesa and Obote were able to work together for as long as they did and achieve the feat of taking Uganda to independence as one united country. Through their ability to transcend what divided them, those two men, warts and all, brought forth on the African continent a new state called Uganda.

Friendship

Where there is friendship between political actors, even what may appear like insurmountable differences can easily be overcome. Mutesa (1967) writes that he did not find Obote particularly likeable and that by end of 1965, all pretence of friendship between them had ceased. This friendship, or lack of it, is what the Americans refer to as the chemistry between two people which creates implicit trust so necessary in relationships whether political or business. Both men failed what the British call "the bloke you'd like to have a pint with" test, somebody around whom you are comfortable, and you would enjoy having a drink with. Indeed, as noted before, these two men reached a point when they communicated only by letter. In the place of friendly cooperation, there was incurable suspicion. That could only exacerbate any differences they might have had and impede their working together to solve jointly the problems that faced their new country just taking its infant steps to statehood.

Age, Hubris, and Experience

Mutesa was born on 19 November 1924 and Obote was born on 28 December 1925 making them 38 and 37years, respectively, at independence, at which age today one would probably be considered too young to chair a Local Council I Committee, the lowest electoral office, in some areas. But here they were, heading a country emerging out of more than sixty years of colonial rule. Their errors may, therefore, be imputed to youth and the pressure of circumstances.

We indicated that Obote was a self-made man; a man who had raised himself from obscurity to the position of prime minister of his country solely by his political skills. It is not unusual for such a man to adore his maker. It is not far-fetched, therefore, to imagine that Obote may have suffered from hubris—that syndrome the ancient Greeks identified as the intoxication of power. Against the odds, given his background,

Secondary Factors and Episodes that Stoked the Crisis

Obote, aged below forty, had become the chief executive of a new nation. Could power have gone to his head causing pride and over self-confidence leading to treatment of fellow leaders with contempt? Owen has this to say:

> Power is a heady drug which not every political leader has the necessary rooted character to counteract: to do so requires a combination of common sense, humour, decency, scepticism and even cynicism that treats power for what it is—a privileged opportunity to influence, and sometimes to determine, the turn of events. (Owen, 2007, p. x)

On the other hand, there was Sir Edward Mutesa, an absolute monarch, whose wish was his subjects' command. Obote and Mutesa, each for his reasons, regarded himself as "king maker" of the other. Kabaka Mutesa was convinced that he made Obote prime minister and Obote believed he made Kabaka Mutesa president of Uganda. Ordinarily, that should have made the two men political friends, if not friends as men, but it was not to be. Instead, there developed a personal animus between the two men which led to their mutual destruction.

There is a Kiganda saying for such destructive mutual regard: *Ezenkanankana nebisiki tezaaka*. (Literal meaning: Logs cannot light a fire. Hidden meanings: first, relations of equally proud parties cannot prosper; and, second, when two equally obstinate people meet, they eventually clash with each other.) Each in his own way, Mutesa and Obote were equally proud men, each with his own group of cronies to edge him on. Their relationship crashed and the institution each represented and cherished suffered.

Chapter 7

POST-REFERENDUM PLOTS AND MANOEUVRES

That there were plots and manoeuvres was neither denied nor disguised. One of the participants explicitly admitted so by titling Chapter 11 of his book, "Plots." In it, he writes:

> Perhaps this is a good moment to disentangle Obote's enemies. The Baganda were hostile almost solidly since the action over the lost counties. This was their main quarrel with him since independence. ... However, he had also alienated at least some of his own party. ... What I know is that there was no collusion between his two sets of enemies. We never plotted his overthrow together. (Mutesa, 1967, p. 183)

That offered Obote cold comfort. The stark reality was that he faced the true meaning of the Kiganda saying: *Gubuze asala ng'akukyaaye awerekedde akubanja,* which translates as, "You know you are in serious trouble when you see your sworn enemy and your creditor advancing towards you in unison." The metaphorical meaning is that it is bad enough to have one enemy; it is worse when two or more of your enemies combine to confront you. Obote felt he was a man besieged. The question lying at the back of Kabaka Mutesa's mind, to put it in the plainest possible language, was: "Obote, how could you do that to me after all I have done for you? I shall not take it lying down!"

While we are putting it thus, it should not be narrowed down to a personal quarrel between Mutesa and Obote. It is being asked in the representative capacity of the two men: as Kabaka of Buganda, on one part, and as prime minister of Uganda, on the other.

Mutesa-Ibingira Partnership

Historically and so far as the 1966 Crisis is concerned, 1965 can be rightly referred to as the year of plots, conspiracies, and manoeuvres.

In collusion or separately, at the very least, Obote's enemies do not deny plotting to overthrow him. One set of Obote's enemies was headed by Grace Ibingira, the secretary-general of UPC and cabinet member; President Mutesa himself led the second set. While both groups had the removal of Obote from power as their shared agenda, each had its separate cause. Ibingira was driven by personal ambition, his objective being to wrest political power from Obote by replacing him as both UPC party leader and consequently as prime minister. Kabaka Mutesa, considering Obote's decision to allow the referendum to go ahead as treachery, sought to exact political retribution by pursuing the removal from office a man he could no longer trust. It is unclear whether Mutesa thought Obote's removal from office would have reversed the referendum results and restored the counties to Buganda or he did not care so long as Obote paid a political price for it by loss of office.

A satisfactory result would be achieved by the two sets of Obote's enemies joining forces or acting separately to overthrow him. UPC now had two factions—the Obote faction and the Ibingira faction. Ibingira and Mutesa working together in a new alliance could only hasten the attainment of their mutual desire. Mutesa was disingenuous in denying that he and Ibingira plotted together against Obote.

Feeling betrayed, President Mutesa decided it was no longer possible "to do business" with Prime Minister Obote. That being the case, what was the way forward for Mutesa? He had two options: either to remove Obote and replace him with someone more agreeable, or resign from the presidency and revert to being just Kabaka of Buganda. The second option was quickly dismissed for two reasons. First, he may have reasoned, if Obote would not protect the interests of Buganda with regard to the two counties of Buyaga and Bugangazzi when he, Mutesa, was president, and thus, influencing him, how safe would Buganda's aspirations be with him out of the presidency? Between mere vengeance and safeguarding Buganda's future interests, we cannot tell what motivated Mutesa more to have Obote removed.

The second reason was deeply personal. Having been president of Uganda and first citizen, how could he just resign? What explanation would he give to those who had edged him on to take up the presidency? And even more heart-wrenching, how was he going to face those who had advised him against taking up the position of president and leaving politics to commoners?

Those two considerations left President Mutesa with one choice: stay the course but force Obote from office by any means available. But what were the available means? The menu of strategies, some of which overlapped in implementation, for Obote's removal President Mutesa and his allies had to choose from had six items:

(a) withdraw KY parliamentary support from UPC to DP and thereby cause a collapse of Obote's UPC-led government through losing a majority of seats,

(b) organise politically to have him voted out in a general election due next,
(c) seek foreign military intervention,
(d) employ physical force by carrying out an armed military coup d'état,
(e) engineer a parliamentary coup through a vote of no-confidence in him as prime minister, and/or
(f) have him voted out as head of his political party, UPC.

And so began the plotting for the downfall of Obote by exploiting his vulnerabilities within his political party, UPC, and the fallout with his previous political partner, Mutesa. He, in turn, began planning his survival. Both Mutesa and Obote must have applied the Kiganda saying, *Atakulekera naawe tomulekera; enyanja ekutta omira,* literally meaning, you give no quarter to one that gives you no quarter; a man drowning in a lake will try to drink it dry to save himself. A person under deadly attack will naturally defend himself by any means available, however hopeless the effort may be.

All six strategies were pursued at different times, concurrently or separately, and not necessarily in the sequence I have outlined. All were tried and either failed, or their time did not come, like denying Obote Buganda support during the 1967 elections. I will set out each separately in no particular order, beginning with KY joining the opposition DP.

The general elections option was quickly dismissed. Scheduled for 1967, they were too far, and the results were uncertain. Mutesa writes, "New elections would solve our problems, but they were distant, and even then, it did not seem likely that Obote would allow elections to be held unless he was sure he could win" (Mutesa, 1967, p. 177). That apart, since KY had no support outside Buganda, winning a general election would have required a new political ally who would lend the necessary support from outside Buganda. This is what Mutesa had to say:

> The idea of joining with DP in opposition, which was greeted as outrageous the year before, was now considered and the name of a KY-DP party mooted— Yekka Democratic—but the Baganda had not forgotten or forgiven what was considered to be the treacherous participation of DP in the election (of 1961) we boycotted. (Mutesa, 1967, p. 178)

In any event, who would KY members be joining when in December 1964, Basil Bataringaya, the leader of DP in Parliament, with a couple of others, joined UPC? It was also the case that neither the Kabaka nor the Buganda Lukiiko had control over KY members once they got to the National Assembly and could do as they wished. Motivated by a variety of causes, most of them had joined UPC.

Mutesa writes:

> Members of KY in the National Assembly were crossing in dribs and drabs to UPC, lured by the chance of office ... and not least by Obote's personal powers of persuasion. Some thought they were strengthening the moderate wing, who would soon tame or, if necessary, dispense with Obote. Others who should have known better—were convinced that an opposition was un-African, a luxury we could ill afford, and so on, that there is something modern and efficient about a one-party State. (Mutesa, 1967, p. 176)

The crossing of KY members to UPC would not have been allowable if the UPC-KY alliance had been tightly structured and formalised. As it were, whereas the Buganda Lukiiko had collectively sent the 21 KY members to Uganda Parliament, Mengo had no hold on them, and they were at liberty to freely exercise their individual judgement. Mengo had failed to foresee and forestall that.

That mixed bag of motives for KY members joining UPC seemed to eliminate the strategy of removing Obote through parliamentary numbers. Still, as the quotation above shows, it also kept alive the hope of removing him from the leadership of the UPC.

What a difference three short years make in politics! Between 1962 and 1964, both years inclusive, DP was transformed from a pariah organisation in Buganda to a prospective partner of Buganda's exclusive Kabaka Yekka. According to Mutesa, by participating in the 1961 elections which Mengo had boycotted:

> The Democratic Party fought the elections in Buganda and gained lasting hatred. They were seen as traitors to Buganda, trying to grab office at the expense of loyalty. 'DP' became and remained the most insulting of swear words. (Mutesa, 1967, p. 158)

He added, concerning the election party symbols:

> These symbols were meant to be neutral. Kabaka Yekka's was a plain chair, which people chose to connect with the throne. UPC had an open hand, and DP a hoe, which they hoped showed a healthy agricultural approach. On the wireless a supporter said that it was useful all through your life and even dug the hole for your burial, but this link with death did not help their popularity. (Mutesa, 1967, pp. 163-164)

So much for today's claim that Buganda is the traditional home of DP. The reality is that political support is not set in stone and parties have no permanent homes or permanent no-go areas. A single act, event or policy can change the alignment of political parties in the country for years to come. For instance, in the USA, the Civil Rights Act introduced by the Democratic Party then in government to abolish racial discrimination virtually washed away that party's support in the south of that county for decades.

After the referendum, the flow of KY members of Parliament to UPC should have been the least of Mutesa's worries. His memory may have failed him when he implied that it concerned him that KY MPs were crossing to UPC when he was part of the plot orchestrated to undermine Obote from within UPC itself. However, it is not surprising to underplay almost to the point of denial of his participation. Some of the objectives of his autobiography could not have been to glorify and amplify his role in the conspiracy but to minimise it and to distance himself from it since it had failed to bear the desired fruit. Success has many parents, but failure is a lonely orphan.

The 1964 UPC delegates' conference provided the backdrop for the plot to remove Obote from the UPC leadership. That year's conference had been convened in Gulu to elect new national party leaders. The most highly contested position was that of the party secretary-general. John Kakonge, the incumbent and founding secretary-general of the party, was challenged by Grace Ibingira, a minister of state for justice.

John Kakonge enjoyed widespread support among the rank and file membership, especially the youth and trade unionists. Obote, the party president, was convinced that Kakonge's popularity within the party threatened his power and position within the party. He was also persuaded to side with Ibingira by those in his cabinet who saw Kakonge as a communist. He, therefore, did whatever was needed to ensure the defeat of Kakonge and to secure the election of Ibingira.

After his defeat in Gulu, which was acrimoniously secured—what, with accusations of election rigging, locking accredited delegates out of the conference hall and replacing them with sugarcane cutters ferried from Kakira 450 miles away—Kakonge and his supporters retired to Kampala. Mretaryany supporters urged him to form a new political party, but he declined. He moved to Tanzania for some period but later returned to Uganda. He was to serve loyally as Obote's minister in charge of planning and economic development until the UPC government was overthrown in 1971.

In favouring Ibingira over Kakonge, therefore, Obote made a grave misjudgement as far as the long-term security of his position was concerned. For Kakonge, unlike Ibingira, future events would show that he had no ambition or plan to supplant him as party leader of UPC and prime minister. (Kakonge was the only member of Parliament who debated and voted against the Ibingira-Mutesa inspired Ocheng gold scandal motion in Parliament, which was designed to bring down Obote's government).

Soon after taking over control of the party as secretary-general, Ibingira began filling positions at the party headquarters with his supporters, especially those from the country's south. Throughout 1965, he also undertook massive recruitment of party supporters in Buganda. Many of the new party leaders from Buganda were former KY supporters. Ibingira's UPC allies in Buganda were led by Dr Emmanuel Lumu, and in the East, by William Nadiope, M. Ngobi and Balaki Kirya. Ibingira and George Magezi led UPC in the West. It became clear that, come the next national party leaders' elections, Ibingira's supporters would carry the day. The balance of power within UPC had shifted from Obote, the party president, to Ibingira, the party secretary-general. Obote knew it. Ibingira knew it. Mutesa knew it. And President Mutesa and Ibingira sought to exploit it as one of the strategies to remove Obote from power.

Under the new Mutesa-Ibingira alliance, if that enterprise succeeded, Ibingira would become prime minister and head of government, and Mutesa would remain titular head of state. The crossing by some KY members in Parliament to UPC and other manoeuvres by both parties have to be viewed in that context.

Obote was also aware of the 1964 UPC delegates' conference and the capacity of his colleagues to mobilise non-eligible personnel to participate in voting at UPC meetings and would take no chances. As far as the UPC's side of the political chessboard stood in 1965, Obote knew he could rely only on one piece on the chess board to maintain his leadership–the northern Uganda vote. But there was yet another chessboard on which the pieces were better positioned in his favour–the military.

Obote's Trump Card

Mutesa and Ibingira did not know, or perhaps underrated, the fact that Obote had the balance of power in the army. They failed in their calculation to realise that having on their side the Army Commander Brigadier Shaban Opolot, who was married from the lower ranks of the Mengo establishment, was not enough to tilt the army scales in their favour. Thanks to the colonial legacy which left the majority of army personnel coming from his ethnic grouping, Obote had the advantage in strife presented as inter-ethnic. Although a more or less similarly composed army overthrew his government on two occasions, on the second occasion in 1985, it was over an intra-ethnic conflict. If push came to shove, the military would be the ultimate determinant. Knowing the forces that were aligned against him, Obote also began planning his political and possibly his very physical survival.

Lwanga-Lunyiigo (2007) writes, "Muteesa II was a trained soldier and a captain in the Queen's Grenedier (sic) Guards and the soldier and the man of action in him was always just below the surface" (p. 108). So, calling the troops to impose a military solution to a political problem came naturally to him.

In 1964, there was an army mutiny in the young Ugandan army. The prime minister had invited the British troops, then stationed in Kenya, to come and quell the rebellion, which they had successfully done. President Mutesa thought that provided sufficient precedent, if not the legal authority, for him to invite foreign military intervention even in the situation. In his view, there was a creeping military coup by Obote. At the beginning of 1966, he writes:

> I sounded out the British High Commissioner and some African ambassadors as to whether it would be possible to fly in troops if the situation got out of hand. ... I had in mind something similar to the successful intervention by the British which Obote had authorised two years before. (Mutesa, 1967, p. 186)

The similarity between the two situations is not self-evident, and it is hard to suppose that a leader of a government worth the name should sit back and allow that to happen.

The conspirators realised that removing Prime Minister Obote through physical force by army intervention was more delicate and carried more risks, but it was not taken off the menu. The two top officers then were Army Commander Brigadier Shaban Opolot and Chief of Staff Lieutenant Colonel Idi Amin. The brigadier was enlisted in the president's camp and the colonel in that of the prime minister.

In his book, Mutesa is careful not to mention the brigadier by name as having been in his camp for fear of exposing him to possible prosecution for treason, as in 1967, at the time of his writing, the brigadier was alive and living in Uganda. But there is sufficient evidence to identify him conclusively. Firstly, he was the only brigadier in the army at the time. Secondly, being married to a daughter of Mugalasi, a minor but well-connected Buganda official, he was as much a Mengo insider as they come. Thirdly, at the 2013 Buganda Kingdom Heroes' ceremony, Brigadier Opolot was awarded a posthumous Buganda Hero medal as a friend of Buganda. Even without looking at the citation for the award, assuming one existed, it is easy to work out the basis of that friendship and how it had exhibited itself. Opolot and Ocheng are Buganda's honoured dead for taking Buganda's military and political side in the 1966 Crisis. Mengo's institutional memory was alive and well after all those years.

Mutesa (1967) writes that at the beginning of February 1966, after observing some unauthorised troop movements in and around Kampala, the cabinet had instructed the brigadier to take a message to Prime Minister Obote requesting him to return to Kampala from his official tour of the north of the country. Narrating the incident, obviously from an account given to him, as he was wont, Mutesa puts it, and not without a touch of drama:

> When he (the Brigadier) arrived to deliver the message, the contents of which he did not know, Obote's party was bathing and several ran naked into the woods, thinking they were being arrested. Indeed, Obote has since accused me of sending them to arrest him, but he has not said in that case what went wrong. If the Brigadier had wanted Obote, he had now got

him. In fact, he was a professional soldier carrying out his instructions. (Mutesa, 1967, p. 186)

Mutesa does not tell whether it was normal practice to deploy the brigadier to deliver to the prime minister cabinet messages, especially those whose contents he did not know.

Others say that the brigadier was indeed sent to arrest Obote, as the reaction of Obote's entourage to the visit narrated by Mutesa above corroborates, in the execution of a military coup but was repulsed by the prime minister's guards. A slightly different but less credible version of the purpose of that mission is that it was intended to arrest Obote, but it was abandoned halfway in favour of the "master card" the plotters were about to play.

Another story regarding the presence of Obote in northern Uganda but again may be discounted as mere speculation, is that Obote had undertaken the tour because, suspecting that a coup against him was imminent, he wanted to be near the border for an easy exit out of Uganda in case it occurred. One thing is clear, the brigadier's unusual visit to the prime minister was not meant to be a picnic. In any event, the brigadier returned to Kampala without Obote. Whatever the correct version was, Obote continued with his tour and returned to Kampala as initially scheduled, to find that Daudi Ocheng had moved his motion and it had been passed.

Parliamentary Option

The plotters had concluded that a neater and probably quicker plan was the passing of a motion in the National Assembly making grave accusations against the prime minister, a couple of his ministers and Colonel Idi Amin, calling for investigations into those accusations. This is what has passed in history as the Gold Scandal, although a scandal it was not. The motion was moved on 4 February 1966 by Daudi Ocheng, a northerner by birth but a Muganda by adoption, a KY member representing Buganda in the National Assembly and a personal school friend of President Mutesa.

The choice of Daudi Ocheng to move the motion could not have been accidental, coincidental or by mere convenience. It must have been calculated that in Uganda's tribally tinged politics, as he belonged to Obote's sub-ethnic group, allegations made in an anti-Obote motion moved by him would be lent more credence.

Those who knew Daudi Ocheng described and characterised him as a huge man, a bulldozer of a man, a force of nature given to hyperbole and tall tales and one who would not allow facts to get in the way of a good conspiracy. He had a relaxed relationship with the truth, for here was a man who, well-knowing that his motion had no factual basis, would still say as he introduced it, "Mr Speaker, if I live to be a hundred years, or if I live for another hundred hours, this motion will be my one and most outstanding contribution to my country." (*The Hansard*, 1966)

The Mutesa-Ibingira camp thought that this motion, when passed, would quickly lead to a vote of no-confidence in the prime minister and the fall of his government. Mutesa informs us that during this period, Daudi Ocheng was a permanent guest at the Kampala Presidential State Lodge (Makindye Lodge), which the two shared. Therefore, it would not be stretching the imagination to assume that the motion was conceived, drafted, assembled and rehearsed within the walls of the state lodge. Prime Minister Obote referred to Ocheng as Mutesa's tool and their connection as the relation between master and servant.

The motion was tabled shortly after Obote had left the capital for a tour of the northern part of the country, but he was aware that it was in the offing. Before he began this tour, the cabinet had decided that the UPC parliamentary group would oppose and block the motion. After his departure, his cabinet colleagues, led by Grace Ibingira, reversed that decision and decided to support it. The motion was passed, with only John Kakonge voting against it.

It is doubtful whether all members of Parliament who took part in the debate and voted on the motion knew of the machinations behind the motion. In fairness to them, in the absence of an adequate explanation from the government side, Ocheng's allegations were grave. If the plotting against Obote by his adversaries were a music piece, this motion was the crescendo. And if it were a game of cards, this was considered the master card. We dwell on this motion in some detail because, together with another supposedly passed by the Buganda Lukiiko on 23 May 1966, it may be said to have immediately triggered the 1966 Crisis.

Daudi Ocheng's motion read:

> That this House do urge Government to suspend from duty Col. Idi Amin of the Uganda Army, forthwith, pending the conclusion of police investigations into allegations regarding his bank account, which should then be passed to the appropriate authority whose final decision on the matter shall be made public. (*The Hansard*, 1966)

Some scholars have suggested that directing the motion against Colonel Amin was a smokescreen; the real target was Prime Minister Obote. Regarding this move, Mutibwa writes:

> This, clearly, was a motion of censure against Apollo Milton Obote and his government. But it was also a

camouflage for an organised group of politicians, led by at least five ministers headed by Grace Ibingira, to overthrow Obote's government. (Mutibwa, 2008, p. 92)

A more likely explanation seems to be that both Amin and Obote were targeted as part of the same project. If the motion succeeded, the removal of Colonel Amin would get rid of Brigadier Opolot's rival in the army and, at the same time, make it easier to stage a military coup should that become necessary.

While he was speaking on the motion, Daudi Ocheng alleged that between 5 February and 2 March 1965, Colonel Amin's bank account had been credited with large sums of money, which were his share of the proceeds of the sale of gold, coffee, and elephant tusks looted from Congo (now called the Democratic Republic of the Congo) during military skirmishes between the Uganda army and the Congolese troops at the Uganda-Congo border, especially the West Nile region. Obote, the prime minister, allegedly shared a larger amount with his colleagues Hon. Felix Onama, the minister of state for defence and Hon. Adoko Nekyon, the minister of information, broadcasting and tourism planning and community development. What was more, Colonel Amin was providing facilities to dissidents who were training in the forests of Mt. Elgon in Mbale District to overthrow the Uganda government, Ocheng asserted.

Daudi Ocheng explained in a press conference on 11 February 1966, shortly after the debate of the motion in Parliament, why he had moved the motion:

> The reason that I have done this is because I have checked and cross-checked my information and have been convinced that the sons of Uganda who were killed in the Congo were killed not in defence of our

territorial integrity, but because certain individuals had personal interests in the conflict that was going on between the Congolese people themselves. (Press conference, 11 February, 1966)

On 13 February, upon his return to the capital from his tour in the north, Obote held a press conference of his own in the presence of his cabinet, during which he not only denied the allegations made by Daudi Ocheng but also announced that a judicial commission of inquiry to investigate those allegations was to be set up to comply with the parliamentary resolution.

Indeed, as ordered by the cabinet, the minister of internal affairs, Basil Bataringaya, former secretary-general of the Democratic Party and leader of the opposition in Parliament, announced the appointment of the commission of inquiry. It consisted of Justice Sir Negeon de L'Estang of the Court of Appeal for Eastern Africa as chairman, Justice Henry Ethlewood Miller, a judge of the High Court of the Republic of Kenya, and Justice Augustine Saidi, a Judge of the High Court of the United Republic of Tanzania. Samuel William Wako Wambuzi of the Uganda Ministry of Justice was appointed secretary to the commission. Mutesa admits that it was an "unimpeachably honest Commission," not the type to be set up by a person who wished to use it to hide the wrongdoing of his colleagues. The commission commenced hearings at the beginning of March 1966, and after many witnesses testifying before it, it concluded:

> We find (1) that the allegations of the receipt by the Honourable Prime Minister, the Honourable Felix Onama and the Honourable A.A.A. Nekyon of gold, ivory and other property from the Congo are totally unsupported by evidence and completely unfounded. (The Commission's report, 1966)

Despite that, the report the commission issued was kept secret by Obote's government. Much has been made of the fact that the report was not published. Mutesa (1967) writes that the report "was said to have been ready by July 1964 (sic). Not even an edited version has yet been published" (p. 191).

During an interview for this work, a former senior official in the Ministry of Justice at the time, who chose not to be named, informed me that there were findings in the report that the government of Prime Minister Obote did not want to be publicly revealed. From my reading of the transcript of the commission's proceedings, I have formed the opinion that this may have had to do with the fact that the heads of government of Kenya and Tanzania at the time—Presidents Jomo Kenyatta and Julius Nyerere, respectively—were fully complicit in Uganda giving support to the Congolese rebels (under the Congolese Revolutionary Government) who were fighting the national government based in Leopoldville (now called Kinshasa). It was diplomatic taboo then, and remains so today, for one African country to interfere in the internal affairs of another. The founding fathers of the Organisation of African Unity had also resolved to keep intact the colonial inter-territorial boundaries.

Amin had been designated to coordinate the assistance to the rebels. The rebel leaders had testified before the commission that the money on Colonel Amin's account was availed to him by them to purchase vehicles and uniforms for them from Uganda, which he had done to their satisfaction. It was not the proceeds of the loot of gold, coffee, and ivory for the personal gain of specific individuals as Daudi Ocheng had alleged.

Indeed, these were not findings that, although they exonerated him and his colleagues from Daudi Ocheng's accusations, Obote's government would have wanted to reveal to the world. But this was not information available to the rank and file members of Parliament. It is safe to say that those in the know twisted the facts and exploited the members' ignorance for their ends.

The commission's report was later published by Amin when he came to power because it cast him in good light and served his political interest to let the world know it. Besides, he was not politically embarrassed by the revelation of the commitments Obote and Kenyatta and Nyerere, who were not his political allies by any stretch of the imagination, had made to the Congolese rebels several years earlier.

It would be naive to assume that the prime minister was a sitting duck waiting helplessly to be slaughtered. Instead, signs were that he was fully aware of what was going on and was prepared to counter it. His strategy involved securing the support of the army. The delivery to him of a cabinet message, as Mutesa called it, by Shaban Opolot, the army commander, had shown him which side the commander was on and alerted him to take appropriate action.

Therefore, it was a confident prime minister who returned to the capital from the north of the country between 13 and 24 February 1966, addressed a press conference in which he denied Ocheng's accusations in Parliament; set up a commission of inquiry into the allegations; arrested five of his cabinet ministers; wrote and proclaimed a new national Constitution.

Power Struggle within UPC

But we cannot take leave of discussion of plots without presenting another angle. In Chapter 1, we contrasted the power struggle within NRM with that in UPC and suggested that while the former was personal, the latter had an ideological tinge. This is a good point at which to revisit that argument.

Besides, to another kind of reader, the narrative or analysis where matters are reduced to a clash between personal ambitions–Mutesa/Ibingira against Obote–or, even more base, between Bantu grouping against Northerners, is rather simplistic and will not do. We now turn to those who would prefer some more sophisticated, nuanced and below-the-surface analysis of the power struggle.

In ideological terms, this was a clash of values or two wings within the ruling Party–the right-wing and left-wing–with the global politics in the mix. It is quite likely, though, that some of the sympathisers of these leaders were not aware and vigorously denied that they were the unwitting representatives of a global ideological battle.

Ibingira represented the right-wing of the party with the support of the American-led Western powers. In contrast, Obote represented the left-wing ostensibly led by the Soviet Union. Ibingira represented the capitalistic values of the market forces determining who gets what from the country's economy. Obote represented socialism premised on the notion that the state has an obligation to help the weak (the common man) stand and the belief that by the weak pooling their resources, for instance, through cooperatives, they can improve their economic lot.

And just below the surface, there was a tension between monarchism and republicanism, with Ibingira and Mutesa on one side and Obote on the other. The victor in these struggles and tensions was Milton Obote. He spearheaded an ideological shift to the left in Uganda's political and economic trajectory, resulting in the abolition of federalism/the kingdoms and introducing a centralised government in addition to what was dubbed *The Common Man's Charter*.

Post-Referendum Plots and Manoeuvres

Kabaka Ronald Muwenda Mutebi II

Sir Edward Mutesa

Daudi Chwa

Mwanga II

Michael Kintu

Sir Apollo Kaggwa

Apollo Milton Obote

Paulo Muwanga

Grace Ibingira

Nekyon Adoko

Abu Kakyama Mayanja

John Kakonge

Shaban Opolot

Benedicto Kiwanuka

Idi Amin Dada

Daudi Ocheng

Paul Kawanga Semogerere

Bishop Joseph Kiwanuka

Sir Andrew Cohen

Joash Mayanja-Nkanji

Ignatius Musaazi

Andrew Lutakome Kayiira

Yusuf Kironde Lule

Godfrey Lukongwa Binaisa

Milton Obote, the Duke of Kent and other guests at Kololo, October 9, 1962

Sir Edward Mutesa in the background, October 9, 1962

STATEHOOD ON TRIAL

The Lubiri before the attack

Ruins of the Lubiri after the attack (1)

Post-Referendum Plots and Manoeuvres

Ruins of the Lubiri after the attack (2)

Ruins of the Lubiri after the attack (3)

Chapter 8

ERUPTION

Prelude to the Attack on Lubiri

Before the commission appointed to look into the gold allegations commenced hearings on 22 February 1966, during a cabinet meeting called purportedly to nominate appointees to the commission of inquiry and formulate its terms of reference, five ministers were arrested.

Obote claimed later that 22 February 1966 was the date that the Ibingira faction of UPC, with the complicity of President Mutesa, had planned to stage a military coup against his government. This was the basis for his assertion that his move was to counter a coup against a legitimate government.

To the Ugandan public, the arrest of the ministers was the first overt and dramatic act of the Crisis. More was yet to come. The 23 February 1966, the day following the arrest of the ministers, saw the promotion of Lieutenant Colonel Idi Amin as army chief of staff. Brigadier Shaban Opolot, his superior, was made army commander and thus effectively removed from direct command of the army, a manoeuvre referred to as "being kicked upstairs." With that move, the prime minister had gained the military upper hand for any battle that might come.

On 24 February 1966, Prime Minister Obote, in a radio broadcast, announced to the nation that he had discovered that Sir Edward Mutesa, the president, and some ministers had been plotting to overthrow the Constitution and the legally elected government by force of arms. Consequently, he had suspended the Constitution and the post of president in the interest of national unity, security and peace.

In so doing, Obote seems to have agreed with Lord Macaulay that:

> ... in such times as those on which his lot had fallen, the duty of a statesman is to choose the better cause and to stand by it, in spite of those excesses by which every cause, however good in itself, will be disgraced. (Macaulay, 1849, p. 160)

The prime minister summoned Parliament on 25 April 1966 and asked it to pass a resolution approving the steps he had taken on 24 February 1966. He also asked Parliament to approve and adopt a new Constitution without the members reading or debating it first. He told the members of Parliament they would find copies of the new Constitution in their pigeon holes after the proceedings on their way out of the parliamentary chamber, hence the name "Pigeon Hole Constitution."

Under the new Constitution, the prime minister became executive president and Milton Obote was duly sworn in as president of Uganda, as all members of Parliament, with the exception of a handful, swore allegiance to the new Constitution (the 1966 Constitution) and four of them voted against it outright.

In contrast to the Independence Constitution, the new Constitution provided for an executive president. Traditional rulers would nolonger nominate chiefs or other members in the Lukiiko of Buganda and the *Rukurato*s (kingdom Parliaments) of Bunyoro, Tooro and Ankore. The members of Parliament from Buganda would henceforth be directly elected instead of the Lukiiko acting as an electoral college.

President Mutesa withdrew from state house at Entebbe and departed, first, to the state lodge at Makindye in Kampala and eventually retreated to his palace at Mengo. With the removal of Mutesa from the presidency, the emotional link between Buganda and Uganda had been severed. From the political and legal point of view, the feeling in Buganda leadership was that, with the abrogation of the 1962 Constitution (the "social contract"), Buganda was no longer bound by the terms by which it had agreed to be part of Uganda. Buganda felt justified in seeking a divorce.

However, if that reasoning was taken to its logical conclusion, one or two other things would have been expected. Either the Lukiiko would have withdrawn the 21 members and those specially elected due to the UP-KY alliance from Uganda Parliament or those members themselves would have returned to the Lukiiko for consultation. None of the two happened.

On 23 May 1966, the Buganda Lukiiko convened and purportedly passed a resolution giving the Uganda government an ultimatum to remove itself from Buganda territory by 30 May that year. The circumstances of this resolution are rather murky. There are some claims that the Lukiiko passed no such resolution, that someone in the public gallery by the name Lwebuga, shouted out the demand that the Central Government removes itself from Buganda soil. However, Kasendwa-Ddumba, in his unpublished letter to The Uganda Human Rights Commission, mentions Kaggwa, a member of the Lukiiko from Kooki County. Others say it was a fellow popularly known as *Ssemakula Ow'Ekitalo* who moved the motion, but that it was not actually debated and voted on as mayhem broke out from the public gallery. Strange as it may sound, these things do happen.

Jared Cohen (2019) narrates the story of the nomination of James Garfield for president. In 1880, at the Republican Party convention for the nomination of the party presidential candidate, James Garfield was present as the chief campaigner for one of the candidates. Contrary to all procedure, the head of one state delegation shouted that Garfield be nominated as a republican candidate for president. Garfield's protestations that a man who did not seek it should not be given the nomination fell on deaf ears. He was not only nominated but went on to be elected 20th President of the United States.

However, Mayanja-Nkangi, the then Katikkiro who attended the Lukiiko session, stated in an interview that they passed a resolution asking Obote "to remove his government from Buganda's soil" (Kavuma-Kaggwa, 2014). He gives the impression that the motion was formally tabled, debated, and voted on. Given the reported chaos in the Lukiiko chamber, the authenticity of his claim is highly questionable.

What Obote probably did not know—and Mayanja-Nkangi would not open up to him about—was that power at Mengo had slipped from the Katikkiro and his cabinet. It had been appropriated by three of the most vocal county chiefs who were Mutesa's closest confidants and big-game hunting mates: Lameka Sebanakitta, the county chief of Bulemezi (*Kangawo*), Kaganda Lutaaya, the county chief of Singo (*Mukwenda*), and Michael Matovu, the county chief of Buddu (*Pokino*).

The draft motion is said not to have been the initiative of the Buganda cabinet which had tried to dissuade the mover from including the part on the expulsion of the Central Government. It is said that within the precincts of Bulange, hooligans were deployed, ready to deal with anyone who dared to speak against the motion. Samwiri Karugire (2010) characterised the Buganda Kingdom as being "so extravagantly endowed with hot-headed mobs" (p. 154).

Who moved the motion, whether or not it was debated and formally passed by the Lukiiko, was an insignificant detail as far as the ordinary excited Muganda at the time was concerned. How much of the circumstances surrounding this motion had been picked up by the Central Government and, therefore, informed its subsequent decisions, is difficult to ascertain. With the conflict cascading into fighting in the Lubiri, there was nobody to render an authoritative record of what happened during that debate, if what took place can pass as a debate. Whatever its real history was, the resolution remains one of the defining moments of the Crisis. Although rather amusing anecdotes regarding the resolution abound, it is better that we leave it at that.

What is certain is that there were riots in some parts of Buganda; trees were cut and culverts in rivers were removed in order to block the major roads. These were overt acts of violence and rebellion.

Attack on Lubiri

Ingham (1994) writes that Obote's first impulse was to ignore the Lukiiko resolution, just as Governor Sir Frederick Crawford had ignored Buganda's declaration of indepence in 1961. However, all signs were pointing to increasing lawlessness, with raw intelligence reporting the stocking of arms in the Kabaka's palace at Mengo and the convergence there of Baganda loyalists, especially ex-servicemen in World War II.

Obote decided to err on the side of caution by dispatching a team of sixty police special force personnel on 24 May 1966 to check out intelligence reports of an arms pile in the Lubiri. Sending the special force was against the counsel of his advisors who preferred the army.

According to Nelson Nkonge, a key figure in the fortification of the Lubiri then, in a Wavah Broadcasting Service (WBS) television documentary titled *Mutesa II ne Uganda*, the special force that was initially sent to the Lubiri was "mowed down like grass." The decision to send in the army to reinforce the police thus took itself, as it were:

> Amin (the Army Chief of Staff), who was in charge of the military operation had, it transpired, ordered the use of heavy weapons. Obote immediately sent instructions to put a stop to what he was convinced must be excessive force. He subsequently accepted, however, that the presence of a large and hostile crowd, together with the rumour that there were thousands of arms in the Kabaka's Palace, might reasonably have led to an error of judgment by Obote in ordering the heavy deployment. In fact, when the Palace was stormed all that was found were a number of hunting rifles. (Nkonge, WBS series, 2003-2005)

Was the threat to national security overestimated? With the evidence that subsequently became available, it is clear that was the case. But most probably to those who lived through the times and cared about the Uganda project, the danger to national unity was imminent.

During the same series of the WBS programme, Prince Simbwa, Mutesa's younger brother who was in the palace at the time, disclosed that he had heard an army commander tell his charge not to shoot him (Simbwa) because they were under instructions not to shoot him (Mutesa). Prince Simbwa bore a very striking resemblance to Mutesa and the commander must have mistaken him for Kabaka Mutesa himself and extended extra protection to him as a result of that mistaken identity. This would render false the allegations that Obote's orders were to capture Mutesa, dead or alive.

What are the circumstances which may have led to this error in judgement leading to the decision to send the police and subsequently the army to Mutesa's palace? There is no clear-cut evidence of the factors which moved the participants during this period. Once again, we are exercising a writer's licence to construct a picture of what went on in their collective mind. We will permit ourselves a digression.

Anyone who closely followed the invasion of Iraq in 2003 by America and Britain, the leading nations of "the Coalition of the Willing," which included, among others, Uganda and another country called Vanuatu, can more easily understand one of the complex psychological phenomena which might have led to the invasion of the Kabaka's palace in 1966. The coalition put out a claim that Saddam Hussein's government had stocked chemical weapons of mass destruction which had to be removed through an invasion. Well, the coalition invaded; Iraq was defeated; and no weapons of mass destruction were found. The puzzle is why, instead of denying and protesting the accusation of the presence of those arms, Saddam's government practically invited the invasion by promising, through its minister of information, "Comical Ali," that an attack on Iraq would be suicidal on the part of the invaders, implying that the weapons indeed existed and would be used against the invaders?

Those who claim that the coalition lied about the presence of weapons of mass destruction in order to justify the invasion have not explained why Saddam made no denial. What would motivate the weaker party to a looming war, portray itself as being militarily stronger than it actually was and thereby attract a physical confrontation? In the case of Saddam, one theory holds that he did not want to have the coalition's claim doubted because he thought it helped him put fear into his internal and regional enemies who might have entertained ideas of challenging his leadership or invading his country. If the presence of weapons of mass destruction was a myth, it was strangely one that served well both antagonists although, ultimately, it hurt Saddam worse by justifying the invasion of his country. Could the same mindset have been behind the omission to deny the presence of arms in the Lubiri? But we digress, although Hugo tells us that "when the subject is not lost sight of, there is no digression" (Hugo, 1862, p. 1972).

Former Ugandan President Godfrey Binaisa once described Kampala as a city of seven rumours a day like what happens everywhere during a period of political tension and uncertainty. The Kampala rumour mill goes into overdrive and produces bigger and more fantastic rumours. At this time, Kampala City, the seat of both the Buganda Government and the Central Government, not to mention the Kabaka's palace, was flooded with rumours and fake news. Although the expressions "fake news" and "alternative facts" have recently gained prominence under the rise of President Donald Trump of the United States, the concept itself is not new.

Battle in Lubiri

The mixture of lies and facts at the time either produced cockiness or induced fear and panic, depending on which side one was. Take the flocking of Baganda ex-servicemen (*Bakawonawo* or *Abaseveni*), the fabled heroes of World War II, into the palace. The underlying cockiness and militaristic chauvinism, on the one hand, and fear, on the other, was based on the fact that the ex-servicemen had fought on the side of the victorious armies of the World War II. Their bravery and skills on the battlefield were, therefore, an unquestionable assumption. The fact that many of these men had not seen any actual fighting, having been effectively deployed as cooks or porters, did not trouble anybody. The fact that of those who had done some actual fighting, few, if any, had touched a gun or done any military drills since they were demobilised from the army more than twenty years previously, was not considered as having blunted their skills.

What mattered to the hot-headed mobs Karugire (2010) referred to was the additional assumed advantage that the ex-servicemen were going to be under the command of Sir Edward Mutesa, a British-trained army officer at the rank of colonel in the Queen's army no less. Therefore, if there was to be any confrontation, the local Uganda police or army would be no match for them. It is the same self-deception that kept alive to this day the rumour that Mutesa had a powerful gun which operated on electricity and that had some traitor not disclosed this fact leading the enemy cutting off power supply to the palace, the result of the fight and the history of both Uganda and Buganda would have been different.

That is the mindset of the people at the time and the cocktail of facts and mere rumours and lies, fears and threats, the air of invincibility and vulnerability on all sides, laced with a dash of ethnic jingoism, started a chain reaction which became hard to stop and which produced the tinderbox that detonated in Mutesa's palace on 24 May 1966.

In the event, the army, led by Colonel Idi Amin, was called in and after some hours' engagement with such armed people it found in the Lubiri, it prevailed. Kabaka Mutesa escaped from the palace during the scuffle and eventually fled into exile in Britain. With that, the course of history of Buganda, Uganda, UPC, and the fortunes and legacy of both Mutesa and Obote, were changed forever.

Chapter 9

AFTER-LIFE OF THE CRISIS

Several things flowed from the attack on the Lubiri and affected institutions and individuals alike. But first, the chaos had to be extinguished. The days preceding the attack had been characterised by civic disorder in Buganda, such as the removal of culverts from roads, attacks on police stations in the countryside, not to mention the infamous Lukiiko resolution. Some measures were direct and taken immediately by the Central Government, while others came eventually, and their effects took time to manifest.

To contain the situation, the Central Government imposed a dawn-to-dusk curfew over Kampala and declared a state of emergency throughout Buganda. The legal and political implications of the state of emergency over an area are that it frees the law enforcement authorities from having to comply with the ordinary laws regarding individual rights. These may include, among others, arrests of individuals without a warrant, detention without trial for periods longer than prescribed by law, and restrictions on the freedoms of speech and assembly. Through those measures, peace, being the absence of war, was restored throughout the country.

Were the measures taken above enough to contain the Crisis? That is the question that has engaged historians, political scientists, commentators, accusers, and advocates of Obote alike, ever since. But Obote did go one huge step beyond those measures. He touched the 1962 Independence Constitution.

First, he suspended it; second, he abrogated it; and finally, he replaced it lock, stock, and barrel.

Abrogation of the 1962 Independence Constitution

While announcing, among other things, the suspension of five of his cabinet ministers, and the suspension of the Constitution on 22 February 1966, Obote called "upon the judges and magistrates, civil servants—both Ugandan and expatriate—members of the security forces, and the general public to carry on with their normal duties." They did.

Was this action by Obote legal? It was certainly illegal under the 1962 Constitution.

> The validity of this Constitution was to become an issue when on September 6, 1966, Michael Matovu filed, through his advocate, a writ of *habeas corpus* under Section 349 of the Criminal Procedure Code of Uganda. Following the revolution, there was some resistance, and some of those who were leading the resistance got arrested. Among those who were arrested was Michael Matovu, the Saza chief of Buddu in Buganda. (Adhola, 2018)

Was the detention of Micheal Matovu, under the 1966 Constitution but outside the ambit of the 1962 Constitution, therefore, illegal and of no effect? That was the issue that fell to be determined by the Uganda High Court in the case of *Uganda v. Commissioner of Prisons ex parte Matovu* concerning the detention of one Matovu under the 1966 Constitution.

In brief, the court ruled that what had happened in Uganda between February and April 1966 amounted to a revolution, which had destroyed the entire legal order of the 1962 Constitution, which was superseded by the 1966 Constitution. The reality was, the 1962 Constitution had ceased to have effect.

In conclusion, Matovu was and continued to be lawfully detained under the 1966 Constitution.

The correctness of that decision has been questioned by many. There have even been allegations of impropriety, including the threatening of the judges who heard the matter. But the judgement also has its defenders. There was no doubt that the entire government machinery was now operating under the 1966 Constitution as Obote had implored all personnel, including the judges, to do. Indeed, some of the judges hearing the petition had sworn allegiance to the 1966 Constitution.

What would be the effect if the court were to pronounce the 1966 Constitution illegal? Logically, it would mean that the court did not even have the authority to entertain that very petition. If the court were to rule that Matovu was illegally detained by Uganda Prisons, an agency of the government it did not recognise under the law, would it have the power to release him? What a legal and political quagmire that would be!

The principle established by the case of Matovu is that a successful coup creates its own legitimacy. Success in this sense means effective control of government.

This case bears some resemblance to the serious disagreement in 1932 the USA president, Andrew Jackson, had with the ruling of the Supreme Court, the implementation of which required the executive arm of the United States government to take some action. President Jackson reputedly remarked about the chief justice of the supreme court, "John Marshall has made his decision, now let him enforce it" (Abraham, 1980, p. 357).

If the Uganda High Court had ruled other than it did, would they have been able to enforce their decision by setting Matovu free? Not likely. We agree that the explanation of

Henry J. Abraham regarding the US Supreme Court equally applied to Uganda High Court in the Matovu case. He wrote:

> ... lacking any source of physical power of its own, the Supreme Court depends on the political branches of the government for the enforcement of its mandates, in particular, the Chief Executive, who has the vital obligation to ascertain obedience to all court orders. If the Court fails to obtain that co-operation in those instances where it is vital for compliance, it necessarily stands helplessly on the sidelines. (Abraham, 1980, p. 357)

Not every offence against the Constitution amounts to its overthrow. Unless an act is explicitly stated to be an abrogation, a distinction should be made between a mere breach and an overthrow of the Constitution. Breaches of the Constitution are judicial matters subject to interpretation by the courts of law. On the other hand, the overthrow of a Constitution and the toppling of a government is a matter of politics ultimately determined by the balance of coercive forces. A violation of the Constitution that does not lead to the changing of government does not amount to an overthrow of the Constitution. It is moot which among the various acts Obote carried out between February and May 1966 were mere breaches of the 1966 Constitution and which were overthrowing it.

It would appear to us that overthrowing the Constitution and toppling the government in a *coup d'état* do not always go together. In our view, over the years, the meaning of *coup d'état* (usually shortened to *coup*) has evolved. It can mean toppling the government, but can also mean a substantial breach of the Constitution without the government itself being toppled. The latter scenario occurs when it is the leaders of the sitting government itself that breach the Constitution.

In Uganda's case, as far as Obote was concerned, in 1966, ngthe question was not so much himself rebelling against a legal government—for he was the head of the government—as his preventing those he perceived to be in the process of overthrowing the 1962 Constitution with dire consequences to himself and the country. In other words, he saw his move as a counter-coup.

Can the overthrow of a country's Constitution or the toppling of a government in a *coup d'état* ever be justified? History has shown that the immortality of a country's Constitution can never be guaranteed. Therefore, the question should not be if the overthrow of a Constitution can ever be justified but when—the setting, the circumstances, the conditions—it can be justified.

In 1961, at the trial of the French soldiers who had rebelled against their government on the question of it granting independence to the then Algerian colony, one of the issues advanced by their defence lawyers was, "when and if it was ever justifiable to rebel against a legal government." de Gaulle, the French president at the time, thought that comparison was being made to his own rebellion and the Free French against the Vichy Government, which had signed a peace treaty with Hitler's Nazi Germany, which they regarded as treason against the French Nation (Jackson, 2018).

The reasons advanced by those who have overthrown Constitutions range from the sublime to the ludicrous. What may be taken as the classic reason is the safety of the state, in pursuit of which, "all laws might with propriety be made to bend to that highest law" (Macaulay, 1849 p. 452). Such spurious reasons as "preventing a bad situation from getting worse" have been given as part of the package for overthrowing the duly established order by Idi Amin in 1971. In 1966, in a broadcast announcing the suspension of the 1962 Constitution and usurping powers vested elsewhere by that Constitution, Milton Obote stated, "I have taken this course of action independently because of my understanding of the wishes of the people of this country for peace, order and prosperity" ("The situation is under control", 1966). When the government of Uganda was yet again overthrown in 1985, a Ugandan roadside jester was heard saying that coup leaders should stop bothering giving reasons for taking over government. They should simply say that they have taken over because they could. The jester might have been closer to the mark than most people thought.

Those who set themselves the hazardous enterprise of overturning a settled government by force of arms have to weigh their chances of success, for the price of failure is high. With all the risks involved, at the end of the day, it is success that counts.

The stakes in a coup situation are extremely high both for those who attempt to take over and those who resist the takeover. In the latter half of nineteenth century Buganda, disobeying the Kabaka, who was the state, was in itself a rebellion for which the penalty was burning alive the offender at a place called Namugongo. That is the fate which befell the early Christians in Buganda many of whom were pages in the Kabaka's palace. They rebelled by abandoning their workstations in order to receive instructions from and listen to the preachings of the early Christian missionaries. When the Christians prevailed militarily and politically over other faiths in the religious wars that followed, Namugongo become a world-famous Christian Martyres Shrine instead. As Charles-Maurice Talleyrand, a French politician and diplomat, once remarked, "treason is a matter of timing."

Modern day failed coup leaders rarely live to be subjected to trial for treason. They are more likely to die trying, at worst, or suffer long-term imprisonment or exile, if they are lucky. Obote simultaneously survived the defence of the coup against his government and the execution of one against his government.

A coup succeeds when the putative leaders of the new regime gain effective control of the larger portion, if not the whole country. That is, the agencies of government answer to the commands of the new leaders: the taxes are collected; the police arrest and detain suspected offenders; the courts of law hear and determine cases; and civil servants report for duty. Conversely, a coup fails when the sitting regime remains in effective control by the government agencies continuing to obey its commands. On both scores, whether he was deemed to have carried out a coup or to have suppressed one, Obote was successful.

Since its independence, Uganda has had five violent changes of government: in May 1966, in January 1971, in April 1979, in July 1985 and in January 1986. What is not clear is whether the removal of President Yusuf Lule in June 1979 and that of Godfrey Binaisa in May 1980 amounted to overthrowing the Constitution. In that regard, Uganda would eminently qualify as a case study of overthrowing of Constitutions.

Between February and May 1966, matters had come to such an impasse that Uganda was breeding a *coup d'état*. There would be a *coup* if Obote did nothing, and whatever he did would be deemed a *coup*. Obote could have argued that in taking the measures that he took, such as the removal of his ministers, and the removal of President Mutesa from office, he was countering a *coup d'état*. In other words, he overthrew the Constitution in order to preserve it by blocking others from overthrowing it. Given the unquiet times in which he governed the country, and his vantage point, who would contradict him?

In our assessment, so far as events surrounding the 1966 constitutional controversies were concerned, Obote's presence was so dominant and pervasive that he personified the concepts of state safety, *coup* success, and survival.

We may now sketch how the Crisis impacted the lives of some individuals or class of individuals and some institutions.

Mutesa, His Dependants and Buganda Officials

When there was a lull in the fighting in the Lubiri, Mutesa and two of his bodyguards managed to climb over the palace perimeter wall to the outside. Eventually, they made their way to Bujumbura, the capital of Burundi. They later flew to London where Mutesa passed on after spending the last three years of his life in a hard exile.

He was a man born in a palace with numerous rooms sitting in grounds stretching into acres, reduced to spending his last days in a single bedroom flat. This was a former Kabaka, who was the chief beneficiary of his kingdom's purse (*Nkuluze*) now niggardly relying on friends and allowances from a foreign government. In a lengthy and lurid narration of Mutesa's life between his escape from Lubiri and his death, Makubuya (2018) writes:

> Upon arrival in England ... his (Mutesa's) party were now faced with new problems. They were penniless and far from the grandeur of the royal palaces and the splendour of State House in Uganda, the trio (Mutesa and his two personal guards, Mallo and Katende) had to put up with a tiny one-bedroom flat offered by a friend .... Given that he was unemployed, the British Government put him on unemployment benefits of 8 pounds, and 1 shilling a week .... As a recipient of

government benefits, Mutesa was required to declare any gifts donated by friends, including birthday presents, to the British Government. His request for a pension from the civil service contingency fund was turned down. Living off the dole (as unemployment benefits are colloquially known) was debilitating for the ex-Kabaka. He and Katende survived on a diet of tea and biscuits. (Makubuya, 2018, pp. 325-326)

We have abridged his narration because we found it unnecessarily diversionary, but we hope someone else might in future comment on its purpose.

Mutesa must have found his life in exile dispiriting and heart-breaking. Unable to get funds from home, he had expected financial support from the British government. Makubuya suggests that during the negotiations for independence, the British government had promised to guarantee Mutesa's interests and those of Buganda in an independent Uganda. Mutesa was allegedly dismayed that when the hour of need came, rather than honouring its promise by coming to his aid, the British government was not forthcoming. Instead, it continued dealing with Obote's government as usual (Makubuya, 2018).

Makubuya does not mention what form that guarantee took. To rely on pre-independence agreements to guarantee his position after Buganda, through Uganda, had become independent, would be taking patronage and plunder to new levels. It would amount to seeking protection under the umbrella of Kipling's Whiteman's burden.

If that was indeed Mutesa's understanding and expectation, it must be attributable to his having forgotten that the morality and loyalty people exercise as individuals is entirely different from that they apply when acting on behalf of their government and country. That was best stated by Camillo Cavour, one of the architects of Italian unification, who said, "If we did for ourselves the things we did for Italy, we would be great rascals." In certain instances, men do for their country or faction what they would never do for themselves.

At some point during Mutesa's exile, Lord Boyd, a close friend and benefactor, observed that Mutesa's situation "was pathetic; he suffered from delusions and sometimes seemed to be nearing a mental breakdown" (Makubuya, 2018, p. 326). Mutesa, no doubt died an unhappy man in November 1969, the cause of his death no less controversial than the life he had lived. The post-mortem report regarding his death stated that he died of "acute alcohol poisoning." Some people, looking for foul play on the part of his nemesis, have labelled the death "mysterious" and twisted that to say that he died of poisoned alcohol. That would mean that the poison which killed him was administered through alcohol as opposed to the simple interpretation of the post-mortem report that the level of alcohol in his blood brought about his death. And the insinuations rage on to this day.

The cause of Mutesa's death having been made to look controversial, his men declined the offer of Uganda government to have his body returned to Uganda for burial. In his friends' assessment of the situation in Uganda, his body might have been subjected to a mock trial for treason. He was, therefore, temporarily interned in London. His proper burial in Uganda did not take place until March 1971, a couple of months after the overthrow of Obote's government.

We have it on some verbal authority that after Mutesa had fled into exile, Obote tried to persuade Baganda elders to select another prince to replace Mutesa as Kabaka, just as Sir Andrew Cohen, then governor of Uganda, had tried when Mutesa was deported to England between 1953 and 1955. As they did then, the Baganda elders refused.

Although it does not appear that he had a direct hand in it, it is inconceivable that would have been undertaken without Obote's knowledge and consent. In contrast to his conduct after 1966, there was an attempt to accommodate by rehabilitating Mutesa's family during Obote's second government in 1980s. Kasendwa-Ddumba writes:

> Sometime in 1984, my Minister (for Security), Chris Rwakasisi, and I became concerned about the welfare of the children of Ssekabaka Mutesa II. Both of us strongly felt that the Princes and Princesses were not a party to the quarrel between Sir Edward Mutesa II and Milton Obote. As our concern grew, one day, in 1984, Rwakasisi expressed the view that instead of endless talk about the plight of the Princes and Princesses, it was better to do something about it .... Therefore, soon afterwards, we invited a leading Buganda Princess who kindly agreed to meet us. The three of us met in Rwakasisi's office and had a very cordial and fruitful discussion. ... It will not be proper to go public about what we discussed with the Princess or her identity. (Kasendwa-Ddumba, 2020, p. 23)

Negotiations of this nature take a long time to come to fruition. It is likely that these were overtaken by events as Obote's government was overthrown again by the army in July 1985.

There were employees of the kingdom who were affected in the aftermath of the fighting. Obote did not perform any better when it came to what many take as small personal matters. The federal arrangement under which Uganda was governed immediately after independence allowed the Buganda Kingdom to appoint its civil service personnel up to a certain level—the *saza* chiefs, the *gombolola* chiefs, and others below. In addition to those, there were non-descript men and women in the palace, not to mention the princes and princesses, who depended directly on the Kabaka for their livelihoods. With the abolition of the kingdom, many of these chiefs lost their jobs, to be replaced by UPC functionaries or those who claimed to be its supporters.

As often happens when the old order gives way to a new one under violent conditions, the men and women who were appointed as the new chiefs in Buganda after the 1966 fighting were not always the most highly regarded and popular members of the communities which they were meant to serve. Given the rather hostile environment in Buganda at the time, those who agreed to serve were daredevil characters and opportunists at best.

A story is told of one sub-county chief who was particularly eccentric and provocative. He was the area's most renowned priest of African religion, more commonly, but inaccurately, referred to as a witchdoctor, and, therefore, presumed to be a non-Christian. One Sunday, he attended service at the local Christian church and ostentatiously took the most comfortable seat in the church, the chair reserved for the church elder. To add insult to injury, when the time came, to the consternation of the shepherd and his flock who could do no more than sigh, he participated in the Holy Communion.

For many people, therefore, the 1966 Crisis changed their way of life and their very livelihoods for the worse—children dropping out of school for lack of fees, loss of shelter for those who lived in institution houses, and social prestige, to mention but a few. This not only affected the people directly concerned and their households but also those who looked up to them.

It is natural for man to sympathise with the misfortunes of individuals, although it is a little harder to celebrate their good fortune. In this case, the individual anger of the few became the collective empathetic indignation of the many against Obote for the hardships that had befallen the few. He called the events of 1966 and after a revolution. He may have followed the dictum that a revolution does not stoop to pick up pins and took the lives of these people to be pins. However, if all politics is local, one may also say that all politics is personal; it is how certain events and policies affect their personal fortunes and feelings that shape people's association with and attitude to the politician who initiates them.

With the benefit of hind sight, one can say that Obote should have attempted to alleviate or mitigate the hardships of the losers that came with his revolution by attending to their immediate personal needs so that they did not suffer a sudden drop in their living standards. We have learnt since the 1986 takeover of power by the National Resistance Movement/Army that many of the leaders of the defeated regime or their offspring can be co-opted into the new order to give the impression that they lost nothing.

The Baganda have a saying: *Abantu magoma, gavugira aliwo*, which literary translates as "Only he who is present can hear the sound of drums." The deep meaning of that saying is that the person who wields power or wealth cannot fail to attract supporters and praise-singers. Similarly, the victorious cause in a contest attracts to itself many supporters influenced by no conscientious principle; many who thought remaining loyal to the losing cause was a danger to them; many who were weary of its restraints; and many who were greedy for the spoils (Macaulay, 1849).

That was amply demonstrated in the 1950s in Buganda. Nsubuga (2013) writes that when Mutesa was deported to Britain, many Baganda, believing that he would never return, had cast their lot with Governor Cohen who had been the chief agent of their Kabaka's exile in the first place. During Mutesa's first exile, the conviction that he would not return was so strong among some people that they went to extraordinary lengths to demonstrate their confidence in his non-return. And they had historic precedence on their side. *Ssekabaka* Mwanga, Mutesa's grandfather, who had been exiled to Seychelles by the same British powers, had not come back to Buganda alive.

A story is told of one Senabulya, a resident Kikandwa, a village a few kilometres from Kampala, who staked his leg to be cut off if Mutesa came back to Buganda alive. Obviously, he had made a poor bargain for there was no counter-bet from anyone if, indeed, Mutesa did not come back. As it happened, Mutesa negotiated his return and came back. A mob trooped to Senabulya's house and demanded "their leg" from him! It took the village Anglican priest to persuade the excited, blood-thirsty mob to accept Senabulya's cow in exchange for his leg. The cow was promptly slaughtered, roasted and eaten in the village square to the accompaniment of music, dance and general merriment. This was another one-sided transaction, for while the villagers could eat the cow, there was not much they would have done with his amputated leg.

In a deal involving possible spilling of blood, if the poor man had been as shrewd as Shakespeare's Antonio in *The Merchant of Venice*, he would probably have saved both his leg and his cow. For Antonio, after failing to repay a loan secured against a pound of his own flesh, was agreeable to his creditor cutting off the pound of flesh from his body but without spilling even a single drop of blood. That condition made it impossible for the creditor to realise the security and the loan remains unpaid to date.

Since 1986, while hurling unsavoury insults at them, President Museveni has given jobs and other material benefits to many prominent people who served under regimes he defeated, or to their offspring. The pain and hardship that come with the loss of office having been obviated, coupled with the realisation that he was not going to vacate power any time soon, have muted their resentment of him. Museveni has profited politically from that approach to no end. There is no strong evidence that Obote made much conscious effort to accommodate his defeated adversaries or those who suffered collateral damage. In the public perception, therefore, he came out as being mean-spirited, winning the battle but losing the war, and yet, it need not have been so.

Milton Obote failed the magnanimity test. The Baganda have a saying, *Tomegga ate n'oluma*. The literal translation is that after wrestling an enemy to the ground, you do not bite him. It also warns against using force in excess of what is necessary to overcome an enemy. The deep meaning is: the vanquished should be spared their dignity.

Obote's Fortunes

Over the next five years, after the arrest of the cabinet ministers, in stark contrast with his archrivals, Mutesa and Ibingira, Obote's political star never shone so bright, before or after. His every desire was realised and every obstacle to absolute power within the party, Parliament, government and country was paved away.

First, he detained five senior party and cabinet ministers who were vying with him for power within the party and government. He also removed Sir Edward Mutesa and Sir William Wilberforce Nadiope from the presidency and vice presidency, respectively. He elevated himself from the position of prime minister to executive president, abrogating and replacing in the short-term the 1962 Independence Constitution in the process. Later, in 1967, he introduced and passed through Parliament-turned-into-a-Constituent-Assembly a Constitution which abolished the kingdoms, federal and semi-federal status, and turned the country into a fully-fledged republic.

On the economic front, through what he termed the Common Man's Charter and the Move to the Left, he shifted the country to socialism. Private foreign enterprises were partially nationalised by the government acquiring a majority shareholding in them.

Politically, he virtually snuffed out the opposition when existing and aspiring political leaders flocked to UPC in droves. For all practical purposes, by 1969, Uganda had become a one-party state, with Obote as its head. At the African regional level, particularly within the British Commonwealth countries, he was the man to go to, when he became the spokesperson on matters of the independence of Rhodesia (now called Zimbabwe), South West Africa (now called Namibia), and majority rule for South Africa.

The only glitch he suffered during this period was in December 1969, when he was shot at in the mouth in an assassination attempt as he was leaving the UPC delegates' conference in Kampala. The year 1970 was a success for Obote on all political fronts, although rumblings of disquiet were beginning to be heard in the distance.

Then in 1971, the accumulated forces of his enemies, created out of his successes, plunged his star into darkness. In January of that year, at the urging of his colleagues who wanted him to lead the campaign for the liberation causes he was spokesperson for, he attended the Commonwealth conference in Singapore. Before the conference came to an end, his government was overthrown by Major General Idi Amin, the army chief of staff. Obote did not return home; he ended up in exile in Tanzania for nine years.

Although he lived to regain power, the glitter had worn off his leadership and he ended up being overthrown for the second time in July 1985, this time never to regain it. He lived the last twenty years of his life in exile in Lusaka, the guest of the Zambian government, with only a couple of aides for company. In October 2005, he died while still in exile.

Such was the fate of Mutesa and Obote, the people who had led Uganda to independence. Such was the personal sacrifice they paid in the after-years for taking up leadership.

Symbolic Buildings and Spaces

After the Kabaka had fled and the resistance put up by loyalists against the Uganda army had been put down, the army did not withdraw from the Lubiri. Under different political leadership at different times, they stayed there for decades, using it as a military barracks. Simultaneously, the army occupied the Bulange—later renamed Republic House—which was turned into Uganda's Ministry of Defence headquarters. Occupying those two monumental buildings in the heart of Kampala constantly served as a symbol of Obote's enmity towards Buganda. It created a solid and visible sense of a victor-vanquished relationship between Obote and the Baganda.

However, it is understandable for a section of Ugandans to reserve their ire for Milton Obote. The Lubiri and the Bulange, among the sites attacked or occupied by the Uganda army, were such powerful symbols for the Baganda as a people. It was difficult for them to direct their rancour to any but that person they perceived as the cause of their misery.

But what authority he had to order the army to vacate the premises after it had taken possession of them is a matter of conjecture. Our guess is that after the Lubiri incident, Obote became beholden to the army and he had to "share" power with it, although as the civilian authority, it was formally answerable to him. The decision as to what use those places were to be put thus got out of his control.

It may be instructive to note that the grass-thatched tombs grounds of equal symbolic value where the previous three Baganda kings were entombed were not occupied by the army. These sit on 26 hectares and lie only three kilometres from the city centre. That would falsify the allegation that Obote was out to wantonly occupy and destroy Buganda's iconic structures just to amuse himself. Be that as it may, the public relations aspect of the post-Lubiri attack was inept, as even the most ardent defender of Obote would admit.

Political Landscape

Beyond the change of personal fortunes, the general elections which had been scheduled for early 1967 were postponed for five years. In 1967, a draft Constitution was circulated, and Parliament was constituted into a Constituent Assembly to debate and pass a new Constitution. After thorough debate, both within the assembly and outside, with several amendments to the draft being made, the new Constitution was promulgated. This is what was known in political circles as the 1967 Republican Constitution.

This work does to seek to compare and contrast the Independenence with the Republican Constitution. It is enough to say that the latter document fundamentally changed the basis upon which the country had been run since independence. For example, the full federal and semi-federal status of Buganda and the other three kingdoms, respectively, were done away with and a uniform unitary form of government introduced in accordance with the slogan of the day, "*One country, one Parliament, one government, and one people.*" As the name of the Constitution implies, the kingdoms of Buganda, Ankore, Bunyoro and Tooro were abolished, and Uganda became a true unitary republic. The administrative buildings of the kingdoms as well as the public land under their administration were placed under the control and management of the Central Government. As far as Buganda is concerned, the demand for *ebyaffe* has been resurrected and has kept alive ever since.

The contest over the Lost Counties by Buganda and Bunyoro was like a nuclear war between the United States and the Soviet Union. It was MAD (Mutually Assured Destruction). The irony of politics is that sometimes the winner and the loser suffer the same fate. Both Bunyoro that regained jurisdiction over the Lost Counties and Buganda that lost it were abolished as kingdoms by the aftermath of the referendum.

As far as Bunyoro was concerned, therefore, the result of the referendum was a disaster disguised as a blessing. The struggle for supremacy between the state of Uganda and the nations in Uganda made it inevitable that the other three kingdoms and the territory of Busoga, together with their kings, which had not been party to the problems, quarrels, and plots that gave rise to the Crisis, suffered the same fate as Buganda.

Sir Charles Gasyonga's fear that, as a result of the ascendency of Kabaka Mutesa to the presidency of Uganda, other crowned heads might be put at risk, hence, came to pass.

Chapter 10

WINNERS AND LOSERS

In every upheaval, whether political, or economic, or even a combination of both, there are invariably those who gain and those who lose as a result, either at an individual or institutional level. However, the loss or gain must be assessed on the basis of the short-, medium- and long-term. When we examine the 1966 Crisis, however, no long-term winners easily come to mind. More easily identifiable are the losers—some individuals and other institutions. We will deal with both types and why we consider them such.

At Individual Level

Although there were five major actors in the 1966 Crisis—three civilians (Mutesa, Obote and Ibingira) and two soldiers (Brigadier Opolot and Colonel Amin) two individual losers may be singled out in this assessment—Kabaka/President Mutesa and Prime Minister Obote. We have chosen those two personalities because they personify and symbolise the two sides to the struggle that is the 1966 Crisis.

As for the other civilians, within days from 20 May 1966, Ibingira and four of his cabinet colleagues were in prison. He played no significant role in Uganda politics after his release in 1971. Apart from moving the gold scandal motion in Parliament, Daudi Ocheng quickly faded out from the political scene, for he died in 1966.

Clearly, Mutesa's loss was the more immediate, dramatic and conspicuous. He lost the presidency, his palace, his throne and, some would argue, his life, the last part of which lived in lonely and uncomfortable exile. He made a major contribution to our knowledge of the history of this period by writing a book in which he left us his insight in the Crisis. In the rather speculative part of this book, he examines what might have been done to avert the Crisis.

It is Obote's more variegated legacy that we shall dwell on. At the immediate and superficial level, Obote appeared triumphant. As it were, politically, he was the only man left standing (but bruised). He not only remained in office but gained more power and prestige when the office of prime minister and that of president were combined to make him executive president of the country. Moreover, he lived to have a second bite on the cherry by heading government again between December 1980 and July 1985.

Obote's stance regarding the referendum gained him popularity in Bunyoro. In Ankore District where the kingship was not universally liked, his abolition of the kingdoms was, on the whole, seen as a popular move. But he, too, lost more still as we shall see.

No major Ugandan politician has been more vilified by a section of the Ugandan population than Obote. He became the politician many Baganda love to hate. For allowing the referendum over the Lost Counties to proceed, leading to Buganda insurrection against the Central Government, the attack on the Lubiri, and the subsequent events all of which he apparently got away with, many Baganda never forgave Obote. Indeed, the vendetta against him became virtually hereditary. Likewise, a little earlier in France, for granting Algeria independence, and for defeating them at every significant political turn, some French people never forgave de Gaulle. Like Jackson (2018) wrote of Charles de Gaulle, for some people, hating Obote gives meaning to their lives.

Some, thinking of it as a fashion to do so, tried to compete with one another as to who would come up with the most derogatory epithet for him. In that vein, extraordinary as it may sound, although not uncommon in the realm of politics, in Wankulukuku, a Kampala suburb, in October 2005, upon his death, some highly inebriated men and harbouring a peculiar attitude, found it fit to hunt down and catch a poor, sick-looking, homeless dog and purported to install it as his heir. Others in Luwero District declared their intention to block the passage of his body through that territory on its way to its final resting place in the district of his birth.

It was the same Obote, a Lango by tribe, whom at independence, the Baganda had honoured by incorporating him into their tribe, inducting him into their *Mamba* (Lung fish) clan and given the clan name *Bwete*, the closest in sound to Obote. Songs of praise and adoration had been composed in his honour by a Muganda artiste at the same time. But I suppose there is an inborn itch within human beings to lower the hubris of their would-be or erstwhile political leaders. He himself seems to have foreseen it when he complained after the passing of the Daudi Ocheng motion, "This is a frame-up to blacken my name and present me as the most dirty (sic) person in Uganda" (Mutesa, 1967, p. 187).

As an aside, it is worth noting that Obote was not the last non-Muganda leader to be first idolised and then later demonised. In idolisation, new heights were reached when it came to President Idi Amin. His role in the attack on Lubiri forgiven and forgotten, Amin was elevated to royalty. In appreciation of his overthrowing of Obote's government in 1971, and in the same year returning the body of Sir Edward Mutesa from London for a proper and befitting burial in Buganda, Amin became the beneficiary of a whispering speculation that he was the secret son of Kabaka Chwa II, the father of Sir Edward Mutesa and, therefore, Mutesa's half-brother.

Amin must have got wind of these whispers and, being a man with a keen sense of the ludicrous, could not wait to return the favour. He promptly rewarded them by naming the son he begat next, Mwanga, presumably after the "great-grandfather" Kabaka Mwanga, the father of Kabaka Chwa. Amin no doubt chuckled at the very thought of being considered a Muganda prince. At the same time, he must have marvelled at a people who derived solace from a falsehood they had themselves created. He probably suspected, though, that this self-deception was too bad to last; that one day they would wake up to his true self. And indeed, soon he would be called *Kijambiya*, the big machete, by the same people (behind his back, of course).

Succumbing to hasty optimism, and not for the last time, only to leave everybody disappointed sooner than later, the British press, on its part, had gone into overdrive when it described him as "a gentle giant" at the beginning of his rule. It later changed its mind and rebranded him (from a safe distance in London well beyond his grasp) "the butcher of Kampala" (with no apology to the innocent Kampala meat dealers).

Every crisis needs a scapegoat. In Obote, some people found an ideal one. Some critics accused him of bringing about the Crisis by holding the referendum on the Lost Counties issue at all or when he did.

No matter when the referendum took place, what choice did Obote have in calling it? It was a constitutional requirement to hold it. Even if it were within his discretion whether or not to hold it, he was between a rock and a hard place. If he ignored it, he risked an inter-ethnic war between the Banyoro and Baganda, which could have dragged in other groups. In fact, there had been skirmishes within the contested counties and between the two before independence. If, as he did, he allowed it to proceed, he risked the anger of the likely loser (Buganda), with unforeseeable consequences to himself or the country. The decision to hold the referendum was a supreme test of the mettle of Obote's leadership.

Using him further as a scapegoat, it is alleged that in order to gain Buganda's support that enabled him to become prime minister, he deceived Buganda that no referendum would be held over the Lost Counties. It is asserted that by appearing to agree to all of Buganda's demands before independence, Obote had used Buganda as a ladder to climb to leadership; and that he threw it away after reaching the top. Hence, Buganda's leadership's sense of being betrayed and tricked by Obote, a man they trusted and had given their support to gain power.

Mutesa himself vindicates Obote on these allegations. He wrote that Obote had wished at the London Conferences that the difficulty of the Lost Counties would be resolved without his involvement. A person who wishes a matter to be resolved without him playing a part certainly cannot be accused of exploiting that very matter to ascend to power.

Obote has been crucified for introducing militarism in Ugandan politics. However, those who hold him responsible for that ignore the fact, as has been shown, that the army was the club he and Mutesa struggled to get hold of and beat the other with, only that Obote got to it before his adversary did. Either way, the military would have found its way into Ugandan politics, as indeed it eventually did in 1971 and remains a player to this day as this is being written!

Whether justified or not, whether it was inevitable or not, it was Obote's misfortune that he clashed with the King of the most populous and the centrally located territory which hosts the nation's capital from where the establishment shapes and propagates all political opinions. This was not the first time that the head of the Central Government had had an altercation with Kabaka Mutesa. In 1953, Governor Sir Andrew Cohen had deported Kabaka Mutesa over accusations including rejecting the East African Federation and seeking independence for Buganda. The response of the Baganda to Kabaka Mutesa's deportation in 1953 differs only in degree from their response in 1966.

Of the 1953 deportation, a lesson learnt was that an attack on the Kabaka always "rekindles Buganda nationalism and cultural consciousness." The Kabaka was the symbol of Baganda's loyalty and pride; humiliating him was an attack at the Baganda (Nsubuga, 2013).

The name Cohen can be substituted with that of Obote, the latter's situation only being made far worse. With Cohen's induced exile, the Baganda had in the end the satisfaction of seeing their beloved Kabaka return to his kingdom in triumph. There was jubilation throughout the country which went on for months and made the Baganda forget the initial wrong. Obote's provided no such relief. To the contrary, their Kabaka returned in a casket, having died in unenviable and, some would insist, under suspicious circumstances.

Man, being both rational and emotional, is governed by the head and the heart. Sometimes, the heart has its reasons which the head cannot understand. However rational Mutesa's subjects may have tried to be, they could not avoid being emotionally affected by what happened to their Kabaka after he fled into exile. The humble existence to which the symbol of their pride and object of their loyalty was reduced, lived, and eventually died could not have endeared Obote to the people who saw him, rightly or wrongly, as responsible for this sad fate. Therefore, long after the guns had fallen silent on Mengo Hill, opinion continued to be shaped by one group of the protagonists to the detriment of the other.

For all that, rightly or wrongly, Obote's legacy as a unifying figure suffered. As a result of the fact that he was not universally appreciated as such, unlike his colleagues in the region—Jomo Kenyatta of Kenya and Julius Nyerere of Tanzania—his mantle as the undisputed "father of the nation" became contested. He became a hero outside his country but without honour at home.

That is how Obote may be viewed in the short- or even possibly medium-term. However, the life of a nation can be long. In so far as the Crisis has been defined as the struggle for Uganda's unity, Obote's legacy should be assessed from that viewpoint by future historians.

Right from the beginning, Obote's commitment was to ensure that Uganda gained independence and remained united. When the issue of the Lost Counties, an issue he had wished to be resolved without his involvement, reared its head to break up Uganda, as the person in charge of the country, he did what he considered necessary to keep it together. And Uganda is still together. Obote's long-term legacy will forever hang on that. As to the actual precipitation of the Crisis, whether he could have kept it together by doing nothing at all or doing less than what he did or by doing things differently, it will remain a matter of debate and opinion since it cannot be reconstructed or re-enacted.

Obote's Second Coming

In the above assessment, we have confined ourselves to activities during the period 1962-1971, prior and immediately after the 1966 Crisis, and their impact; but there is a sense that

that is not the parameter within which a good number of ordinary Ugandans view Obote's legacy. We are aware that even within that period for many political observers, the things which define Obote's rule are the 1966 Crisis and his relationship with Kabaka Mutesa. But we are convinced, that there are Ugandans both in Buganda and outside who think that there was more to his legacy than the 1966 Crisis and the period we have tried to confine ourselves to. It would have been safe to do so if Obote's public service had been limited and isolated to that period and had not been extended beyond it.

As far as his legacy is concerned, it was Obote's misfortune that he sought and assumed the country's leadership for the second time between December 1980 and July 1985. However, it is not our purpose in this writing to make an exhaustive over-arching evaluation of the totality of Obote's legacy. Other writers have done a good job painting Obote's picture on a wider canvas: writers like Ingham (1994). However, it would be remiss of us to totally ignore everything else apart from the 1966 Crisis that shape people's opinion of him. Even then, our task in this section of this work is only to briefly lay out the broad context within which Obote's performance during his second term may be evaluated. But not to let it cloud the main theme of this work.

Although it is common to talk of Obote I, meaning the 1962-1971 period of his rule and Obote II, referring the period 1980-1985, as representing the two periods he was in power, to the ordinary person his legacy cannot be so compartmentalised or segregated into time frames or particular episodes but is looked at as a whole. Many people can isolate the Amin period and not hold Obote accountable for it, although there are those who, for political expediency, mention Obote and Amin in the same breath. Fewer still will leave out of consideration his second rule in assessing how they view him.

It is known that Idi Amin was president of Uganda from January 1971 to April 1979; and Obote's second coming was from December 1980 to July 1985. It is also a fact that Amin was the very antithesis of what Obote stood for. His rule was characterised by horrendous human rights abuses and economic stagnation. Obote II witnessed great insecurity of person and property, especially in the internationally more visible and vocal south of the country and more especially in the Buganda region where the physical part of the 1966 Crisis mostly played out. If all the negative things (and the negatives stick to memory more than the positives) that happened from 1962 to 1985 are aggregated and placed at Obote's door, though unfairly, an entirely different picture of Obote emerges.

Whether it is acknowledged or not, the Uganda that Obote took over in 1980 was a broken state morally, physically, economically, and with barely functioning institutions. The people had been traumatised by the near lawless nine-year rule of Amin and the war that dislodged him. Their faith and confidence in government had been badly bruised during the short-lived and chaotic administrations that followed the fall of Amin's government—Yusufu Lule's that lasted 68 days from 12 April 1979, and Godfrey Binaisa's that followed only to be removed eleven months later. Binaisa was replaced by the Military Commission headed by Paulo Muwanga and deputised by Yoweri Museveni, under cover of the headless, powerless and clueless Military Commission. This was in charge of the country until December 1980 when Obote took over. The entire army and police had been disbanded following the war that removed Amin and were being rebuilt in the midst of an on-going insurgency against his government in and around the capital, which started even before he assumed power.

It was this new army in formation, still lacking in training and discipline, that was deployed to fight a guerrilla war, a new type of war employing war methods which up till then were unknown on Ugandan soil. Unlike in wars fought before that, it was hard to tell a combatant, including child soldiers, from innocent civilians going about their normal lives. Value systems have since changed. If the Rome Treaty had been in force at the time the insurgence war was fought, given the way they conducted the rebellion, some of the NRA commanders would have been seen in entirely different light: not hailed as freedom fighters but as international law criminals subject to trial before the International Criminal Court (ICC). The Rome Treaty brought into effect the Rome Statute, which created the international crimes of genocide, crimes against humanity, and war crimes. It established the International Criminal Court to try individuals charged with such crimes.

Incompetent staff, the competent ones either having been killed or fled into exile, were in charge of what remained of the government. The formal economy had virtually collapsed. The international community (called development partners) which had left during Amin's rule was yet to be persuaded to return to Uganda to lend a helping hand.

To capture the environment in which Obote struggled to rebuild Uganda, one has to factor in the following: the manner of his assumption of power this second time—the controversial elections of December 1980, which left bitterness and resentment against the government in their wake; the fact that even before the elections were held there was a group of militarists, driven by ambition that knew no bounds, who were ready to exploit anything and everything in order to acquire power at any cost; a ruling party (UPC) which had been moribund for ten years and was divided between leaders who had gone into exile and those who had stayed in the country during Amin's rule. A more different Uganda from the one he inherited at independence in 1962 and one he left in 1971, when power was grabbed from him, could not be imagined. That was the situation he freely walked into to make Uganda rise and shine again and hoped that history would be kind to him.

Whether Obote's legacy is viewed purely from the context of the 1966 Crisis, as was part of the aim in this work, or in the broader context of his works in the entire period he was in leadership, as some people would wish, there are a few things we can be certain of. The jury is not out yet. The statute of limitation does not apply to the assessment of a leader's legacy; it can be visited and revisited any time and any number of times. Therefore, no one can claim to have the last word. And even more important, assessment is a free port. Anyone is at liberty to enter, make, and hold their evaluation and leave.

Obote's admirers and detractors alike should be comforted by the immutable fact that the evaluation of the success of great men and women can rise and fall and rise again over time. The question that is rarely asked, though, is: who assesses the assessors? But that is another matter. Having examined closely the entirety of his rule, we are persuaded to conclude that Obote, like Macaulay (1871) describes one Clarendon: "… in every respect a man unfit for his age, at once too good for it and too bad for it" (p. 223).

At Institutional Level

Uganda Peoples Congress

At institutional level, UPC, an innocent bystander, lost. Yes, UPC was an innocent bystander, unless, due to a refusal the or failure to distinguish an individual from an institution, one chooses to equate Obote—the individual—with UPC—the institution, the party he led—and visit his perceived failings upon it. Unfortunately, that is how it has turned out. It became the victim of misplaced indignation in Buganda which was the main theatre of the clash. It was deemed guilty by association with Obote, its leader. What is ignored is the fact that, as with the formation of the UPC-KY alliance before, between 1964, when UPC held its last delegates' conference in Gulu, and 1967, when the Republican Constitution was passed, no UPC organ— whether the delegates' conference or the national executive council meeting—had ever sat to discuss, let alone make a resolution, on the issue of either. And no party organ ever sat to discuss the arrest of the cabinet ministers, the presidency of Mutesa, or the abolition of Buganda Kingdom and other kingdoms, for that matter. In fact, during this period UPC was not sufficiently cohesive to organise the convening of a meeting of any of its decision-making organs. In addition to that, it would have been imprudent on the part of Obote to call any such meeting when he clearly knew that a section of his party membership had joined with the sole purpose of deposing him from leadership. It is important to remember that all the ministers who were detained were members of UPC top leadership. These included, among others, Grace Ibingira, the party secretary general and Dr Emmanuel Lumu, the chairman of UPC Buganda Region. Therefore, whatever their merits or demerits, the measures taken in the first half of 1966 could not have been in execution of the collective UPC project as a party.

As stated before, this was a contest between the state of Uganda, represented by Obote, and the nation of Buganda, represented by Mutesa arising from holding a referendum to resolve the issue of the Lost Counties. On the back of this contest, the UPC leadership wrangles rode, and UPC as a whole suffered. Obote was merely the common factor in the two contests.

Buganda Kingdom

Buganda's loss is obvious: the centuries-old kingdom folded and, until recently, only remained in the hearts of its adherents. However, at a deeper level, a kingdom cannot suddenly die like a human being. A kingdom as old as Buganda is a way of life "bred into people's bones and a part of their national tradition" (Kennedy, 1940, p. 27) guiding its subjects from the cradle to the grave, and possibly beyond the grave.

The monarch may be prohibited from presenting himself as such. The royal regalia may be confiscated and kept away in museums; and the pomp and ceremonies may be barred and banned. But with or without the Kabaka on the throne, there are institutions and practises which are intrinsically part of the kingdom that went on without hindrance. Examples of such institutions include clan heads. Practises like celebrating last funeral rites and the naming of offspring in accordance with kingdom practices and traditions were carried foreward. Such institutions and practices cannot be killed with the mere stroke of a pen. They remained functioning despite the legal abolition of the kingdom.

That notwithstanding, although all kingdoms, except that of Ankore, have been restored and indeed new ones have been created, three different types of people hold different views regarding the restored Buganda Kingdom: the purists, the pragmatists, and the incrementalists. The purists maintain that what was restored was *byoya bya nswa* — a heap of worthless white ants' wings, all volume and no weight, a meaningless pretence. They want all-or-nothing.

To call the type of kingdom that was restored *byoya bya nswa* is, in my view, an illusion. It assumes that the abolition of the kingdoms, and particularly the Buganda Kingdom, under the 1967 Constitution, represented a mere freezing of time: that, it was like pressing the "pause" button on a Video Camera Recording (VCR) electronic device and that the restoration of the kingdoms in 1993 under the Cultural Institutions Statute was the equivalent of the pressing the "play" button to allow life to continue as from 1967. To this type of thinking, anything that differed from life before 1966 was *byoya bya nswa*. Yet, so much water had gone under the bridge. Like the Bourbons, the purists seem to have learnt nothing and forgotten nothing.

The pragmatists admit that, although a restoration can never be as good as the item in its original form, it is better than nothing. They are willing to live with the kingdom in its debased form.

On the other hand, the incrementalists believe that *akanyama akatono okayana kakuli mu nkwawa* — if meat is being shared out, especially after a hunt, you first grasp firmly to the little that you have been given as you demand for more. The incrementalists essentially say, "This is not the type of kingdom we wanted, but Buganda will incrementally realise its full demands."

The incrementalists, who prevailed, may not be awake to the fact that by agreeing to the gratification of their demands in undefined instalments at non-specified intervals and content, and no date for closure, they had reduced themselves to supplicants over what they deem to be theirs by right. They have played in the hands of the powers that be who are in the position to give or withhold what they demand.

As long as they hope for more, they lend political leverage to the giver who is enabled to dangle some of the remaining demands, especially land titles, whenever it is most politically profitable, say, at election time. Those who demand more have thus, become the hostages whose political support, explicit or implicit, is demanded as the ransom. To whatever school of thought they belong, it is undeniable that something was lost in 1966/1967.

Uganda

On an even wider platform was Uganda's loss. As a result of this conflict, Buganda became, once again, a reluctant partner in the Uganda Project. This hostility of Buganda to the Obote government because of the 1966 Crisis made the 1971 coup against the Obote government gain easy acceptance in the central province from which political opinions largely originate, to the great loss of the country as a whole. Idi Amin's seizure of Obote's government and the Baganda's ready acceptance is easily attributable to the 1966 Crisis. As a result of that seizure, many projects which were in the pipeline were affected. A few of them, which either stalled or were cancelled, may be cited:

(a) Construction of the Karuma Dam for the generation of electricity was due to start in 1971. It was restarted forty-four years later.

(b) A well-planned universal primary education (UPE) scheme was already on the drawing board and a pilot scheme was due to kick off before 1975. It was hurriedly announced years later in 1996 and implemented immediately before proper preparations were made. The consequences of its hurried implementation are yet to be fully assessed but there is a strong opinion that the children under the present UPE get largely "a good-for-nothing education."

(c) Grand housing projects like the one at Bugolobi, a suburb of Kampala, which were about to be expanded and rolled out in major towns throughout the country were halted.

All those plans were shelved because of the instability traceable to the 1966 Crisis.

Uganda also suffered intangible losses. The path for the departure of many Ugandans into exile we see today was opened in 1966. The political turmoil that has followed since then has only made it worse. It is often the best trained or the most adventurous and innovative people who usually go away, and few ever return during their productive years, with the resultant loss of a big portion of the best manpower of the country. In terms of loss of manpower, Uganda continues to pay the price for the Crisis.

A progressive regime, so popular in and outside Africa, apart from Britain with which it disagreed over issues of democracy in Rhodesia, South Africa, and South West Africa (Namibia), was later replaced by a regime that became a pariah of Africa and whose economic policies destroyed almost all the progress Uganda had achieved under Obote.

Kiwanuka, a former head of the Information and Public Relations Department in Uganda's Ministry of Foreign Affairs, in his autobiography titled *The Son of a Rat Catcher* hints that Uganda's loss might even be greater than we imagine. He writes:

> Other writers have spent considerable space and time on Milton Obote's politics and the upheavals he deliberately created or was forced to create during his two terms as President of Uganda. I will, therefore, confine myself to what I saw and thought of a man who, if he had lived under different circumstances could have probably much earlier turned Uganda into a first world country like Singapore, just like his friend, Lee Kuan Yew, gradually did. (Kiwanuka, 2014, p. 127)

Kiwanuka's observation should give Ugandans, friends and foes of Obote alike, cause to pause and ponder what Uganda might have become if Obote's administration had not been disrupted.

Chapter 11

COULD THE CRISIS HAVE BEEN AVERTED?

In his contribution to the debate on the Uganda Independence Bill in the British House of Lords, Viscount Ward of Witley reminded members that the commission which had been appointed to look into the dispute between the Buganda Kingdom and the Bunyoro Kingdom had recommended that the two counties should be returned to Bunyoro and the other four should remain in Buganda. Having said that, he continued:

> The Omukama of Bunyoro, although disappointed that we had not recommended the return of all the territory, generously agreed to this compromise in the interests of peace, stability and the unity of Uganda as a whole, and he renounced all claim to the four remaining counties. And if there could have been an equally magnanimous gesture by the Kabaka of Buganda the problem could have been solved and the dispute settled for all time. But unfortunately, the Kabaka doubtlessly with the Kabaka Yekka breathing down his neck, refused to cede any territory at all. (*The Hansard*, 26 July 1962 col. 145-172)

The Crisis thus became inevitable because of the intransigence of one of the parties to the dispute. In Chapter 7, we covered the factors which inflamed the Crisis. Here we try to imagine the actors and factors which could have tempered the Crisis before or after it manifested itself in iron and blood.

Could the Crisis have been Averted?

If our only concern here was whether the Crisis could have been prevented, the starting point would have been tackling the cause of the Crisis itself: the Lost Counties. If the counties had not been "lost" or if their "loss" had been accepted or they had been returned peacefully to where they belonged, the Crisis would not have arisen. But that would be like arguing that there would have been no crisis if its actual cause had been removed before it arose. Faced with such logic, we have to admit that the word avert is used here not in the sense of how the Crisis could have been prevented but how its ill effects could have been mitigated. In much the same way as a car safety belt does not prevent an accident from occurring, wearing it does reduce the injuries that might be suffered in case an accident occurred. Avert is also used in the same way here in the sense of a shock absorber which limits both the force of the impact and the effect of that impact.

What inflamed the Crisis is a certainty. It is known because it existed. What is not known and is unknowable is what could have mitigated the Crisis. What might not have happened or might have happened differently is unknowable because, well, it did not happen. That is a question that takes us into the realm of what historians refer to as "the might-have-beens" or "the what-ifs." However, speculation is unavoidable both in history and economics. I will, therefore, indulge in some speculation, if only to reduce the burden of responsibility for what happened from the shoulders of the main protagonists in this saga.

We cannot conduct controlled experiments, to see what the situation would have been if a certain issue had not arisen or if certain personalities had not occupied certain offices, or if they had acted differently (Stiglitz, 2012). In other words, there are no tools for telling what would have happened historically or economically.

As is the case in economics, so it is in history. History is a social science, not a physical experimental science. There are no controlled laboratory experiments to tell with precision in advance how a particular decision will work out. It is easy to critique certain decisions many years after they were taken, and their effects have shown themselves.

It bears repeating that the primary cause of the Crisis was the issue of the Lost Counties on the resolution of which hinged the independence of Uganda as one country. The transfer of those counties from Bunyoro to Buganda planted the seed which germinated in 1966. Throughout history, at the end of inter-state wars, some territory has been gained and some territory has been lost between the loser and the victor. Mutesa (1967) says as much when he refers to the Lost Counties issue during the Lancaster House Conference. "To the victor, the spoils," he wrote. Indeed, Buganda originally consisted of three counties of Kyaddondo, Busiro, and Mawokota. It had gained its size at the expense of Bunyoro during various wars. As we noted earlier, this war, at the end of which Buganda gained the Lost Counties, was entirely different from the earlier wars between Buganda and Bunyoro in many ways. Kabaka Mwanga, the deposed king of Buganda, fought on the side of Bunyoro and its Omukama Kabalega. Buganda was in assistance of a power not even from within Africa but a colonising force from outside Africa, which was in quest to bring Bunyoro under its colonial rule.

What if the Issue had been Resolved before Independence?

Several attempts had been made by the British colonial government towards that end but to no avail. As far as Buganda was concerned, it had a special relationship with Britain; it had not been colonised but had invited Britain to come in and "protect" it. Any return of the counties to Bunyoro without its consent would have been seen as an act of betrayal on the part of Britain, to which it had rendered service in the colonisation project.

Regarding the delusion of invitation of Britain, Buganda does not seem to have been aware of Theodore Roosevelt's advice to would-be colonisers, "Speak softly but carry a big stick." At the time these "invitations" were going on, the Kabaka's palace at Mengo was within shooting range of Captain Lugard's Maxim gun and Nubian soldiers stationed at Old Kampala Hill.

When the transfer of territory was being made, no one knew that there was going to be created an entity called Uganda of which Buganda and Bunyoro were going to be composite parts. History had imposed it and there was no running away from it. As we have seen, a decision was made during the London conferences that a referendum would be held so that the people living in the area might determine under which jurisdiction the counties were to fall. The first "if" we have to deal with is, what if the referendum had not been held? Unfortunately, this is an issue which did not lend itself to compromise or flexibility.

What if Obote had not Gone Ahead with the Referundum?

Some people assume that if Obote, the prime minister, had not gone ahead with the referendum, and thereby incurred the wrath of President Mutesa and Buganda, the machinations which led to the Crisis would not have taken place. Those who advance that view ignore the fact that as far back as 1921, the Bunyoro-Mubende Committee had been formed by the

Banyoro living in the Lost Counties to struggle for the return of not only those counties but also Buwekula, Singo, Buruli and Bugerere to the jurisdiction of Bunyoro from Buganda.

If there had been no referendum, it is not too far-fetched to imagine that there would have been in that area fighting between the Banyoro and Baganda of the type we saw between the Rwenzururu (Bamba and Bakonzo) and the Batooro or the Sebei and the Bagisu before independence and well into the 1960s. For how would the Banyoro have been expected to fold their hands and not fight to regain the lost Buyaga and Bugangaizi, the very centre of their ancient kingdom, where "lie the graves of Banyoro Bakama, where every creature, hill, rock and blade of grass cries aloud to those interested that they are Banyoro?" (Dunbar, 1965, p. 102).

Obote as Prime Minister of Uganda had other constituencies to mind apart from Buganda. People from other areas expected him to observe the constitutional provisions. Calling that referendum was one of them.

What if Mutesa were not Kabaka of Buganda and the president of Uganda at the same time?

It may be argued that the Baganda would have sulked at the loss of the counties. Probably there would have been a scuffle but perhaps not the conflagration of the magnitude witnessed in May 1966. But definitely, there would have been less opportunity for Mutesa and Ibingira to reinforce each other in a conspiracy which compelled Obote, facing an existential threat, to respond the way he did.

If Mutesa were not president, it would not have been his duty to sign the referendum instruments, the refusal of which opened him to the accusation of dereliction of his presidential duty to the benefit of his kingdom. This hypothesis falls on its face because, like it or not, Mutesa had to be president. It is worth repeating what Mutesa wrote regarding the decision to elect him for the five-year term as president of Uganda,

> ... there was little choice either for Obote or me. He was not in a position to snub the Baganda, who would have been enraged if any other ruler were chosen, as the new President would have precedence over the Kabaka even in Buganda. (Mutesa, 1967, p. 172)

Mpambara, as quoted before, also reports that Mutesa was elected at the insistence of Obote in order to make Baganda feel part of Uganda. It was the unity of Uganda that was at stake. It may be remembered that Buganda had had to be coaxed into remaining part of Uganda after independence. Therefore, the question of if the Kabaka were not also the president of Uganda does not arise. He had to be. Sadly, in Mutesa's mind, the line between the person of the Kabaka of Buganda and the person of the president of Uganda became blurred when the time came to decide between the two roles.

Mutesa seems to suggest that if Prime Minister Obote had fallen on his sword, as Buganda's Premier Mikaeri Kintu had done after the referendum or if he had been successfully removed from office by whatever means, the Crisis would not have happened. In a rarely quoted paragraph, Mutesa writes:

> ... I do not pretend that at this stage I would have been heartbroken to see a man who now represented no one but himself and was determined to *destroy my kingdom* [Emphasis added] forced from office... Such an event would be satisfactory and would avoid the crisis we were otherwise approaching. (Mutesa, 1967, pp. 187-188)

Of all the "might-have-beens" we have encountered, this is the novelest. How realistic is the suggestion that if Obote had resigned his position as prime minister in "atonement" for having allowed the referendum to take place, the return of the Lost Counties would have gone without further incident? I leave that to the reader to decide. Suffice to say that a person who had risen to the top of the political heap in the manner that Obote had done rarely yields his position at the first encounter with adversity but holds on to it with tenacity. It would have been expecting too much to think that such a man would fold his tent and quietly walk off into the sunset. As his two-time loss of office would later show, in 1971 and 1985, respectively, Obote was not a man who went out with a whimper; he went out with a bang!

An equally important "if" is that the Crisis would not have come about if the advice of Archbishop Joseph Kiwanuka had been heeded to. In his September 1961 pastoral letter, Archbishop Joseph Kiwanuka advised that the Kabaka should remain a constitutional monarch and should not engage in politics. That advice was in the context of Buganda, but Mutesa went on to engage in the even broader Uganda politics. The Archbishop wrote:

> When a country with a king reaches the stage where its government is ruled by its people, such a country may still want to keep its kings and for that reason it takes its kings out of politics. When political parties are established in a country, if the king still mixes up in politics, the kingship is on the way to digging its own grave. (Kasozi, 1996, p. 147)

It is intriguing to observe that Archbishop Kiwanuka died on 22 February 1966, the very day of the arrest of the five ministers that sparked off the events of the 1966 Crisis. His death was drowned out by the unfolding of events leading to the eventual abolition of kingdoms, an outcome he had more or less predicted.

What if Mutesa had Looked a Little Farther?

In my opinion, by far, the most intriguing and fanciful "if" of all is what if Sir Edward Mutesa had lifted his horizons a little farther, cast his gaze a little wider and had had a little more political ambition to preside over a political territory bigger than his native Buganda? Things would have been different.

During his earlier exile in Britain between 1953 and 1955 following his disagreement with the colonial power, Mutesa met Sir Sereste Khama, king of Bechuanaland (present-day Botswana), who was another reluctant guest of Her Majesty's government. The two monarchs got talking about their plans. Sereste Khama informed Mutesa that he planned to abdicate his throne and form a political party. That is indeed what he proceeded to do and not only led his country to independence but established the foundation for one of the most politically stable and economically prosperous countries in Africa. He became a revered father of his nation.

Mutesa took a completely different path upon his return from exile. Despite the yearning for Uganda-wide leadership and the political and financial support he had received from outside Buganda to bolster his return, Mutesa, edged on by his cronies, rather than form a political party himself, actively discouraged the formation of any in Buganda. Mutesa chose to remain just the Kabaka of Buganda (for a while) and to encourage the formation of Kabaka Yekka movement which had no presence outside Buganda.

Some scholars have posited that in the unification of Uganda and possibly that of East Africa, for that matter,

Buganda and Mutesa were positioned to play the same role Prussia and Otto von Bismarck did in the unification of Germany, namely, respectively, being the driving force and the centre around which the neighbouring territories coalesced to form a new, bigger, and more powerful nation behind that project. Buganda may have been like Prussia but, sadly, Buganda's Mutesa was unlike Bismarck.

We are persuaded that Mutesa's presidency in the form it took was part of the problem. His presidency in a different formation, shorn of the kabakaship, as an elected president through universal adult suffrage, would have been part of the solution. Better still, if he had cast his gaze even wider as leader of East Africa, the Lost Counties would have assumed a far less significance in the general scheme of things and diminished their impact on the politics of Uganda. There were opportunities and openings which, if he had exploited, would have made not only his fate but the history of the region different.

Beyond Uganda, the Kikuyu Mau Mau leaders from Kenya who were then fighting for independence saw Mutesa as a possible ally and a figure around whom to rally in their struggles. Their representatives attended celebrations to mark his return from exile. Even Jaramogi Oginga Odinga, a prominent Luo politician from Kenya, paid a courtesy call on the Kabaka. Kimenye (2015) reports that Mutesa was on very friendly terms with the Charles Mutara III, *Umwami* (king) of Rwanda and Mwambutsa, *Umwami* of Burundi who paid regular visits of pleasure to his palace. Mutesa enjoyed some goodwill even in Tanganyika.

Around the period when the colonialists partitioned the territories around the Great Lakes into the present-day states, Buganda was the supreme power in the area. Although

Buganda may not have exercised formal suzerainty over these territories, tribute was exacted from chiefs in Bukoba region, in present-day Tanzania. Even after the colonialists had created the colonial states of Kenya and Tanganyika, but before their independence, the chiefs from those areas, particularly from Tanganyika, used to make courtesy calls on Sir Edward Mutesa, as to his father, Chwa II, before him. With Buganda as his base, given the necessary political skills and if he was possessed of, and had exhibited bigger ambition, Mutesa would have started out with the great advantage of not only monarchical prestige but also having the widest name recognition among the emerging African leaders within the region.

It is not improbable that these influential people, who partied and played together, would have embraced him as the political leader of a united East Africa. He had the gravitas as *Bwana Kubwa* (the Big Boss), the (former) king, who had suffered exile for his people but who had in turn relentlessly struggled to have him returned home by the colonialists. He had the looks and vigour of youth (being in his early thirties) and military training with a formal rank. Myths around great leaders have been built around far less. Inevitably, this would have involved his abdication of his crown to the kabakaship of Buganda just as Sereste Khama had done with regard to his crown in Bechuanaland. That would have been a tough call but one which, if answered boldly, leads men to found new nations and find greatness.

As Shakespeare wrote in his play, *The Twelfth Night*, some men are born great; some achieve greatness and others have greatness thrust upon them. He should have added that "and yet other men shirk greatness."

To the question whether the resolution of the Lost Counties issue had, inevitably, to end in bloodshed, the answer is, therefore, a paradoxical "definitely, maybe." That there would have been rancour and that the loss of the counties would have left a bitter taste in the mouths of Baganda, there is no doubt. But whether a military confrontation would have been inevitable at the end of it all, no fair-minded person can tell.

There would have been trouble if the referendum were not held. And there was trouble because it was held. Whichever solution was devised, disaster loomed. Such is the stuff that Greek tragedies are made of. No matter which way one chooses or acts, tragedy strikes, for the gods have so ordained it. And as for Obote and Mutesa personally, the gods raised them high only to smite them low.

Absence of Experienced Statesmen

As if the indirect causes of the Crisis were not inauspicious enough, the gathering Crisis found no reservoir of experienced statesmen and institutions around—either at the Central Government level or at Mengo—clothed with sufficient authority and willing to broker a deal that might have averted the catastrophe. Obote and Mutesa, with no one to consult in the country over the unprecedented problems they faced, relied on their own devices and their inexperience showed.

That should not be lost sight of either in assessing the performance of the two main disputants or in speculating whether the presence of experienced statesmen could have mitigated the Crisis. Beyond the events that preceded the actual fighting, this reservoir of experienced statesmen would have helped in advising the government on how to manage better the "victory" and what remained of the Mengo establishment on how to manage the consequences of "defeat."

Chapter 12

LESSONS LEARNT

There is a saying that "a crisis should not be wasted." We understand that phrase to mean that a crisis should be seized as an opportunity to introduce long overdue reforms of the system which, but for the crisis, would have been met with insurmountable resistance. It should not be business as usual after the crisis. A crisis is wasted if not followed by reforms. At the very least, there must be lessons learnt from it. Uganda did not waste the 1966 Crisis. Ugandans are, if not wiser after fifty years, acutely conscious of the Crisis, as a reference point.

From the trauma of the Crisis, a number of lessons seem to have been learnt. Since then, some changes have been introduced in the governance of the country as a whole and within UPC in particular to address the mischief perceived to have contributed to the Crisis.

Conflict of Interest
One of the most glaring problems was that the Kabaka of Buganda was at the same time the president of Uganda. To avoid a person being placed in positions with potential conflict of interest as the Kabaka was, The Institution of Traditional or Cultural Leaders Act, among other things, prohibits a traditional leader from engaging in partisan politics. This is buttressed by Article 80 of the 1995 Constitution which disqualifies a traditional or cultural leader for election as a member of Parliament and, impliedly election as president of the country.

Sudden Change of Equilibrium in Parliament

To avoid the destabilising of government by the sudden change of parties by members of Parliament, the framers of the 1995 Constitution proscribed the free movement from one party to another during the life of the Parliament in which they are serving.

It provides in Article 83:

1. A member of Parliament shall vacate his or her seat in Parliament—
   - (g) If that person leaves the political party for which he or she stood as a candidate for election to Parliament to join another party or to remain in Parliament as an independent member;
   - (h) If, having been elected to Parliament as an independent candidate, that person joins a political party;

The absence of restraint in 1960s on members to switch parties contributed to the political turmoil of that period. Since the promulgation of the 1995 Constitution, no member of Parliament has taken the plunge and resigned their seat, although clearly some would have wanted to change parties.

Prime Minister vis-à-vis President Conflict

From 1966 until 1980, the position of prime minister ceased to exist in the Ugandan cabinet. There was only an executive president. Even when the position was re-introduced in 1980, it was more of a public relations stance than a reflection of real power. Even then, it was not constitutionally provided for. The 1995 Constitution did not initially provide for it. It came into existence in 2005 through the Constitutional Amendment Act, which added a new Article 108A. This article creates the position of prime minister and also provides for the duties and how that office may be vacated. Today's prime minister is appointed by the president like the rest of the ministers and can be dismissed with as much ease as other ministers. Under this set-up, it is not easy for the prime minister and the president to clash the way Obote and Mutesa did.

Power Struggle within a Political Party

In order to forestall a power struggle within UPC between the party secretary general and the party president, the party constitution was amended in 1970. Formerly, all top party officials were elected by the party's delegates conference. An official elected by the party delegates, the way Ibingira was, could not be removed by the party president no matter how difficult it became for the two to work together. The amendment provided for the election of only the president. He/she then appoints the other officials, such as the secretary general, vice president, treasurer and others and only submits those appointments to the party delegates conference for approval.

Under such arrangement, the president has a free hand to make quick adjustments in his team should they see any tension in the way it is functioning. Within UPC, the danger of the secretary general developing their own power base from which to undermine the party president can easily be nipped in the bud. Some political parties in Uganda have belatedly become alive to this reality and to the wisdom of UPC's solution to the problem of the power struggle between the party president and the party secretary general and have scampered to put it right.

It may not look democratic, but it is certainly effective. It is inconceivable, for instance, that in the event of the party winning power, the cabinet to make up the government would be elected by the party members. The leader picks their cabinet, but it would be an insensitive leader who does not consider the sentiment of the party membership in so doing. A cabinet is a team, and a team requires cohesion. By the same principle, a football team line-up for a match is not chosen by the club fans, and not even by the owners of the football company. A team is selected by the hired manager or coach who takes responsibility for its performance. In a nod to democracy, however, the regional leaders of the party should be elected by the regional party membership.

Conflict Between Nation and State

For the sake of clarity, we need to go back a little in history. In a 1953 speech, the British secretary for colonies made some remarks to the effect that an idea was being mooted to merge Kenya, which was a colony, Tanganyika, which was a trusteeship, and Uganda, which was a protectorate into an East African Federation along the lines of the federation among Nyasaland, Northern Rhodesia and Southern Rhodesia (present-day Malawi, Zambia, and Zimbabwe, respectively).

When Buganda Lukiiko got wind of that speech, it sought to have the affairs of Buganda transferred from the colonial office to the foreign office which handled matters to do with the sovereign independent states. The disagreement that ensued between the Kabaka and governor ended up with Kabaka Mutesa being deported to Britain. In order to resolve the impasse and as a condition for Mutesa's return to Buganda, the second Buganda agreement of 1955 was concluded between Britain and Buganda. That agreement turned the Kabaka of Buganda into a constitutional monarch with an elected Katikkiro. It further embedded Buganda into Uganda. Buganda was required to send representatives to the Uganda Legislative Council. However, as negotiations to grant Uganda independence commenced, Buganda renewed its demand to be granted independence as a state separate from Uganda. However, reality prevailed and they understood that it would be too costly to extricate itself from Uganda.

In the Lancaster Settlement, therefore, a compromise was reached whereby Buganda remained part of Uganda but as a federal kingdom. That compromise formed part of 1962 Uganda Independence Constitution.

Going by the apparently entrenched opinion that on 23 May 1966, the Lukiiko of the Buganda nation, feeling that the 1962 constitutional arrangement had been breached by the Uganda government, issued an ultimatum ordering the Uganda state government to remove itself from its territory. It is highly unlikely that such a resolution, even one shouted from the gallery, would be passed today by that body or any other local government chamber. The Crisis confirmed the supremacy, apparently for good, of the power and authority of the Central Government in Uganda, which is the state, over any other authority of a local government of any nature or form, and which may be a nation. In the case of Buganda, many responsible political actors from that area today speak consistently of a united Buganda nation in a united Uganda state. But the nuts and bolts are yet to be fixed to make that talk a reality and ensure that a part (a nation) does not wag the whole of Uganda (the state). A dog wags its tail. The tail does not wag the dog. In 1966, the tail tried to wag the dog.

Today, there seems to be a consensus that, without any conscious act by either unit, Buganda, and Uganda, have evolved and are so embedded into each other that they are, and must conduct themselves, like conjoined twins. They have no choice but to coordinate their movements or stumble together.

The confidence of the state of Uganda that it is presently strong enough to withstand the tremors that may come from the nations must have informed the decision to restore the kingdoms/cultural institutions in 1993. No doubt there were political advantages to be harvested by the group that instituted the restoration of the kingdoms. In our view, that would not have been undertaken if there was a perceived real threat of tearing the state apart.

Inter- and Intra-Territorial Claims and Divisions

The Lost Counties issue, where one political unit in Uganda (Bunyoro), claimed as part of its territory, an area belonging to another political unit (Buganda), solely on the ground that it historically belonged to it, appears to have been a one-off situation brought about by peculiar historical circumstances. What we see today is pressure for intra-territorial divisions. Essentially, it represents a desire or an arrangement to place people of similar ethnic make-up under one administrative unit. While we need not narrate again how the Lost Counties issue arose, which was an inter-territorial claim, it must be placed in the wider context of Africa's colonial history. In drawing the colonial borders, many tribes were split into two or more territories. Indeed, it is said that the Great Kabalega himself, omukama of Bunyoro, was born on the western side of Lake Albert in what today is called the Democratic Republic of Congo where a good number of Banyoro still live.

Within the individual colonial countries, many administrative units created put together different ethnic groups. These units were inherited by the post-independence governments, including Uganda. The founding fathers of the Organisation for African Unity (now called the African Union), established in 1963 after a majority of African countries had attained independence, resolved to leave intact their countries' colonial boundaries. In their wisdom, redrawing the boundaries in order to cater for ethnic groupings and to create more natural borders would have opened a pandora box. We believe that it is in that spirit that at the dawn of independence, Bunyoro did not demand the re-establishment of the territorial boundaries of the pre-colonial greater Bunyoro-Kitara, part of which was now in Congo. But it was a different matter when it came to territory "lost" within Uganda, which was also a colonial imposition. Was it because this territory was acceded to Buganda, which was Bunyoro's "traditional enemy," as Mutesa put it?

In Uganda, even after the transfer of the disputed counties to Bunyoro, other internal administrative units remained unchanged. However, over time, national leaders have bent to pressure from local leaders to rearrange the districts, in some cases based purely on ethnic composition. These may be described as intra-territorial divisions. This has resulted in the creation of some districts which are not economically viable. Lately, we have seen the rising of claims for separate kingdoms to be curved out of existing ones. These claims are often encouraged for political expediency. Coupled with the decentralisation, which encourages local recruitment of labour, an inward-looking society and tribal enclaves are being promoted instead of building a nation called Uganda. To that extent, no lessons have been learnt from the inter-territorial-claim-generated crisis.

On the whole, however, the Crisis offered an opportunity for political reforms. In our opinion, that opportunity was not squandered. It enabled measures as we have set out above to be put in place in order to consolidate the state and make Uganda stronger. These measures were designed to stave off the repletion of some of the events which contributed to the Crisis.

Chapter 13

STARTING ANEW

Let us overleap these many years since the Crisis to the present time. We must think anew to bring long lasting solutions to the fundamental problems which confront the country. Some lessons have been learnt and solutions devised, as we have seen, but some questions remain unanswered and others have emerged and demand to be addressed. Uganda is not settled in the best possible position yet.

One of the issues crying out to be attended to is that of governance and the quality of our elections. A sizeable number of citizens is of the view that holding elections has become a mere ritual. If it is in fact so, is it not time we restored meaning to elections, Uganda, moving forward? How do we deal with the citizens' complaint that the raiding of the treasury by the party that may be in power is tantamount to buying the electors with their own money? Should we not address the issue of disputed elections of 1980 that led to a devastating rebellion? We must begin by coming to terms with what brought us where we are. However, each of those questions and others not asked merits a separate piece of work.

In this chapter, our intention is merely to sketch the problems we perceive as demanding redress and leave others to fill up the outline but not to paint a finished picture and give a complete prescription.

As a nation we must face the many structural problems we have either been too busy with other urgent matters to attend to, ignored and pretended they did not exist or, lacking the necessary courage to address them squarely, we have delicately kept in the "too hard tray." Some answers must be embedded in a new constitutional order. Others need to be tackled from outside the Constitution. But one would ask: why call for a new Constitution when a long time and vast sums of money were expended on making one as recently as 1995? Let us go back to the beginning of our nationhood.

A New Constitution

We are yet to come up with a Constitution that is robust enough to last without being overthrown or amended almost beyond recognition. Whilst a Constitution should not be etched in stone, it should not be written in sand either. Since no constitutional text can cover every eventuality, it should be short and "obscure" enough to be a living document that can be adapted to different circumstances that might arise in the future without a need for a fresh document.

One of the casualties of the 1966 Crisis was the 1962 Independence Constitution. The architecture of the country, carefully crafted by the peoples of Uganda with the guidance of the departing colonial power, crumbled under the weight of the 1966 Crisis. Since that time, three attempts have been made to re-establish a fundamental law of the land that would enjoy widespread lasting acceptability by the people of Uganda.

In 1966 itself, a new Constitution was hastily passed to replace that of 1962 that had been overthrown. It was in reality a stop-gap measure meant to cover the situation that had just arisen with the departure of the president, Sir Edward Mutesa, and the merger of the office of president and that of prime minister. It is said to have been the product of a single all-night effort by the attorney general and ministry of justice lawyers. It was discussed neither by the people of Uganda nor their representatives in Parliament. It has since enjoyed the dubious moniker of "The Pigeon Hole Constitution," as earlier clarified.

In 1967, Parliament constituted itself into a constituent assembly and passed what is known as the Republican Constitution after considerable debate. Its main features were the abolition of the kingdoms and the introduction of a uniform centralised system of government throughout the country. In the end, it was seen as the Constitution of the victor in the 1966 Crisis.

Yet again, in 1995, a new Constitution was promulgated by the representatives who had been elected and some nominated to compose the constituent assembly. Never in Uganda's constitutional making history was more time and treasure ever expended or personnel involved as in the making of the 1995 Constitution. We give the 1995 Constitution a little more coverage than the previous ones because it is the most recent and current Constitution.

To begin with, there was a constitutional commission consisting of 21 members, whose appointment was announced in February 1989 to, among other tasks, make a draft Constitution. During a period of four years, the commission traversed the country mingling with the mighty and low, seeking their views on what the portrait of the new Constitution should look like. It concluded its assignment by coming up with a draft Constitution and an accompanying report, which two documents were presented to the president on 31 December 1992.

In its report, the commission recommended that a constituent assembly be established solely to scrutinise and debate the draft Constitution and enact and promulgate a new Constitution. The government decided to set up a constituent assembly composed of 288 delegates, 214 of whom were to be elected to represent constituencies while the rest would represent various interest groups (Odoki, 2014).

Although the elected members had been required to campaign and be elected on their individual merit, without regard to their political affiliations, soon after the constituent assembly deliberations had commenced, various caucuses emerged, the major ones being the multiparty, the cultural institutions, and the NRM caucuses. After debating the draft Constitution for 16 months, the constituent assembly delegates enacted it on 22 September 1995, and it was promulgated on 8 October 1995.

One would expect that the acceptability and durability of the Constitution, whose making cost so much would be in proportion to the inputs in its making. But is it?

Two remarkable things characterise the 1995 Constitution. First, although the signing of the new Constitution was not a formal requirement for the delegates to signify their approval, a number of the constituent assembly delegates, upward of 70, declined to do so. Some of those delegates gave the reason for their refusal to sign as being the fact that the Constitution did not cater for their interest to establish a federal system of government.

Subsequently, according to Makubuya (2018), the Buganda Lukiiko passed a resolution rejecting the new Constitution. But the Mengo establishment has never shied away from invoking that very Constitution when it suits them. For their part, UPC and DP were not happy that multiparty politics was not introduced immediately but would be subject to a referendum in later years. Consequently, the two parties boycotted the 2001 general elections as a sign of their protest against the 1995

Constitution, which denied them their wish to participate in elections as political parties.

Secondly, according to Odoki (2014, p. 277), "The NRM had more than two-thirds of the delegates in the Assembly." By the president's own assertion, the 1995 Constitution was passed by the constituent assembly, the majority of whose members belonged to the NRM.

It is, thus, perceived as a faction document, an NRM document, and a document that its members consider open to alteration at will by any means possible. In that spirit, since its promulgation in 1995, the Constitution has been amended and expanded from the original 216 to 295 articles, it is a patchwork document. It will go down in history as the quilt Constitution, to add to the names of the previous three Constitutions.

The process of making the 1995 Constitution was touted as the African model for scholars in contrast to those of the United States of America and France (Odoki, 2014). The Constitution that was the product of that process which received so much praise might now be enjoying the dubious reputation as a study in how not to operate a Constitution. Why does the 1995 Constitution stand on such wobbly legs?

Probably, too many subjects, which by their nature change over a short span of time, and should not call the Constitution home, were included in the Constitution. One example will suffice. The president, who was in power at the time of making the Constitution, once revealed that the amendment of the article relating to the administration of the capital city, Kampala, was motivated by the desire to curb the sitting mayor of the city, who is a member of the opposition. One wonders if the city were to elect an NRM mayor, while the NRM is still in power in national leadership, the article would be restored to its original form.

But more importantly, some of the issues which have dogged the nation, over the years were, yet again, not satisfactorily resolved by the constituent assembly in the 1995 Constitution. We now need a Constitution of the people of Uganda for the people of Uganda by the people of Uganda, whose representatives convene as a national convention. Sketched out below are some of what we consider the most important matters the new Constitution should lay out in broad principles while leaving the details to be set out in separate acts of Parliament.

Governance

Governance is the glue that binds the various resources of the country, both visible and invisible. It is to the country what management is to a business enterprise. The quality and quantity of material production of a business enterprise largely depend on the quality of its management. So does the prosperity of a country depend on the quality of its governance.

More than ever before, Ugandans today question the quality of their governance and fervently debate what needs to be done to improve, nay, overhaul it moving forward. In our observation, the following areas, in particular, are exercising their minds the most.

Presidential powers. The 1995 Constitution gives the president power to appoint over 300 individual heads of Ugandan commissions and directorates. For instance, the president appoints directly all the resident district commissioners of the districts. It is contended that anybody with that magnitude of power is bound to abuse it. Apparently, referring to such power, one of the leaders of the opposition is reported to have said, "Even if you elected me under this system, nothing stops me from acting like Museveni (president). I would only be different from him because of my personality and good will" (*The Independent*, 2014).

It is taken as a given that the presidential powers to appoint so many different office holders are bound to be abused and the solution lies in minimising them. My view is that the solution is in building strong institutions which counterbalance or check each other. The ultimate disincentive to abuse power, the inbuilt corrective measure if it occurs, is the fear of being voted out in a free and fair election.

Term limits and age cap. If there is a matter the collective political opposition in Uganda is agreed on regarding the Constitution, it is the question of term limits and the cap of the age of the president. Almost without a dissenting voice, the opposition argue: Restore term limits; Do not remove the 75-year limit on the age at which a person can be elected president. But there is a solitary voice with a different view on this matter.

The 1995 Constitution introduced a presidential term limit of two five-year terms from the election of 1996. In 2005, when the two five-year terms of the first holder of the office of president under that Constitution was about to expire, a constitutional amendment was passed controversially removing the term limits. Ever since that amendment, the clamour for the restoration of term limits enlists new adherents and grows louder by the day. Indeed, after over thirty years since 1986 with one man at the helm, every outrage that breaks out in the country recruits new supporters for term limits.

It is argued that most of Uganda's governance problems largely hinge on the absence of presidential term limits; that given the advantages of incumbency in Africa, the absence of term limits is equivalent to life presidency and a recipe for stunted development, if not the regression we see around us. It is assumed that Uganda is in the sorry state it is because the term limit experiment has never been tested. To reinforce their argument, its proponents further argue that presidential terms limits is international good practice.

Since the idea of a presidential term limit appears to be borrowed from America, where constitutional term limits probably began, a brief look at the history of the American presidential term limit should be helpful. For 150 years since the founding of the United States, two terms had been the practice by convention, started by George Washington, the first president. He stepped down after two terms as some of his countrymen were urging him to become a king of America. However, between 1830 and 1864, one term had been the norm.

The presidential two-term limit was introduced in 1947 through the Twenty-Second Amendment of the Constitution and was ratified in 1951. That was two years after President Franklin Roosevelt had died in office during the first year of his fourth term. He had been first elected at the beginning of the Great Depression in 1932 and was considered by a good majority to have done a good job in nursing the economy back to health. As the depression was subsiding, World War II broke out in 1939. The Americans followed the wisdom that lies in the saying that "horses should not be changed midstream" and decided to keep Roosevelt on the job so he could steer the country through this fresh mortal difficulty. We understand the horse metaphor to mean that tried and found to be true leadership should not be changed at a trying and testing time. Roosevelt's was such a leadership. World War II running into their American Great Economic Depression was such a time. Those were the unusual circumstances which led the Americans to elect him to an unprecedented third and fourth term.

But even without that amendment to the American Constitution, it is unlikely that another person would have sought election or been elected beyond two terms in the future. In other words, our argument is the term limits do not have to be embedded in the Constitution. Given free choice in the elections, the voters can be trusted to decide when a leader has served long enough and should not be returned. The Kiganda saying testifies to that: *"N'azina obulungi ava mu ddiiro."* (Even a good dancer must yield the floor for others to demonstrate their dancing skills or also to have fun. Do not overstay your welcome.)

But if age limit and the number of terms a president may serve are too important to be left to the good sense of the electorate, as expressed in periodic elections, term limits and age cap should be embedded in the Constitution with a proviso that changing them should be subject to a referendum. That way, belief in direct democracy, trust in the judgement of the electorate, and constitutional guarantees would be equally assuaged.

Term limits is a coin with two sides: the negative and the positive. Our first objection to term limits is that the argument is based on a negative: limiting the harm a bad president can inflict on a country. It does not consider the positive: the continuity of the benefits a good president can bring to the country. In the case of Uganda, we have a suspicion that the argument has a desperate angle to it as well. The opposition having failed to dislodge from power a man who has been president of the country for over thirty years and those within his party apparently wishing to replace him, having waited too long in the queue, have grown impatient. Both may be looking for a convenient shortcut. How easy it would be to sit back and see the back of him, if there were term limits, by just watching the clock tick towards his departure from office!

In the East African region, term limits as has been tested in Tanzania, for example, is not what, we believe, the proponents of term limits have in mind. Since the introduction of term limits in that country, the practice has been for one incumbent party-man being replaced by another man of the same party after two more-or-less guaranteed terms of five years each. To all intents and purposes, theirs is a one term of ten years with a "commercial break" after the first five years. If the two terms are that automatic, why not call it one term of ten years? We would like to see a situation where it is feasible to vote out a non-performing leader even after one term and being replaced by another whether of the same or another party solely on the basis of how they had performed in that office. It is not reckless to argue that the people should be free to replace a leader for no better reason than that they are just tired of her/him. The creation of conditions that make that possible is of far more importance than the clamour for term limits as such.

Although it may be argued that the principle of term limits should be dealt with first, in our view, it is of equal importance to give serious consideration to the length of a term. For example, in the United States of America, the term of the president is four years. Uganda's is five years; and in neighbouring Rwanda, it is seven. Possibly longer or shorter terms exist elsewhere. In effect, one term of the Rwandan president is just one year short of two terms for the American president. And two terms for the Rwandan President are equivalent to three and half terms for the American president. If, as we have shown, a single term in one country can be almost as long as two terms in another, where is the merit in the term limit argument? Where does the potential injury to the country lie? Is it in the length of the period one serves? Is it the number of times one is elected to a particular office that is the problem? We believe Ugandans are barking up the wrong tree.

We think the concern of Ugandans should be the quality of service the president delivers and the way they assume power. It is the quality of elections, which puts them in power that should be our major concern. Ugandans should be prepared to live with the leader that emerges out of a free and fair election and governs by the rules.

In a system of parliamentary democracy we are trying to build, the failures and dictatorial tendencies of the executive can be ameliorated by meaningful elections, and they should be made aware that they can be turned out of office at any time on any issue. If we undertook a vigorous election civic education programme, those who elect the leaders should become conscious of the power of their vote and realise their responsibility to hold accountable, not only the chief executive, but the entire spectrum of their political leaders.

Emphasis on term limits is, therefore, in our view, misplaced and diversionary. There is definitely no single magic bullet to democracy and development. But if you want to see development with the participation of the citizenry, the correct emphasis should be placed on conducting regular free and fair elections as the starting point.

Free, fair, and transparent elections. One of the issues crying out to be attended to is that of governance and the quality of our elections. What determines the quality of governance is the ability of citizens to freely elect their leaders and hold them accountable. We know it is humanly impossible to run a faultless election anywhere in the world. But we also know that there is conduct which marks a line that divides free, fair, and credible elections and sham elections.

Throughout 2015, Ugandan political parties in opposition, civil society organisations, and individual eminent persons traversed the country campaigning to rouse the citizens to ensure that the next elections would be free and fair. In June, those groups, joined by the youth and women, assembled in Uganda's capital city and crafted a twelve-point document titled *Citizens' Compact on Free and Fair Elections*. It was presented to Parliament with a demand that it should be the basis for amending the various laws relating to elections scheduled for 2016.

The government's only response to the Citizens' Compact was to pass an amendment to the relevant law to, rather cynically, add the word 'Independent' before the current name of the body responsible for conducting elections. It would now be called "Independent Electoral Commission" instead of just "Electoral Commission," as if that word by itself would make that body independent! The Supreme Court in two presidential election petitions rulings ten years apart (2006 and 2016) has pointed out the need to plug the gaps in Uganda's electoral laws.

We need to have elections, not selections. We need an electoral process at the end of which the winner is determined by counting votes, not by allocating votes. We need to have a situation where the losers of an election feel they have lost honourably, and the winners feel proud of their victory.

The 2016 elections were commenced under widespread suspicion that they would be neither free nor fair. International election observers have since pronounced them as greatly flawed. Internal observers who have followed Ugandan elections since independence have expressed the view that the just concluded elections reached lows never seen before.

Free and fair elections are not an end in themselves. They serve a purpose beyond reflecting a free expression of the citizens' will. They provide a sense of ownership and participation in the affairs of the country by its citizens. They also impose a moral and political obligation on those elected under such conditions to attend to the needs of the voters who have placed them in the positions of power and responsibility. When elections are free and fair, they cease to be a mere ritual. They also introduce political stability.

We saw earlier on that Mutesa, having lost trust in Obote, considered mobilising politically against him in the next general elections. But he had no confidence that those elections would be free and fair. Thus, in his pursuit to bring about change in national leadership, he allied with Ibingira to depose Obote from UPC leadership, and considered a military *coup*, even through foreign military intervention.

In a country where free and fair elections are the norm, the questions of term limits, in the sense of how long a leader may hold office, and presidential powers, meaning the prudence with which a leader exercises their power, are routinely taken care of. Therefore, as Ugandans we should insist on it. We should not allow anybody to push off the political agenda in the struggle for a near-perfect electoral system until it is realised.

So, to borrow the elegant phraseology of Martin Luther King, *One day in the future, the children of Uganda will ask, What is election-rigging?* and their aged parents or guardians as they walk into their sunsets will answer, *That used to happen a long time ago before you were born, but the word has now slipped out of usage and is just a word in the dictionary.* And to paraphrase Kwame Nkrumah, Ugandans would be urged, therefore, *seek ye first free and fair elections and the rest will be added unto you.*

The Power of the sword. Uganda was forged by the sword or the threat of use of the sword. The Crisis entrenched militarism, which had been amply demonstrated during the army mutiny in 1964, in Uganda's body politic. Both protagonists in the 1966 Crisis relied on the army for support—Obote on Colonel Idi Amin and Mutesa on Brigadier Shaban Opolot, although Mutesa had a wider range of political options to choose from, according to the menu we set out above earlier. From that time up to today, Ugandans have been infatuated with the coercive part of politics and the army has become a constant factor; in fact, the arbiter, in political calculations. Kasendwa-Ddumba writes:

> In the sixties and eighties, I had the privilege of observing the army from close range. This letter is not the right forum to discuss details of what I was able to learn from that close relationship with the army. But one thing I want to mention herein is that I clearly detected a mentality which drove soldiers to think that they had divine right to impose their will on Ugandans; and they looked at themselves as the senior partners in coalition governments of Uganda. (Kasendwa-Ddumba, 2020, p. 70)

One cannot fail to note the infatuation of Ugandans for things military—uniforms and titles—especially among the presently ruling NRM leadership who even attend their seminars and retreats adorned in military fatigues and a visit to the shooting range is considered a compulsory part of the programme. Hardly any presidential candidate on a campaign trail fails to mention the army. One candidate may go as far as claiming the entire national army as their own. Others may be satisfied with just mentioning the high percentage of support they assume to command in the army. The more modest ones settle for asserting that the army is a professional body which will respect the outcome of the election. The electorate, their freedom of choice devalued, weigh whether their preferred candidate might be able to protect their victory, in case the army intervened.

It has become a permanent feature of Uganda's political life that statements of soldiers are examined closely for political message content. Apparent dissident soldiers are viewed as possible liberators by the disenchanted population and their utterances and moves make instant and constant news.

Since the creation of the standing army, history has shown that the one who wields control over it has great sway on the course of events in the country. They can use it to protect the country, but they can also use it to oppress the people. Right from the army mutiny in 1964, to the high visibility of army personnel and heavy armour in virtually all the major towns immediately before, during and after the 2016 elections, and the many incidents in between, the army has had and continues to have great influence over who governs Uganda.

Given the way power in Uganda has often been acquired, retained and lost, more attentive re-consideration should be paid to the institution of the army—the checks and balances in its recruitment, training, promotion, deployment and control. Just to dare that nothing is left unsaid, an even more radical conversation should be held on whether Uganda should have an army at all.

Federalism and the Buganda question. One of the major issues—that of a federal system of government—was supressed during the debate. The restoration of kingdoms —also called "cultural institutions"— effected before the election and inauguration of the constituent assembly, would have benefitted from being subjected to the rigours of debate by a large representation of the people of Uganda. Of late, new kingdoms have been created in an apparently surreptitious and opportunistic manner without known transparent procedures being followed. Ugandans must collectively and openly determine whether to restore or recreate the kingdoms and the federal system.

The Buganda question refers to the extent of Buganda's self-governance within Uganda and the authority of Uganda government within Buganda. Despite appearances of peace and harmony, the Buganda question still festers. The Baganda have a metaphor which aptly captures the situation, *Obusa bw'embogo, bukala kungulu nga munda bubisi*; literally translated as, "Buffalo dung may appear dry on the outside while it is still fresh on the inside." Therefore, appearances, especially of innocence, peace, and calm that give one a sense of security, may be deceptive. Beneath the appearance of peace often lurks danger.

Specifically, with regard to the popular return of Buganda land, the Central Government and the leaders at Mengo seem to have embarked on a "muddle through" approach in the hope of establishing a behind-the-scenes reality on the ground, which, in time, will be assumed to be legal. Apart from legal niceties, the return of assets raises serious concern about the parties' methods of work, especially with regard to transparency and democratic practices.

Despite the slogan of *obwerufu* (transparency), all we see is opaqueness. Such an approach as they have adopted only transfers the problem to future generations. The method adopted, although opaque, has yielded immensely popular results. However, popularity is not a test of legality. Something may be popular but that does not make it legal. For instance, mob justice is popular in Uganda, but it remains unlawful. We do not believe the practice of politics demands that one should grab or give what one can—a kingdom here, a chunk of land there—while others are not looking or have no platform from which to express their views and be taken to account.

A solution imposed through force or fear as under the 1967 Republican Constitution or incrementally by subterfuge and employing backdoor methods as since 1993 when the kingdoms were "restored," will not last. We believe only an open and above-board conversation will lead to an enduring solution.

In that context, the *ebyaffe* need to be crystallised in content, shape and size under a new constitutional arrangement. Presently, *ebyaffe* appears to be a code word. Like all codes, it is a secret which only a select few have an iron-clad knowledge of. That would not be a problem if it were not meant to be for public consumption. Presently, it is a problem to Baganda and non-Baganda alike.

Buganda has the most ethnically diverse population of all regions of Uganda. For Ugandans who are not Baganda but live in Buganda and even those outside Buganda, the call for *ebyaffe* elicits suspicion, fear and in some cases mockery. If, as it does, *ebyaffe* means what belongs to us, it carries with it a whiff of exclusion. For where there is *us* on one side, there must be *them* on the other. Which raises the questions: who is *us* and who is *them*? Is *us* the Baganda or is *us* the people living in Buganda? The answer can make a world of a difference.

When pushed to extremes, the *us* and *them* divide can lead to inter-group bloody conflict. That happened during the "90 days of madness" in the Rwanda genocide of 1994. The same happened in the 1995 Bosnia genocide. It was also at the core of the holocaust. In September 2009, the Kayunga riots, triggered by the blocking of the Kabaka by the Central Government from touring Kayunga Town in Bugerere County of his Buganda Kingdom, brought Uganda to the very edge of the cliff.

The *us-them* divide was largely based on such anatomical matters as the shape of one's nose or hips, and unverifiable cultural ability and ease to recite one's family lineage to the third generation. What saved the day was that those who presumably fell in the *them* category had the power, the instruments, and the will to silence the means of mass communication. They shut off the FM radio stations which were indirectly fuelling the riots before they reached the dehumanisation of *them*, the point from which inflicting physical harm starts.

Later, people joked about the Kayunga riots not realising how close Uganda got to the abyss. That is the road on which we would rather not take even a single first step. What makes the *us* and *them* division so potentially dangerous is that no one knows the rules for setting people apart, and who sets them. Other than for purely social matters, we would much prefer that political interests be determined on the basis of the more clearly defined common human needs of people who live in a shared geographical area. After all, the Kabaka has never been the Kabaka of Baganda. He has always been the Kabaka of Buganda.

If you are a Muganda, you are assumed to know what *ebyaffe* consists of, even without being told, as if you were hard-wired as part of your DNA to know. Seeking clarity is taken as a clear sign that you are either not a true Muganda and a traitor, or something is wrong with your head. You are likely to be slapped with a question: *Obuuza nga atali Muganda?* (Are you asking that question as if you are not a Muganda?) The implication is: a true Muganda does not have to seek explanations to issues concerning Buganda. They understand them instinctively by virtue of simply being a Muganda.

To avoid being branded as either a non-Muganda or one having a problem with one's head, some Baganda whose understanding of *ebyaffe* may be at best tenuous and patchy are prompted and are likely to cheer the loudest when the demand for *ebyaffe* is made in public.

But again, like all codes, attempts can always be made to break it. It would appear to me that *ebyaffe* encapsulates the interests of Buganda as they are presently or as they may emerge or are perceived by Mengo from time to time. The need for a clear definition cannot be over-empathised. In the interest of all Ugandans, it would be far better if this word were decoded by those in whose custody it is entrusted. All parties would be left relieved and released from the emotions that are associated with a word that seems to have assumed a life of its own.

But the big elephant in the room, which everybody is tiptoeing around, is the election, rather than the selection, of the leadership in Mengo by the people living in Buganda. For how long will the personalities at Mengo hide non-democratic practices under the cloak of culture? Cultural norms are erroneously equated with development issues.

Whereas there may be little dispute about culture, there will definitely be different approaches to development issues. There was a kind of assumption that the issues and solutions to a country's development were so clear that alternative views were not possible. That assumption drove the single party agenda in Africa in the 1960s. It was thought that having opposition parties was unAfrican. That view, although no longer strongly advocated, has not been entirely erased.

The theory of the opposition being unAfrican, spouted by those leaders already in power, was obviously self-serving. The strangling of democracy in the name of culture is no less often advanced by those it serves. This is not to say that democracy is a perfect form of government. We associate ourselves with the remark of Winston Churchill that democracy is the worst form of government but for the alternatives.

Ebyaffe are either elastic and, therefore, capable of accommodating new demands, or evolutionary, and change over time, or circumstantial, depending on the situation as it arises. According to Abu Mayanja, during the Lancaster House negotiations for independence, *ebyaffe* meant the place of Kabaka and Buganda in Uganda.

In our research for this work, we asked one highly placed official of the Buganda Government (name withheld) what *ebyaffe* means. He informed us that today, *they refer to assets that were appropriated by the Uganda state in 1966/67, including land, artefacts and cultural regalia.* Yet, in 1961/62, during the independence negotiations, *ebyaffe* were not material objects but consisted of rights and privileges, such as the position of the Kabaka and the place of Buganda in an independent Uganda.

From some quarters, sometimes, the demand for *ebyaffe* sounds like a call to go back to the pre-1900 Agreement status, minus the land distribution arrangement, of course. Shooting at a moving target can be very hard. *Ebyaffe* is a moving target. What *ebyaffe* were yesterday may not be what they are today or might be tomorrow. The fact that people continue to talk about it means that it remains unsettled. A platform needs to be provided to articulate it and address it meaningfully and formally.

In his book, *Buganda ku Ntikko*, Katikkiro Charles Peter Mayiga states the fundamental demands or requirements (*Ensonga Ssemasonga*) of Buganda to be:

(a) *Obwakabaka n'ekitikkiro kyabwo, nga ye Ssaabasajja Kabaka;*
(b) *Ettaka n'Ensalo za Buganda yonna gye ziyita;*
(c) *Okugabana Obuyinza mu nkola/enfuga eya Federo;*
(d) *Okukola Obutaweera;* ate
(e) *n'Okubeera Obumu.* (Mayiga, 2013, p. 31)

We have taken the liberty to translate the above in their order as:

(a) To preserve, protect, and defend Buganda Kingdom and the king;
(b) To preserve the land and boundaries of Buganda;
(c) To share power under a federal arrangement;
(d) To work tirelessly; and
(e) To be united.

It's not clear whether that is in addition to *ebyaffe* or a substitution thereof. *Ebyaffe* literally means "what belongs to us." *Ensonga ssemasonga* means "fundamental reasons." But the literal meanings will not do. *Ebyaffe*, therefore, means "our demands" and *Ensonga ssemasoga* simply means "our objectives or aspirations" or better still "our concerns." On the assumption that the concerns are a substitution of the demands, there has been a shift for the better. Where the demands (*ebyaffe*) are elastic and fluid, Katikkiro Mayiga appears to have codified and concretised them.

That is the good news. The opposite is that much as the concerns have been articulated by Katikkiro Mayiga, it is not clear this far whether they are, and remain the individual vision of one leader or have been adopted and become the collective concerns of Buganda. In the meantime, Mengo matters remain as murky as before. It is not clear what Mayiga's objectives were or are in stating the concerns. Whether he intended to reconcile the rival packs regarding *ebyaffe* and nature of the restored kingdom or to divert them, he succeeded in leaving many confounded. If he were a Katikkiro elected on the platform of *ensonga semasonga*, those questions would not arise.

Coalition Governments and Government of National Unity

Throughout Uganda's independence history, single party government, coalitions, and what may pass as government of national unity, have featured frequently and prominently. A new Constitution should provide specific guidance to the formation of coalition governments when the need arises without having to demolish the whole Constitution.

Truth-telling and reconciliation

This is a one-off matter which should have no place in the Constitution. It is said that history is written by the victors. In Uganda's situation, where there were no clear-cut winners, history has been written by the loudest. But a bitter taste remains in the mouth. A way forward can only be forged if the facts of what really happened are laid out.

For our purposes, truth-telling relates to particular episodes, periods and locations. In our opinion, these include: (a) the 1966 Crisis in Buganda, and particularly in the Lubiri at Mengo; (b) the war in Luwero between 1981 and 1986; (c) the war in northern Uganda, which includes Teso, Lango, and Acholi (and spillover) between 1986 and 2006.

We are aware that there are those with deep and entrenched interests in the murky status quo. Kasendwa-Ddumba observes:

> Hardly a month passes without nasty references to the 1966 Crisis. That should be a serious cause for concern to Ugandans. It should be a serious concern because political opportunists seem determined to continue to exploit it in complete disregard of the common good of all Ugandans. (Kasendwa-Ddumba, 2020, p. 31)

"… and of the facts," he should have added.

We agree with Kasendwa-Ddumba (2020) who insists that the truth must be revealed in spite of opportunists who want to cling to their prejudices like the people of Israel during the days of Prophet Isaiah who shouted him down, saying,

> Do not tell us about what is right.
> Tell us what we want to hear.
> Let us keep our illusions. (Isaiah 30:10)

They hold on to their illusions as if they would lose their very identity if their illusions were unmasked. The 1966 Crisis is the bogeyman, the stick with which some people politically batter UPC and its leaders over the head. If the facts about it were known, they would lose their political tool. Maybe, they are afraid of the truth for fear it will disarm them. There is a nagging suspicion, too, that keeping the 1966 Crisis murky provides some people with an opportunity to indulge their perverse pleasure in contrived victimhood and martyrdom in an "ongoing" attack on Lubiri.

As an extension of that, it would appear to us that a small but influential section of traditional Baganda may be suffering from "status anxiety." That phenomenon is most likely to emerge when a group's social status, identity, and a sense of belonging are perceived to be under existential threat. The White supremacists in America who, seeing the dwindling numbers of the White race compared to that of the coloured races, perceive themselves to be "strangers in their own land."

That perception may not be very different from that of a group of Baganda.

Buganda nation, being centrally placed in Uganda and hosting the political as well as the commercial capital of the country, has attracted a lot of *others* from outside Buganda. Those *others*, assisted by political power, among other things, have acquired large tracks of land, which originally belonged to Baganda, besides other forms of wealth.

If we may adopt a mental health term, some Baganda are descending into a schizophrenic mode. They see non-Baganda immigrants into their territory as people to be assimilated, which they consider an asset. At the same time, they see these non-Baganda immigrants as diluting the Baganda, which is a threat. One people cannot embrace the two positions—an asset and a threat—at the same time and remain one people.

It offers no comfort to them that there should be no good cause to feel "status anxiety." For, whereas their "hard power" may have waned, their "soft power" has been on ascendancy for some time, as exhibited in the use of Luganda. In many parts of Uganda, Luganda is the language commonly used in political communication and entertainment, be it in songs, plays or comedy. *Agataliiko Nfuufu*, a Bukedde Television newscast in Luganda, is widely watched even by the people who have only a smattering knowledge of the language. Culturally, the marriage introduction ceremony throughout Uganda is increasingly taking the Kiganda format. No politician of whatever origin worth their salt will give a press conference in English without a Luganda version of it being rendered or demanded at the end. Yet, a sense of political insecurity vis-a-vis the rest of Ugandans lies just below the surface of this group.

Rather than enhancing their self-esteem, the use of their language by the non-Baganda has enhanced the Baganda's sense of being under siege. They say that even their language has been taken over from them and they can no longer keep their secrets to themselves since *others* now understand their language. This has led to a deliberate concealment of facts regarding Uganda's history as a way of self-preservation.

We have to allow that the scene we have painted above has not been in existence for long enough to lead to a conclusion that it represents a permanent change in behaviour and attitude. We are not even certain that it will continue on the same path or in the same direction. But it is serious enough to merit our comment. This departure of the Baganda from their ancient practice of assimilating outsiders instead of seeing them as a threat, even though it may be temporary, calls for some explanation.

To one who has been attentively observing events in Buganda over the past several years, it is not difficult to read what has led to the feeling of Baganda being under siege. It is land grabbing. It takes two forms: forcible acquisition of and eviction from land. In the past, people who moved into Buganda from other countries (including territories now within Uganda) came either singly on their own, in small groups as refugees, or as seekers of greener pastures. Others were target workers who came to raise cash capital to invest back in their places of origin. They were not considered a threat to their hosts and were easy to absorb and assimilate. In the context of this work, hosts mean people indigenous to the area. That is not the situation today.

In the recent past, people have moved into Buganda in apparently large organised groups arriving in vehicles in the middle of the night with their herds of cattle and have occupied large empty parcels of land. That has been the case in Kyankwanzi. The new migrants are either armed or guarded by armed personnel. Where the undeveloped land is privately owned, such people begin clearing the land and cultivating it, as happened in Namutamba in the Mityana-Mubende areas and elsewhere. The owners who run to the police or the courts of law to complain against the trespassers obtain no assistance.

There is a strong conviction that this movement of people is evidence of an effort which is underway to deliberately change the demographics in the sparsely populated areas of Buganda.

The second form of land grabbing involves the eviction of customary tenants or squatters from large privately-owned pieces of land. There are landowners of big chunks of land who cannot utilise it because it is occupied by customary tenants and squatters. These occupiers are either unwilling or unable to pay the land owner to obtain a certificate of title for the portion they occupy. The land is consequently of no value at all to the owner.

The annual rent of 1,000 Uganda shillings prescribed by law as payable to the landlord by the customary tenant regardless of size or location of the land occupied is undeniably unrealistic and hardly any landlord bothers to collect it. Some landlords find it more profitable to sell their land to anyone willing to buy it as it is. Such buyers have tended to evict the occupiers they find on the land, often without paying them any compensation. In the more blatant cases, the land grabber will come and evict the occupants of the land regardless of tenure and under no cover of right.

What the two forms of land grabbing have in common is the presence of state security operatives to back up the occupiers and the evictors. This has led to fear and resentment of the newcomers who seem to be above the law and enjoy protection from the authorities. That has turned the people of the region from the welcoming people of the years-gone-by into suspicious, involuntary, and sullen hosts.

It so happens that the only people with both the money to buy such land and the audacity to evict the customary tenants in such a manner are the *nouveau riche* and largely belong to the ruling class; hence, the bitterness and resentment by the hosts.

A commission of inquiry headed by a Court of Appeal judge, was appointed to look into land wrangles in 2017. Unfortunately, it has gradually turned itself into a perpetual land police, court, and prison. Hopefully, by the time this book is published, its findings and recommendations will have been made public.

To those tempted to think that a military *coup d'état* is the way to address the injuries of the past, the advice is that there is a better way. In his column in *The Daily Monitor* newspaper, Augustine Ruzindana, then deputy secretary-general, policy and research, Forum for Democratic Change (FDC), wrote:

> ... the incitement by coup talk could have unintended consequences. The coup talkers would rather engage society in wide ranging talks (national conference) to find a solution to the current impasse. This is the way to go for a stable Uganda. (Ruzindana, 2013)

If we may revert to the issue of some prominent Baganda wishing to conceal certain facts regarding Uganda's history, *The Daily Monitor* newspaper in its issue dated 16 November 2013 reported that during the hearings of the Judicial Commission of Inquiry into the violation of human rights in Uganda between 1964 and 1985, Commissioner John Nagenda, irritated by what he saw as an orchestrated plan to mislead the commission, wrote: "had . . . warned that some individuals in Buganda had been coached on what to say and threatened to name the perpetrators if the witnesses to the Commission did not tell the truth of what they saw" (Nagenda, 2013). "Being coached" is the polite way of saying being trained to lie under oath.

Nagenda seems to have detected a carefully calibrated plan by the Mengo establishment to deflect from certain personalities and institutions' responsibility for historical events that took place during the period under review by the commission. However, the commission was not able to come to the bottom of what and for whom the establishment was covering up. So it is also possible that it was itself not interested in probing too deeply for its *raison d'être* was to compile all human rights abuses since independence on Obote and Amin. That is where political capital lay.

One way of getting out of the impasse is to get to the truth of the 1966 Crisis, the most divisive episode in our nation's history, through a truth-telling and reconciliation commission, the findings of which will be official, final and, hopefully, incontestable. This view is widely shared across the political divide.

While addressing the nation on the occasion of lying in state in Parliament of the body the late President of Uganda, Milton Obote, President Yoweri Museveni said:

> I would like to end by re-emphasising the need for continuing to search for a national consensus and reconciliation. We have not had time to deal with all aspects of our turbulent history... There may be need, therefore, to look at additional interaction that may help us to close this sad chapter of our country: Truth and Reconciliation Commission, Reconciliation National Conference. (*The Hansard*, 2005)

Sadly, after more than fifty years, the numbers of those with first-hand knowledge of what happened, either as first-hand participants or observers, are fast getting depleted. In the absence of those whose memory can be excavated, any inquiry instituted today might largely depend on evidence of researchers.

That certainly is not the case with other episodes which equally demand looking into. We must deal with the five-year Luwero war and the twenty-year war in northern and eastern Uganda. The world needs to know from an impartial commission what really happened instead of taking as the truth the version which the victors have put out.

The truth commission is not an end in itself. Its purpose is to find the truth of what really happened during these painful episodes of our national history by separating it from myths and outright lies, hold accountable those responsible for the wrongs committed and reconcile the wrongdoers with the wronged. Then, the healing process of the different communities will start, and Uganda will become a normal country with no community feeling vanquished awaiting its turn to load it over the others.

Different peoples respond differently to military defeat and triumph. On their part, the people of Mengo seem to have decided to cultivate a culture of mourning, especially centred around the attack on the Lubiri on 24 May 1966.

As a start to the journey of reconciliation, Mengo should reconsider its recent practice of marking 24 May in remembrance of the fighting at Lubiri and awarding honours to those, alive or dead, deemed as having been active on its side of the conflict. Obote himself never celebrated that day, much as his side came out triumphant. Should that day be marked or celebrated? The losing side marking it as a day of mourning or the winner celebrating it as a day of victory only helps to keep the old wounds open. Should it be a day to commemorate? This was a family contest and family contests are and should not be celebrated whoever the victor was.

There is no good reason to keep 24 May 1966 alive. Uganda should learn from the way other countries, particularly the United States, which went through almost a similar situation, handled such comparable events. Momentous as it was in their history, it would be inconceivable, for instance, for the American people to commemorate 9 April, the day General Robert E. Lee, commander of the confederacy army, surrendered to General Ulysses S. Grant, commander of the union army, to bring an end to the American civil war. For, as President Abraham Lincoln put it, that was not a war between independent nations.

Chapter 14

IN CONCLUSION

We must conclude, although we are loath to. We do not have the capacity, nor the time, nor the space to say everything there is to say about the 1966 Crisis. Therefore, this work does not contain everything you ever wanted to know about that Crisis but did not know where to look. In any event, if everything were to be said, the volume of this work would be such as to give the Ugandan reader, who is not renowned for a great reading culture, an excuse to put it, unread, in the empty part of their bookshelf. This writing is not an encyclopaedia on the 1966 Crisis; any writing is necessarily based on a selection out of the materials on a given subject available to an author at a given time. It represents the judgement of the writer.

The history of this episode is yet to be settled and may not be settled by any single piece of work, let alone this one. But as we close, let us first go back to our definition of the Crisis for in it we set our task. It was our thesis that the Crisis was about the struggle for the unity of Uganda.

Have we answered all the questions relating to the Crisis? No. Some questions have not been asked yet and many cannot be anticipated. Just before we went to press, we encountered Makubuya's questions. He asks:

> Indeed, if Buganda or Mutesa were the problem, why did Obote unilaterally abolish the Kingdoms of Toro, Bunyoro, Ankole, and the Kyabazingaship of Busoga. [His ending] What wrongs had the rulers of these kingdoms committed? Were they also guilty of the

treasonous activities Mutesa was accused of? (Makubuya, 2018, p. 313)

There are two answers. Truth be told, for good or ill, those other kings and kingdoms have often ridden on the back of the Kabaka and the kingdom of Buganda and have fallen together. On the surface level, therefore, those other kingdoms and territories together with their heads may be likened to bystanders, who get killed by stray bullets in a scene in a town movie gun-fight. They are not combatants, but they get killed, nevertheless. But this was not a movie. At a deeper level, those kingdoms were fodder for historic forces for reasons beyond their knowledge or control.

The fact that those other kingdoms were abolished at the same time as the Kingdom of Buganda went to prove that the 1966 Crisis was not a personal quarrel between Obote, on the one hand, and Mutesa and Buganda, on the other. Rather, it was an institutional contest between the state of Uganda and the nations in Uganda. The state of Uganda sought to establish and confirm its supremacy over the nations and their representatives, and the nations strove to render subordinate to the state of Uganda.

In our view, those other kingdoms were abolished together with the Buganda Kingdom because they were perceived as nations aligned on one side in the battle for the supremacy over the state of Uganda. At that moment in history, Obote happened to represent the emerging state of Uganda and to protect it against all forces which, singularly or collectively, threatened its survival.

However, in answer to his own questions, Makubuya's considered opinion is:

> ... that the real problem was not what Mutesa did or did not do. The tribally minded, dishonest and power hungry Obote was prepared to destroy anyone who stood in his way to obtain power in Uganda. (Makubuya, 2018, p. 314)

Makubuya (2018) offers no explanation as to how the other kings stood in Obote's way to attain absolute power in Uganda but the supposedly non-tribal Makubuya finds it "odd" that when a case, *Uganda v. Commissioner of Prisons ex* parte *Matovu*, was filed challenging the legality of the 1966 Constitution, "... among the lawyers who defended Obote's action, were two of Buganda's leading legal minds at the time, namely Godfrey L. Binaisa QC and Peter James Nkambo Mugerwa" (Makubuya, 2018, p. 314). Incidentally, Binaisa and Nkambo Mugerwa were respectively Uganda's attorney general and solicitor general in the then Obote's government. Makubuya's statement could be interpreted to mean that since they were Baganda by tribe, they were not expected to defend the government they served in a matter in which Buganda had an interest and what cases a lawyer takes on should be determined by that lawyer's tribe, even when taking it on lies in the lawyer's line of duty. On the other hand, Obote was confident that the government lawyers would carry out their duties responsibly regardless of their tribe.

The 1966 Crisis was the closest independent Uganda had ever come to a revolution, although some call it such, or a civil war. The execution of revolutions and civil wars leaves a lot of debris and they tend to be interpreted and remembered differently at a superficial level according to which side one was on. The 1966 Crisis has proved to be no exception. One civil war and one revolution which were fought earlier in other countries, such as the United States of America and England, respectively, clearly illustrate the point.

In America, some people remembered the American civil war for the hardships it caused and, mostly, the destruction of the southern way of life (read slavery) and could not forgive Abraham Lincoln who led the union government, to the extent of refusing to sleep in the bed he once slept in. In his essay on John Milton, Lord Macaulay tells us that the Englishmen who were on the side of the

In Conclusion

deposed King Charles wished to remember the offspring of the civil war or revolution or the great rebellion, as it was variously called, for only major-generals and soldiers swindling their districts and celebrating their ill-gotten gains (Macaulay, 1849).

Many people in Buganda, as Kabaka Mutesa himself did, would like to remember the 1966 Crisis narrowly for the desecration of the Buganda Kingdom; for loss of office by some individuals; for a stint in prison or, at worst, the death of a beloved one and perpetually hold Obote to blame for all. There are people still busy fighting the battle of Mengo in their heads.

Fundamentally, Obote and Mutesa were merely the human agents and symbols of something bigger—the contest for supremacy between Uganda the new state and Buganda the old nation, one trying to establish its roots and the other struggling to survive in the new environment. Much as they were so, it was inevitable to delve into their individual roles in this contest while leaving it to the reader, if they finds it necessary or even possible, to assign to the two men their responsibility for the tragedy. In that regard, therefore, if a reader was looking in these pages expecting us to set out the right and wrong about the Crisis, we confess to have disappointed. In any case this work is not about those two personalities. It is about the causes they represented: state versus nation.

At a deeper level, Macaulay wrote of the English civil war: "Many evils, no doubt, were produced by the civil war. They were the price of our liberty. Has the acquisition been worth the sacrifice?" (Macaulay, 1849, p. 39). We may adopt Macaulay's majestic language and say, "Many evils, no doubt, were produced by the 1966 Crisis. They were the price of Uganda's unity. Was it worth the sacrifice?"

Before we sit in judgement of the main protagonists in the 1966 Crisis, we would do well to remember that old cliché: with the benefit of hindsight, it is easy to be wise. To trigger off the actual fighting, maybe there were miscalculations; maybe some things were done that should not have been done; maybe some things which should not have been done, were done. Ultimately, in exercising one's judgement, it is not always a matter of one decision being correct and another being wrong. It is often a matter of one's standpoint and value system.

Time did not stand still to allow actors to make decisions informed by facts, checked and cross-checked. Hard choices had sometimes to be made on the run-in conditions of uncertainty, with or with no advisors.

We have tried to present facts in a manner that we hope will make it easy for an ordinary reader to appreciate the complicated story that is the 1966 Crisis. We do hope that at the end of this narrative, people's opinions about the Crisis and the main protagonists in this saga will have some link with the hard facts even if those facts are inconvenient. In the psycho-analytical parts of this work, we tried "to enter the skins" of Mutesa and Obote in order to understand the forces that leaned on them and made them act the way they did. Once one understands those forces, you begin to appreciate that in spite of their own statements, Obote might not have been a man who "was determined to destroy my kingdom" (Mutesa, 1967, p. 188), as Mutesa viewed him, and Mutesa was probably not part of the forces that were determined to drag the country back into feudalism, as Obote implied. Clearly, both men personalised their differences.

As the passage of time fades out those who personally witnessed the 1966 events, from whatever vantage point, and those who were merely told about them, with whatever degree of authenticity, history will do its job to fairly apportion to each their share of responsibility for the Crisis. We also tried to make the

In Conclusion

reader appreciate the loss of the innocent bystanders, namely UPC and the kings and kingdoms of Ankore, Bunyoro and Tooro. Above everything else, effort was made to persuade the reader of the imperative need for Ugandans to forge a new beginning.

We recognise how hard it is for the majority of mankind to admit that they had passed the greater part of their lives in error and to have the courage to embrace new facts. It is uncomfortable for people to risk losing their life-long heroes and villains by reviewing their positions. We are mindful of Kennedy's observation that "It takes time to change men's minds, and it takes violent shocks to change an entire nation's psychology" (Kennedy, 1940, p. 14).

Britain got its shock when it came to the brink of defeat by Germany which deployed the air force in World War II. That changed its concept of national security. We do not know whether fifty years is not long enough or whether it takes a thousand shocks of tsunami proportions to change Ugandans' psychology with regard to the 1966 Crisis. That notwithstanding, if, as a result of this narrative, anyone has been persuaded to pause and reconsider their earlier position on these events which have shaped our history, our effort has been worthwhile. And if there is someone Winston Churchill called a fanatic who cannot change his mind and will not change the subject, that is too bad. In any event, as for us, there was pleasure in its telling. It was a labour of love.

If we were asked who the greatest winner from the 1966 Crisis was, my unequivocal answer would be, "Uganda. Because it survived."

References

Abraham, H. J. (1980). *The judicial process: An introductory analysis of the courts of the United States, England, and France* (4th ed.). Oxford University Press.

Adhola, Y. (2018, August 19). The 1966 Revolution and the Constitution. *Sunday Monitor*. https://www.monitor.co.ug/OpEd/Commentary/The-1966-revolution-Constitution-Milton-Obote-Mutesa/689364-4719770-hcms9wz/index.html

Barungi, B. N. I. (2011). *Parliamentary democracy in Uganda: The experiment that failed*. AuthorHouse.

Carter Centre. (2014). *Election obligations and standards: A Carter Centre assessment manual*.

Cohen, J. (2019). *Accidental presidents: Eight men who changed America*. Simon & Schuster.

Dunbar, A. R. (1965). *A history of Bunyoro-Kitara*. Oxford University Press.

Fellman, M. (2003). *The making of Robert E. Lee*. Johns Hopkins University Press.

Golooba-Mutebi, F. (2016). Five reasons Museveni's son won't succeed him (and five he will). *The East African*. https://www.theeastafrican.co.ke/oped/comment/Five-reasons-Museveni-son-not-succeed-him-and-five-he-will/434750-3223454-cl9kb7z/index.html

Hansard HL Deb vol. 242 col 145-72 *(26 July 1962)*. https://api.parliament.uk/historic-hansard/lords/1962/jul/26/uganda-independence-bill

Hansard, The. (1966). Uganda Parliamentary Debates, Fourth Session of the First Parliament of Uganda, (Emergency Meeting), 15th April, Kampala.

Hansard, The. (2005). Uganda Parliamentary Session, 20th October, Kampala.

Hofstadter, R. (1965). *The paranoid style in American politics and other essays.* Harvard University Press.

Hugo, V. (1862). *Les mserables.* Planet eBook

Independent, The. (2014, May 09-15). Issue No. 316, p. 8.

Ingham, K. (1994). *Obote: A political biography.* Routledge.

Jack, I. (2018, November 17). The people's vote: why didn't we heed the lesson of 1979? *The Guardian.*

Karamagi, V. (2005, October 24). Milton Obote: Telling his own lifetime story. *The Daily Monitor.* https://www.upcparty.net/memorial/life_story.htm

Karugire, S. (2010). *A political history of Uganda.* Fountain Publishers.

Kasendwa-Ddumba, C. (2020). The land of freedom (Revised ed.). An unpublished letter to the Uganda Human Rights Commission.

Kasozi, A. B. K. (1994). *The social origins of violence in Uganda, 1964-1985.* Fountain Publishers.

Kasozi, A. B. K. (1996). *The life of Prince Badru Kakungulu: The development of a forward-looking Muslim community in Uganda 1907-1921.* Progressive Publishing.

Kavuma-Kaggwa. (2014, June 29). Why Baganda celebrated on May 24. *The Independent.* https://www.independent.co.ug/baganda-celebrated-may-24/

Kennedy, J. F. (1962). *Why England slept.* Sigwich and Johnson.

Kimenye, B. (2015, November 1). How Kabaka, UPC marriage was hatched. https://www.monitor.co.ug/Magazines/PeoplePower/How-Kabaka-Yekka--UPC-marriage—was hatched/689844-2936918-85kslez/index.html

Kimenye, B. (2015, September 26). Tales from Mutesa's palace. Unpublished book serialised in *The Daily Monitor*.
Kirunda-Kivejinja, A. M. (1995). *Uganda: The crisis of confidence*. Excel Vision Education.
Kiwanuka, J. (2014). *The son of a rat catcher*. MK Publishers.
Kiwanuka, M. S. M. (1974). The diplomacy of the lost counties and its impact on relations of Buganda, Bunyoro and the rest of Uganda, 1900-1964. *Mawazo*, 4(2). p. 125.
Lwanga-Lunyiigo, S. (2007). *The struggle for land in Buganda, 1888-2005*. Wavah Books.
Lwanga-Lunyiigo, S. (2015). *A history of the Democratic Party in Uganda: The first thirty years (1954-1984)*. Fountain Publishers.
Macaulay, L. (1849). *Critical and historical essays*. Longman.
Macaulay, L. (1871). *The works of Lord Macaulay*. Longman.
Makubuya, A. N. (2018). *Protection, patronage or plunder? British machinations and (B)Uganda's struggle for independence*. Cambridge Scholars' Publishing.
Mayiga, C. P. (2013). *Buganda ku ntikko*. Prime Time Communications.
Mpambara, S. M. (1967). *The gold allegations in Uganda*. Milton Obote Foundation.
Mutesa, E. (1967). *Desecration of my kingdom*. Constable & Co.
Mutibwa, P. (2008). *The Buganda factor in Uganda politics*. Fountain Publishers.
Nagenda, J. (2013, February). One man's week. *The New Vision*.
Nsubuga, G. E. N. (2013). *Sir Edward Mutesa: His life and politics*. Nissi Publishers.
Odoki, B. J. (2014). *The search for national consensus: The making of the 1995 Uganda Constitution*. Fountain Publishers.
Owen, D. (2011). *In sickness and in power: Illness of heads of government during the last 100 years*. Methuen.

Owen, D. (2012). *The Hubris syndrome: Bush, Blair and the intoxication of power*. Methuen.

Owen, J. (2014). The establishment uncovered: How power works in Britain. *The Guardian*. https://www.theguardian.com/society/2014/aug/26/the-establishment-uncovered-how-power-works-in-britain-elites-stranglehold

Ruzindana, A. (2013, February 1). The way forward is a national conference instead of coup threats. *The Daily Monitor*, OpEd/Commentary, p. 8.

Shakespeare, W. (1996). *The twelfth night*. B.E.S. Publishing.

Stiglitz, J. (2012). *The price of inequality*. Penguin Books.

The situation is under control. (1966, February 23). *Uganda Argus*.

Truman, H. (1955). *Years of decision*. Doubleday.

Uganda Independence Bill (Hansard, July 26, 1962) (October 9, 2018). 1962: How Buganda tested Ugandan, British Politicians. *The Independent*. https://www.independent.co.ug/independence-how-buganda-tested-ugandan-british-politicians-ugat56/3/

WBS series. (2003-2005). *Muteesa II ne Uganda*.

Wrigley, C. (1988). Four steps toward disaster. In H. B. Hansen, & M. Twaddle (Eds.). *Uganda now: Between decay and development* (pp. 32-33). James Currey.

Appendix

Five different acts have been passed as of 2018:
(a) Constitutional Amendment Act 2000 Act No. 13 of 2000
    i. Very 1st Amendment
    ii. Articles 88 and 90 repealed
    iii. Articles 89 and 97 amended
    iv. New article 257 came into existence.
(b) Constitutional Amendment Act 2005, Act No. 11 of 2005. 47 Amendments made on this occasion, including:
    i. Removal of term limits
    ii. Swahili adopted as a 2nd national language
    iii. Return to multiparty democracy
    iv. Creation of office of Leader of Opposition in Parliament
    v. Office of Prime Minister and Deputy Attorney General created
    vi. Establishment of Anti Corruption Court
    vii. Instituting an independent office of the Auditor General.
(c) Constitutional Amendment No. 2 Act, 2005, Act No. 21 of 2005 8 amendments around article 178
(d) Constitutional Amendment Act 2015, Act No. 12 of 2015. Amendment of Articles 60, 83 and 148.
(e) Constitutional Amendment Act 2017 signed into law on 27th December 2017. Amendments to articles 61, 77, 104, 105, 181 and 185.
    i. Replacement of articles 102, 289 and 291
    ii. Insertion of Articles 289(A)

Index

A

Acholi, *51, 54, 55, 56, 254*
African leaders, *220*
Amin, Idi, *xix, 54, 56, 55, 87, 112, 114, 142, 144, 146, 147, 149, 150, 161, 166, 170, 176, 187, 192, 194, 195, 200, 201, 202, 203, 244, 260*

B

Baganda, ix, x, xi, 3, 5, 12, 13, 16, 17, 18, 19, 21, 30, 34, 35, 46, 47, 49, 52, 53, 54, 55, 56, 58, 62, 63, 67, 72, 77, 81, 87, 98, 108, 110, 111, 112, 118, 126, 132, 136, 166, 169, 181, 184, 186, 188, 189, 193, 194, 196, 197, 198, 207, 214, 215, 216, 221, 246, 248, 249, 255, 256, 259, 265, 271
Bakopi, ix, 60
Banyoro, *ix, x, xi, 24, 34, 35, 39, 63, 67, 70, 72, 73, 74, 81, 196, 214, 229*
Berlin Conference, *11*
Binaisa, Godfrey Lukongwa, *15, 112, 113, 168, 178, 201, 265*
Britain, *xviii, xix, 1, 11, 12, 14, 18, 23, 33, 38, 75, 77, 84, 95, 96, 104, 167, 170, 184, 208, 213, 218, 226, 269, 273*
British, the, *xvii, xviii, xix, 11, 17, 19, 23, 29, 34, 35, 37, 38, 39, 49, 63, 77, 84, 87, 89, 91, 92, 93, 95, 104, 114, 123, 130, 142, 169, 179, 180, 185, 187, 195, 210, 213, 226, 272, 274*
British government, *12, 17, 38, 39, 123, 180*
British High Commission, *xix*
Buganda indepence, *ix, x, xi, xiii, xvii, xviii, xix, 1, 2, 3, 5, 6, 7, 8, 10, 11, 12, 13, 14, 15, 16, 17, 18, 19, 20, 21, 22, 23, 24, 25, 26, 28, 29, 30, 31, 33, 34, 35, 36, 38, 39, 41, 42, 43, 44, 45, 46, 47, 48, 49, 50, 51, 56, 57, 58, 61, 62, 63, 64, 65, 66, 67, 68, 69, 70, 71, 72, 73, 74, 75, 76, 77, 78, 79, 80, 81, 82, 85, 87, 89, 90, 91, 92, 95, 96, 97, 98, 99, 100, 101, 102, 103, 104, 105, 106, 107, 108, 109, 110, 111, 112, 113, 115, 116, 117, 118, 119, 121, 126, 127, 128, 133, 134, 135, 136, 137, 138, 140, 143, 145, 146, 162, 163, 164, 165, 166, 169, 170, 171, 172, 176, 177, 178, 180, 182, 183, 184, 185, 188,*

189, 190, 191, 193, 195, 196, 197, 199, 201, 204, 205, 206, 207, 210, 212, 213, 214, 215, 216, 217, 218, 219, 220, 223, 226, 227, 228, 229, 234, 246, 247, 248, 249, 250, 251, 252, 253, 255, 256, 257, 259, 263, 264, 265, 266, 267, 272, 273, 274
Buganda nationalism, 48, 104, 197
Buganda Question, the, 8, 45, 46, 49, 53, 56, 67, 76, 91, 93, 117, 126, 132, 171, 175, 203, 211, 216, 221, 236, 237, 246, 249
Bugangazzi, xi, xvii, xviii, 7, 28, 35, 36, 39, 61, 65, 66, 76, 81, 134
Bulange, ix, 18, 120, 165, 188
Bulemezi, 35, 165
Buluuli, 36
Bunyoro, ix, x, xi, xvii, xviii, 1, 2, 7, 8, 19, 22, 23, 25, 28, 29, 31, 33, 34, 35, 36, 37, 38, 39, 61, 63, 65, 66, 67, 68, 76, 79, 81, 97, 121, 162, 190, 193, 210, 212, 213, 214, 228, 229, 230, 263, 268, 270, 272
busuulu, 25
Buwekula, xvii, xviii, 35, 214

C

Chwa, Daudi, 24, 195, 220
colonialism, 23, 24

Common Man's Charter, 152, 187
coup d'état, 135, 175, 178, 259
Crawford, Frederick, 166
cultural institutions, 228, 234, 246
cultural norms, 126

D

Democratic Party (DP), x, 57, 88, 137, 138, 148, 272
Duke of Kent, 17

E

East Africa, 219, 220
East African Federation, 96, 197, 226
ebyaffe, 8
elections, 26, 41, 44, 48, 57, 62, 73, 88, 90, 91, 94, 97, 98, 113, 124, 135, 137, 140, 189, 202, 231, 235, 239, 241, 242, 243, 244, 245
England, 4, 9, 10, 179, 181, 266, 270, 272

F

federalism, 152
Forum for Democratic Change (FDC), x, 88, 259

G

Germany, 9, 10, 58, 175, 219, 269

Index

Ghana, *38, 112*

I

Ibingira, Grace, *xix, 20, 27, 129, 133, 139, 146, 147, 204*

K

Kabaka, *x, xi, xiii, xvii, xviii, xix, 2, 3, 4, 5, 6, 8, 18, 19, 20, 21, 22, 24, 26, 28, 33, 34, 43, 44, 45, 46, 47, 48, 49, 50, 51, 57, 58, 60, 61, 62, 63, 64, 67, 68, 71, 72, 79, 80, 82, 94, 95, 100, 101, 103, 105, 109, 110, 111, 115, 117, 118, 119, 120, 126, 127, 128, 129, 131, 132, 133, 134, 136, 137, 138, 166, 167, 168, 169, 170, 176, 179, 181, 182, 184, 188, 191, 192, 195, 197, 198, 199, 205, 210, 212, 213, 215, 216, 217, 218, 219, 223, 226, 248, 251, 252, 264, 266, 272*

Kabaka Yekka (KY), *x, 43, 44, 101, 109, 110, 137, 138, 210, 218*

Kabalega, Omukama, *19, 23, 24, 29, 117, 213, 229*

Kakonge, John, *22, 81, 91, 101, 106, 139, 140, 146*

Kakungulu, Badru, *60, 271*

Kalule, Miria, *44, 53*

Katikkiro, x, xiii, 35, 80, 103, 116, 117, 118, 119, 120, 127, 164, 227, 251, 252

Kenyatta, Jomo, *112, 149, 150, 198*

kingdoms, *6, 11, 22, 23, 24, 39, 60, 66, 97, 152, 187, 190, 193, 204, 205, 206, 217, 228, 230, 233, 246, 247, 264, 268*

L

Lancaster Conference, *41, 75, 98*

Lancaster Settlement, *227*

land, *ix, x, 12, 13, 14, 19, 22, 24, 34, 63, 66, 72, 190, 207, 232, 247, 251, 252, 255, 256, 257, 258, 271, 272*

land allocation, *14*

land grabbing, *257, 258*

land leased, *12*

land owners, *12, 25*

land wrangles, *258*

landlords, *258*

Lango, *15, 23, 51, 54, 55, 123, 125, 194, 254*

London Conferences, *196*

Lost Counties, *xviii, xix, 1, 2, 20, 22, 23, 25, 26, 28, 29, 30, 31, 34, 35, 37, 38, 39, 40, 62, 67, 70, 71, 73, 75, 78, 79, 80, 85, 104, 116, 117, 118, 121, 126, 132, 190, 193, 196, 197, 199, 211, 212, 214, 216, 219, 221, 228, 272*

Lubiri, x, xiii, xix, 7, 11, 30, 31, 58, 120, 161, 165, 166, 168,

245

169, 170, 171, 178, 179, 188,
189, 193, 195, 253, 254, 261
Luganda, *x, xii*, 13, 24, 55, 103,
125, 255
Lukiiko, *x*, 6, 13, 17, 18, 42, 44,
81, 97, 115, 118, 127, 136,
137, 146, 162, 163, 164, 165,
166, 171, 226, 227, 234
Lumu, Emmanuel, 113, 140,
204
Lutaaya, Kaganda, 165

M

Mailo, x
Magezi, George, 140
Marlborough House
 Conference, 33
Matovu, Micheal, 172
Mau Mau Movement, 123
Mayanja, Abu Kakyama, **16,**
 118, **121, 251,** 156
Mayanja-Nkangi, Joash, 118,
 119, 120, 164
Mbabazi, Patrick Amama, 26,
 27
Mengo, *xiii, xix*, 5, 12, 13, 14,
 15, 17, 21, 43, 49, 57, 68, 70,
 72, 74, 75, 76, 79, 84, 91, 92,
 94, 95, 96, 98, 100, 102, 103,
 108, 109, 110, 116, 118, 119,
 120, 126, 137, 141, 143, 163,
 164, 166, 198, 213, 221, 235,
 247, 250, 253, 259, 261, 266
Mengo and Obote, 68
Mengo and UPC, 98

Mengo establishment, 12, 13,
 14, 43, 49, 79, 92, 95, 96, 98,
 100, 102, 108, 109, 110, 141,
 222, 235, 259
Mengo government, 18, 120
Mengo leaders, 94
Mengo matters, 253
Military Commission, 201
monarch, 125, 131, 205, 217,
 227
Muganda, xi, 15, 16, 17, 23, 46,
 47, 48, 53, 54, 56, 111, 145,
 165, 194, 195, 249
Mwanga II, Kabaka, 23, 24, 25,
 185, 195, 212

N

nation, *xx*, 5, 9, 10, 22, 25, 35,
 40, 49, 84, 98, 116, 120, 131,
 161, 197, 198, 199, 205, 218,
 219, 227, 230, 232, 236, 255,
 260, 267, 269
National Assembly, 36, 41, 42,
 44, 50, 62, 71, 90, 96, 119,
 136, 144
National Resistance
 Movement (NRM), 26
nationhood, 232
Ndaiga Development Scheme,
 62, 66, 72, 73, 74
Ndaiga Project, 75
Nekyon, Adoko, 154

O

oligarchy, *109*, *110*
Omugabe, *xi*
Omukama, *xi*, *19*, *23*, *29*, *39*, *60*, *68*, *117*, *210*, *213*

P

political actors, *xiv*, *90*, *129*, *228*
political alliance, *89*, *95*
political capital, *13*, *58*, *260*
political crisis, *3*, *7*, *8*, *19*, *31*
political history, *xvii*, *xx*, *85*, *271*
political institutions, *7*
political interest, *150*
political leaders, *110*, *112*, *187*, *194*, *241*
political organisations, *92*, *101*
political parties, *33*, *43*, *44*, *45*, *87*, *88*, *90*, *96*, *109*, *110*, *111*, *112*, *138*, *217*, *225*, *235*, *242*
political support, *2*, *43*, *138*, *207*
post-independence, *28*, *80*, *103*, *229*
post-independence government, *80*
post-independence history, *28*, *103*
power, *xiii*, *xvii*, *xix*, *xx*, *8*, *9*, *12*, *14*, *17*, *19*, *20*, *21*, *23*, *26*, *27*, *30*, *31*, *33*, *37*, *47*, *55*, *57*, *62*, *77*, *85*, *86*, *91*, *92*, *95*, *96*, *101*, *102*, *105*, *106*, *107*, *108*, *109*, *115*, *120*, *127*, *128*, *130*, *131*, *133*, *139*, *140*, *141*, *150*, *151*, *164*, *170*, *173*, *174*, *184*, *186*, *189*, *193*, *196*, *197*, *200*, *201*, *202*, *213*, *218*, *220*, *224*, *225*, *226*, *227*, *231*, *232*, *235*, *236*, *237*, *240*, *241*, *243*, *246*, *249*, *250*, *252*, *255*, *265*, *273*
Presidential Commission, *201*

S

Scotland, *77*
Singo, *35*, *165*, *214*
Ssekabaka, *xi*, *181*, *185*
state, *xix*, *xx*, *2*, *7*, *10*, *11*, *17*, *33*, *37*, *40*, *45*, *47*, *48*, *49*, *50*, *61*, *69*, *85*, *86*, *89*, *92*, *95*, *96*, *97*, *100*, *111*, *113*, *114*, *115*, *117*, *122*, *129*, *139*, *140*, *145*, *147*, *151*, *163*, *164*, *171*, *176*, *178*, *187*, *190*, *201*, *204*, *212*, *227*, *228*, *230*, *238*, *251*, *258*, *260*, *264*, *266*
state of emergency, *xix*, *171*
state *of* Uganda, *2*, *264*, *265*
state *within* a state, *97*

T

traditionalist, *81*

U

Uganda, *i*, *iii*, *xi*, *xiii*, *xiv*, *xvii*, *xviii*, *xix*, *xx*, *1*, *2*, *4*, *5*, *6*, *7*, *8*,

*10, 11, 12, 13, 16, 17, 18, 19,
20, 21, 25, 26, 28, 33, 34, 35,
36, 37, 38, 39, 41, 45, 46, 47,
48, 49, 50, 51, 52, 53, 54, 55,
56, 57, 60, 61, 62, 63, 64, 66,
67, 68, 69, 71, 73, 76, 80, 82,
83, 84, 85, 86, 87, 88, 89, 90,
91, 92, 93, 95, 96, 97, 99, 100,
101, 102, 103, 104, 108, 110,
111, 112, 113, 114, 115, 117,
118, 119, 123, 129, 131, 133,
134, 137, 139, 141, 142, 144,
145, 146, 147, 148, 149, 152,
162, 163, 166, 167, 170, 172,
173, 174, 175, 176, 177, 178,
179, 181, 182, 187, 188, 190,
191, 192, 194, 197, 199, 200,
201, 202, 204, 207, 208, 209,
210, 212, 213, 215, 216, 217,
218, 219, 223, 224, 225, 226,
227, 228, 229, 230, 231, 232,
233, 236, 237, 238, 240, 242,
244, 245, 246, 247, 248, 251,
253, 254, 255, 256, 257, 259,
260, 261, 263, 264, 265, 266,
267, 269, 270, 271, 272, 273,
274*

Uganda Human Rights Commission (UHCR), *68, 164, 271*

Uganda National Congress (UNC), *xi, 86, 110, 123*

Uganda Peoples Congress (UPC), *xiii, xix, 2*

UPC/KY alliance, *85, 91, 92, 93*

UPC/KY coalition, *45*

www.ingramcontent.com/pod-product-compliance
Lightning Source LLC
Chambersburg PA
CBHW052048220426
43663CB00012B/2484